CW00543118

Contents

Diver with a champagne bottle recovered from the site of the former pier at Plymouth.

Preface

Without the help of the leading divers of Devon, this guide would not have been possible. All gave freely of their time and knowledge to provide readers of this guide with more diving information about Devon than has ever been collected together before.

Certain areas of expertise have been attributed to those named, but many supplied material for other areas too. From east to west, the thanks of all who dive Devon go to:

- Derek Cockbill, a BSAC vice-president, who provided much of the basic material for earlier editions and without whose great knowledge of diving Devon the first Devon diving guide would not have appeared.

- Nick Chipchase and Wellington BSAC divers for the LSTs and other shipwrecks in Lyme Bay.

- Colin Davies, Ray Kirkland and John Ledger for diving from Axmouth and Seaton.

- Maurice Webb, skipper of *Grace*, and the divers of Exedive BSAC, for invaluable wreck material.

- Colin Ayres, Richard Smith, Alan Hartshorne, Peter Lord, Derek Boustred, Jack Stoneman, and the divers of Exeter BSAC for giving all their vast experience in Devon waters.

- Carol Brandie, Peter Milner, Adrian Hughes, Reid Fleming, Dave Tipper, and the divers of Torbay BSAC for details of their patch and elsewhere.

- Ken Breeze and Dave Baker of Paulanda for a vast amount of wreck diving detail from Brixham and beyond.

- Tony Hoile, Martin Cox, Dave Crockford and the divers of Totnes BSAC for immense amounts of diving information.

- Graham Bush, skipper of *Maureen,* for diving from Dartmouth.

- Tony Aylmer, President of Torbay BSAC, for priceless information from Berry Head to Start Point – and even further afield.

- Mike Holbrook, Dave Shaw and other members of the BSAC National Diving Committee for details of deep wrecks off Dartmouth.
- Stephen George for the *Gossamer*, the *Venerable*, and many other South Hams wrecks.
- David and Muriel Murch and Len Fairweather for wreck information out of Salcombe.
- Bill Bunting for the Bolt, Head and Tail and all about.
- Roger and Suzanne Race, John Saltmarsh, and the divers of Bigbury BSAC for that coast and Start Point.
- Roy Wardle for a Bigbury Bay cannon find.
- Geoffrey Moles for other cannon almost in the same gully as the one above!
- Terry Crocker for Prawle.
- Neville Oldham with Mick Palmer and the divers of Northampton BSAC for the Erme Estuary shipwrecks and the Bronze Age tin ingot site.
- Alan Bax and Jim Gill for diving out of Fort Bovisand.
- Andy Barber and the divers of Bovisand BSAC for the reefs to Stoke Point and Plymouth Sound.
- Glen Peacham, Martin Buckle, Bob Michael, Paul Bustard, Roger Dadds and the divers of Plymouth Sound BSAC for a huge input of wreck and other diving information, both in and out of the Sound.
- Dave Wybrow for much diving in Devon waters.
- Barry Mason, the marine artist, for shipwreck detail and research.
- Lieutenant-Commander J.D. Pugh, RN, formerly of the Wreck Section of the Hydrographic Department of the Ministry of Defence, for his generous help.

The above all made major contributions to this guide, but there are scores of others whose enthusiasm and help can only be acknowledged by the author in a general way. Hopefully they will think their reward comes from this guide and the increased pleasure it will give to all who *Dive South Devon*.

KENDALL McDONALD

Acknowledgements

The photographs on pages 74, 92, 94, 139–47, 152 (top), 155–67, 190 and 207 were supplied by the author. The photograph on the front cover was taken by Frank Allen and the photograph on page 170 was taken by Bernard Eaton. All the remaining photographs were taken by Roy Smallpage, except for the following, which are reproduced with the kind permission of:

- Brian Worth (page 182)
- Dartington Rural Archive (pages 84, 103)
- Imperial War Museum (pages 54, 191)

- Plymouth News Pictures (page 121)
- Salcombe Museum (pages 122–138)
- United States Navy (page 39)

The transit markings that appear on pages 49, 119, 144, 165, 168, 189 and 192 have been redrawn with kind permission from the BSAC Wreck Register.

The information on decompression accidents (page 19) and the Diver's Code of Conduct (pages 207–9) have been included with the kind permission of the BSAC.

Some of the casemates at Fort Bovisand are now used as classrooms.

How to use
this Guide

In this guide the coastline of south Devon is divided from east to west into seven areas. Each area has a chapter to itself, containing a guide to diving – spot by spot, wreck by wreck, and backup information of vital importance to divers. This includes details of launch sites, parking places, routes, harbour information and usage, addresses and contact telephone numbers, Admiralty charts and Ordnance Survey maps. Appendix 1 gives details of dive boats, air supplies, dive shops and BSAC branches to contact for local help.

Depths are given in metres; distances in yards and miles. Dimensions of ships are shown in feet and all tonnages quoted are gross. References to Admiralty charts are to the metric versions. References to Ordnance Survey maps are to the 1:50,000 Landranger series. Positions are not metric – they are shown in degrees, minutes and seconds.

Most Devon diving is boat diving – in this guide boat diving should be taken to cover inflatable and hard boat diving. This does not mean, however, that all the boat diving sites can be reached safely by inflatable. In the same way, shore dive sites are intended only for a strong swimmer on a very calm day.

Each dive site is given a number, which will be found on the area map at the start of each chapter. Over 360 dive sites are detailed in this guide, and some may be new even to veteran divers in the area.

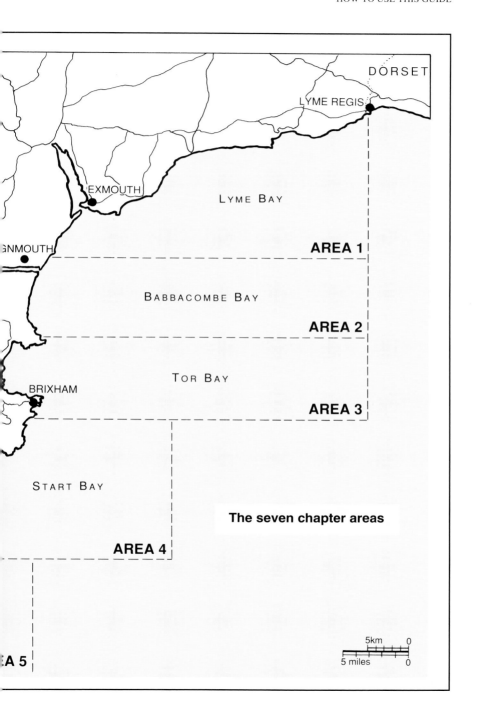

DORSET

LYME REGIS

EXMOUTH

LYME BAY

 GNMOUTH

AREA 1

BABBACOMBE BAY

AREA 2

TOR BAY

BRIXHAM

AREA 3

START BAY

The seven chapter areas

AREA 4

A 5

5km   0

5 miles   0

Cliffs to the east of Bolt Tail, where the Jebba (Site 249) and the Ramilles (Site 250) lie.

About South Devon

If you ignore all the inlets – and there are some lovely, deep inlets difficult to ignore – there are some 150 miles of south Devon coastline in direct contact with the open sea. It is this coastline that provides some of the finest and most varied diving in Britain.

The south Devon coast starts just to the west of Poker's Pool, near Lyme Regis. The county border comes down to the beach almost opposite Virtle Rock. All to the west is Devon until you come to the great anchorage of Plymouth Sound, on the west side of which Cornwall begins.

Devon is the third largest of all the English counties: its total area is 1,671,613 acres and some 1,049,200 people call it home. To cross its widest part, from Ilfracombe to Prawle Point, you would travel 70 miles, and it is 66 miles across from east to west. Exeter is the county town, but the biggest city is Plymouth with a population of 259,000.

Access by road

In the summer holiday season, Devon's population certainly doubles and may even treble as the holidaymakers flood in. In the early days of tourism, after the railway first reached Exeter in 1844, everyone came by train and the railway spread its tentacles all over the county. Many of these local lines were axed following the Beeching Report of 1963, and now the only practical way to travel around the county is by car. In the high summer months the resulting congestion is enormous. Divers must make allowances for this when timing diving trips. Remember that most of south Devon's roads are narrow and that close to the coast – particularly in the South Hams – they turn into little lanes with occasional passing places. Hold-ups for divers towing boats will occur at peak times, and even on the main roads traffic jams can be expected.

The best approach road, even in high summer, must be the M5 (M4 then M5 from London) though roadworks, which always seem to take place in the peak

5

holiday periods, can and have brought even this great artery to a standstill. Many divers coming from London take the M3 and then the A303, which is shorter and dual carriageway for much of its length, but takes longer than the all-motorway route. Some motorists stick to the A30, but this will take even longer, despite a great deal of traffic having deserted it for the motorways.

Once on Devon soil and settled in, divers, particularly those towing boats, would be well advised to study the largest-scale map they can lay their hands on, to try and ensure that their trips to and from the dive sites are as jam-free as possible. There are some sites where there is only one sensible method of approach by car. Wherever possible in this guide parking places near popular dive sites are pinpointed. Please use them. In many cases it is not possible to park right beside the sea.

It is a pity that some of the best launching places for divers' boats are at the edges of popular beaches catering for the ordinary "bucket-and-spade" holidaymakers. This not only means that divers must be careful not to spread their equipment, but that they must take exceptional care when bringing boats in or taking them out from these beach sites, which can become crowded with holiday swimmers. If you know that your launch site is a popular beach, an early start in the morning will give you a clearer run to it through the narrow lanes – the south Devon non-diving holidaymaker rarely makes a move before 10am!

It is not only the non-divers who crowd the beaches. Divers visit Devon in large groups and "diver saturation" is no idle phrase at some very popular sites. Hope Cove and Brixham are areas that have suffered from too many divers in times past. Divers must follow local signboarded instructions to divers in sensitive areas.

The BSAC coach for the South-West Region is always willing to help, and can be contacted through BSAC Headquarters (tel. 0151 357 1951).

Physical features

A large chunk of the south Devon coastline – from Exmouth to Start Point –actually faces east. Another section – from Bolt Tail to Stoke Point – almost faces in a westerly direction. This nearly always enables decent diving to found somewhere whatever the wind direction.

White chalky cliffs are striking from the Dorset border to near Sidmouth, particularly at Beer and Branscombe, backing the shingle beaches. The red sandstone cliffs, which many imagine are everywhere in Devon, in fact occupy only a short stretch from east of Sidmouth to Exmouth with some other outcrops further west. The great cliffs at Berry Head are limestone; further west granite and slate take over. It is slate that provides the walls of many gullies running straight out from the shore. Granite and quartz make up the rugged cliffs of the Bolt, both Head and Tail.

Bigbury Bay is thought by holidaymakers to be a sandy area, and so it is on both sides of the River Avon (which has its mouth at Bantham) and at the great sweep of Thurlestone Sands. But though there are some more sandy smaller beaches at the mouths of estuaries, steep cliffs are the main feature of the coast there and on to Plymouth. This lack of sandy beaches gives this area the best visibility in south Devon.

View of Dartmouth from Kingswear, on the opposite bank of the river.

Wrecks

Devon has always been famous for its seamen – Drake, whose statue is on Plymouth Hoe, and Raleigh who was born and spent his boyhood in East Budleigh are two good examples. The county has always been famous for its ports. Plymouth means the Royal Navy.

Yet over the centuries of Devon's maritime history there have been other ports almost as well used – including Dartmouth, Exmouth and Teignmouth – and in early days ships could get up the River Otter at Budleigh. They used Salcombe, despite its Bar, went into the Avon at Bantham, ran up the Erme and into the Yealm.

Mycenaean pottery has been found near Salcombe, clear evidence that Devon was a port of call for Greek traders of long ago. Earlier evidence of shipping in the area is provided by the Bronze Age swords found on the sea bed at Moor Sands and the more recent discovery by divers of ancient tin ingots in the mouth of the Erme Estuary. There is an Iron Age fort on Bolt Tail and a very early settlement on Bantham Ham at the mouth of the Avon may well have been the site of early tin trading.

It was from Devon, glorious Devon, that men crewed the first ships to America, went cod fishing on the Newfoundland Banks, sailed round the world, and fought the Armada, the Kaiser, Hitler and the Falklands War.

The coast of south Devon has seen ships of all times and of all kinds. Many of them have come to grief in these waters. War took its toll of some but parts of the coast in certain winds are quite unforgiving of mistakes. Close to the sheltered haven of Plymouth, Bigbury Bay provided a deadly trap for ships running before a westerly gale. In poor visibility they were caught before they knew it and few escaped. Classic examples of this are the wrecks of the Armada's *San Pedro el Mayor* and of the *Ramillies*, both close to Hope Cove. Not far away the grim cliffs of Bolt Head have taken their share of vessels and not all by any means were sailing ships. Prawle Point is Devon's most southerly tip, which may account for all the wrecks there. Parts of Lyme Bay have no hiding place for ships caught in trouble in onshore winds. Even right in Tor Bay ships are never safe – during one day in January 1866 a gale wrecked thirty.

Many of the ships littered on the sea bed around the coast are the victims of U-boats of both World Wars. Time and time again in U-boat commanders' logs there are references to Lyme Bay and Start Point as favourite killing grounds. So yet another maritime activity has sprung up along the coast – the provision of large, often very powerful boats to cater for wreck divers.

South Devon is famous for its wrecks. Can there be a diver who has never heard of or dived the *Maine*? But almost as popular are the *Persier*, the *Elk,* the *Soudan*, the *Riversdale*, the *Medina*, the *Picton Castle*, the *Sevilla*, the *Bretagne*, the *Galicia* and the *Empress of India*. The list of dived and exciting wrecks runs into hundreds.

Depths vary and there are many shallow inshore rummages for divers to enjoy. However, many of Devon's wrecks are very deep and for this reason are often in a better state of preservation than those elsewhere around Britain.

Deep wreck diving can be dangerous and divers should use great care. Remember that while 50m is the recommended depth limit for sports diving. many experts feel that this should really be 40m. Medical evidence shows that decompression sickness is more likely on dives deeper than 50m even when the tables are strictly followed. When diving deeper than 30m extra care with planning is essential, especially when wreck diving.

An additional hazard on wrecks to the east of the area covered in this guide is that most are very heavily silted. Finning quickly raises a great deal of sediment, then visibility, which can already be poor in this area, is quickly reduced to nil. For this reason no diver should enter a wreck without being sure that he can find his way out by means of a line.

The danger of wreck netting is detailed in the next chapter – divers are reminded to look out for such lethal traps on every wreck they dive.

In most parts of the country no amateur diver would wish to dive in harbours for pleasure. But Devon is different – Plymouth Sound, for example, is a enormous harbour – and in this guide you will find the rules and regulations concerning such places in the appropriate section. But to dive areas that come under a Harbour Master's jurisdiction, you must have permission and must get this before the dive. And once permission is given you must dive where you said you would. Otherwise there are no restrictions on the amateur who wants to dive Devon.

Dive Planning

Weather

Divers who want to get the most out of diving Devon should adopt the "have lung, will travel" approach. This is the key to dealing with the variable weather. Sometimes a trip of only a few miles by car from a wind-lashed beach can produce flat calm water in the shelter of one of Devon's great headlands. A good example of this occurs when you leave the surf of an onshore wind at Beesands and find perfect peace at Thurlestone Sands in the shelter of Bolt Tail.

South Devon's weather has one thing in common with the whole of southern England. The wind rules the diving. For example, south-westerly winds bring mainly cloudy, and what Devonians call "dampy" weather. These winds are often accompanied by periods of rain and strong winds, particularly in winter. North-west winds bring showers and bright periods. But take care – squalls often come at the same time. Winds from between east and south bring warm and mainly dry periods in summer and very cold times in winter.

Divers out in small boats should be aware that they may suffer the worst of the weather close in. This is due to the wind funnelling down off those apparently protective great headlands or spilling out from river mouths. Wind speeds in these "funnel" areas, which are sometimes at the entrance to, or even in, ports, can be 20 per cent higher than in areas only a short distance away.

Winds from the west are the most common throughout the year and those from the south-east are the least frequent and the least persistent. North-east winds are most common in spring.

Gales come most often out of the south-west and west and usually last for four to six hours or even less in the summer. Divers should note that when a gale dies down this does not mean that the windy weather is over. Gales can follow one another almost immediately. Series of gales have been recorded with speeds of over 90 knots – a hurricane on the Beaufort Scale.

Generally speaking, the whole of Devon enjoys a mild climate. Spring comes early, which must account for the mass migration of divers to the South-West at Easter! The south coast of the county enjoys the best of the spring weather and that of the summer. On average there are usually only five days in June, July and August on which there is no sun at all. Over the same period temperatures on the south coast are between 18 and 20°C. These temperatures and the mild winters – the average daily temperature in January at Torquay is 6.3°C and at Exmouth only slightly lower at 5.6°C – make south Devon an ideal place for the elderly to live in their retirement, as you will notice from some of the driving!

The moors – Dartmoor and Exmoor – often have a totally different weather system from that of the coastal regions. In winter this is seen in the form of massive snowfalls and blizzards. The moors play an important part in the summer coastal weather – particularly Dartmoor, which has a dramatic effect on the weather of the South Hams (roughly, the area south of Totnes). The name comes from the Old English "ham" or meadowland and has been used for centuries to describe the fertile land between the River Dart in the east and the River Erme in the west. The South Hams are backed by the grim hills of Dartmoor and this "wall" often means that great grey clouds are piled up over the moor while the South Hams are bathed in brilliant and tranquil sunshine.

This very tranquillity has been known to lure divers into thinking that the whole area is suitable for diving. Be warned if you see large trawlers idly swinging at anchor in Bigbury Bay. They are not there to admire the view. A short drive to Start Bay will show you the reason. A violent east wind will bring surf crashing down on Torcross, Slapton, Beesands, Hallsands and will cripple diving in Start Bay and Tor Bay. Some idea of the violence of such a wind comes when you see the size of the trawlers sheltering inshore near Bigbury. Big as they are their skippers are not prepared to bash them round Start Point and back to Brixham.

Diving coxswains should watch out for the development of cumulonimbus clouds. These indicate that squally showers are likely, perhaps with hail and thunder. Sudden changes of direction and dramatic increases in wind force will come with them, strong enough to put small diving boats into trouble.

The whole area enjoys higher temperatures than normal, but once again the wind affects it. South-westerly winds in summer cause a fall in temperature to slightly below average. A north-west or north-east wind will not affect the temperature, but an east or south wind will boost the warmth considerably. The air is slightly colder than the sea from October to March and slightly warmer from April to August. In September air and sea seem to match.

Thunderstorms are common during warm spells in the summer. It is odd to note that these storms usually form over France and drift north during the night before bursting forth after the dawn on Devon. The importance of this to the diver is that in such periods sudden squalls sweep across the sea inshore and there are sometimes waterspouts swirled up from the sea. How these waterspouts might affect small boats is not properly recorded. Any diver coxswain caught up in such turmoil should report it to the Accidents and Incidents Officer of the BSAC!

Fog is always a great hazard for small diving boats and is most common in spring and summer. This is because the mild westerlies are then blowing over the colder waters of the sea. Fogs can persist for two or three days but usually last only for 6 to 10 hours. Keen night divers should note that in summer fog often drifts in after sunset. Fogs are most likely when the wind veers westerly; then fog spreads across the whole area. Winds from the south also produce fog, but because the wind is less moist the fog is least over the eastern part of the area. In south-west wind conditions extensive banks of fog may form at any time of the year.

Swell, particularly in the eastern part of the region, can inhibit diving for several days. This generally comes from the south-west and west, although divers in the east will tell you that after a spell of windy weather they suffer from a particularly nasty easterly or north-easterly swell. In the same area southerly or south-westerly winds can make the whole of Lyme Bay very rough indeed in a very short time.

Weather services The Meteorological Office offers several services of use to divers in south Devon. The general weather forecast for Devon and Cornwall is available by telephoning Weathercall on 0891 500404. More important to the diver is Marinecall on 0891 500458. This gives the sea weather for coastal areas from Hartland Point, right round Land's End and up to Lyme Regis and 12 miles offshore. It includes the Isles of Scilly and is followed by a forecast for the next three days.

MetFax, including surface pressure charts and two-day printout forecast, is also available for the area by dialling the Met Office fax number 0336 400458. A 3- to 5-day Channel Waters forecast and charts are available by fax on 0336 400471.

Visibility

This varies from place to place, but generally the further west you go the better the visibility. However, this does not mean that the east of the region is cursed with permanent poor visibility, and divers do find 20m in the area from time to time. Much of the reputation for poor visibility given to the wrecks out in Lyme Bay is really due to the amount of silt present. These deposits are very fine and the poor visibility is often almost entirely due to the first divers on the wreck stirring up the silt. It is sometimes possible to see a "wall" of silt rolling over the wreck – entirely due to the careless fin-work of the first divers down.

But the western parts of the region do have the best visibility. It is not unknown for divers on the bottom to be able to see the diving boat, tiny but clear, 30m above them. A diver on the surface can sometimes, too, see the whole of a wreck spread out below him. River mouths can often be blamed for poor visibility in their areas, and divers say that dredging of Exmouth Harbour has affected visibility in that area.

In Plymouth Sound visibility is totally qualified by the most recent rainfall. It is interesting to note that marine life will be found higher up in the Sound due to short penetration of sunlight. Visibility there is usually in the 3-4m range. Deep it can be nil!

Marine life

Devon's marine life can sometimes make you wonder if you are is diving in British waters or those of the Mediterranean – or even tropical waters. The reason for this is not simply because of the splendid visibility, but because some of the fish should not be in British waters at all. Divers have seen brightly coloured triggerfish that would be more at home on a coral reef. Local crab fishermen regularly found them in their pots a few years ago. More recently, divers have reported seeing gilt-head bream, whose real home is the Mediterranean. The presence of these fish away from their normal haunts is due to the influence of the Gulf Stream and the Lusitanian current, which wells up off the western coast of the British Isles.

Devon marine life is varied enough without such strangers to our shores. Fish seem to grow to enormous sizes in the rich Devon waters. Pollack look huge to the diver and wrasse of over 5 kg and half a metre long are not uncommon. Large bass and salmon are often encountered near the entrances to estuaries.

Large skate, plaice and soles inhabit the flatter sand and mud plains all along the coast, particularly in Lyme Bay to the east and further south on the Skerries, where outlines in the hard mud of plaice and turbot and brill – so perfect that the rays of each fin are quite clear – are of such a size that the cruising diver can only hesitate then push on convinced that such a monster must be waiting in the next depression!

Lobsters are not as common as crabs, and at one time, particularly in east Devon, might be called rare, but lately divers have noticed that the lobster is making something of a comeback. Crawfish, after being almost common some years ago, are now a rarity and are usually only seen below 30m.

The famous Mayflower Steps on the Barbican, Plymouth.

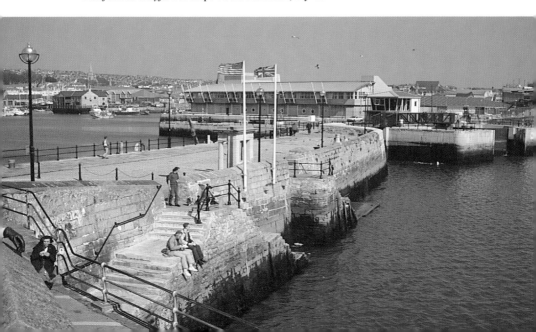

Spider crabs come inshore in May and June and form breeding heaps in late summer. Edible crabs of great size are found out in the open in late summer too. Crabs tend to move westward along the coast, so the really large ones seen by divers probably set out from Kent!

Beds of scallops, queen scallops and cockles are to be found in some of the most unlikely places. Over-fishing does occur; trawlers are known to have cleaned out one huge bed in two days. There is also over-fishing by divers. An example of this is the present lack of scallops in the Beesands area, where some visiting divers have taken more than their fair share.

Basking sharks come inshore during warm summers and divers have reported seeing other sharks on rare occasions. Cuttlefish are common. So are congers, which are often seen out in the open among the ridges and gullies that are such a feature of much of the south Devon inshore underwater landscape.

Jewel anemones and Devonshire cup coral make rock faces glow and sparkle. Sponges are common. Large clumps of rose coral are such an ordinary sight that no diver bothers to pick them up any more. For the underwater photographer the clarity of the water and the marine life in it make south Devon waters something close to paradise!

Fishing regulations

If you wish to take fish or shellfish for your own supper during any dive, you must conform to the same rules as those that apply to professional fishermen, such as minimum fish sizes. Such rules are laid down by the Devon Sea Fisheries District in the form of by-laws. The area controlled by the Devon Sea Fisheries District extends three miles out to sea and starts in the east from "a line drawn true south from the seaward extremity of the boundary between Devon and Dorset near Lyme Regis", which is the western boundary of the Southern Sea Fisheries District. The western limit of the Devon Sea Fisheries District is "a line drawn true south from the seaward extremity of Rame Head in the County of Cornwall" (the Cornwall Sea Fisheries District starts from Rame Head). The Devon Sea Fisheries District also includes the coast of north Devon and around Lundy, not within the scope of this guide.

The Sea Fisheries district does not extend above a line drawn across the mouth of every river, or stream flowing into the sea, or estuary. In Plymouth Sound for example, this means in the case of the Tamar, a line drawn across the river true south-east from the southernmost point of the quay at Cotehele, another drawn across the Tavy along the crest of the weir at Lopwell, and yet another across the Plym along the seaward side of the Laira Bridge at Plymouth. At Salcombe this means a line drawn across the mouth of every river and stream flowing into the estuary at high water spring tides; for the Dart the line is drawn along the weir at Totnes; the line for the Exe goes along the crest of St James's Weir at Exeter. In case you think that no one has authority higher up than these invisible lines, please think again, for above them the National Rivers Authority has probably more power than a local fisheries committee.

The Devon Sea Fisheries District has a good relationship with branches of the BSAC, but say that they have experienced considerable aggravation from "breakaway" diver groups. As a result they have drawn up a "Code of Practice for Underwater Swimmers" as follows:

1. Underwater swimmers should keep well clear of fishermen and their buoys, nets and pots, and other equipment, making allowance for tidal movements. They should also refrain from using pot markers as diving buoys. Apart from the risk of damage to potters' catches and equipment, there is a danger that divers' air cylinders may become entangled in pot marker lines.

2. Underwater swimmers must not remove or interfere with fish or shellfish from the nets, pots, traps and other instruments used by fishermen for the catching or storage of fish or shellfish. Legal action may be taken against persons committing this offence.

3. Underwater swimmers should not take crabs lobsters or other shellfish by means of spears, tongs or other instruments that are likely to damage shellfish.

4. Underwater swimmers are reminded that it is an offence to land shellfish of less than the minimum size specified in the Sea Fishing Industry (Crabs and Lobsters) Order 1966, and in the by-laws of the local Sea Fisheries Committees. They should make sure they know what minimum sizes apply in the areas in which they operate.

5. Underwater swimmers are strongly recommended, in the interests of safety, when diving to exhibit on their boats (and on their diving buoy and/or shore diving base) the "Diving Flag", namely the International Code flag

This ceramic bottle was found by a diver under Paignton pier.

"A", which is the flag generally recognised by the Royal Navy to indicate that skin divers are at work.

6. Underwater swimmers should observe the guidance given in this Code of Practice. They should in turn be accorded by other fishermen reciprocal consideration and freedom from interference.

No Devon Sea Fisheries District by-law has a direct bearing on diving, but divers' attention is drawn some of them. By-law 7 refers to scallops: "No person shall remove from a fishery any escallop measuring less than 100mm across the broadest part of the flatshell." By-law 8 says: "Any person who takes any shellfish the removal of which from a fishery is prohibited by any of the by-laws, or the possession or sale of which is prohibited by or in pursuance of any Act of Parliament, shall forthwith re-deposit the same without injury in the water and as near as possible to the place from which they were taken."

By-law 9 gives the Committee the power to close any bed or part of a bed of shellfish so that it can recover when severely depleted. Notices of such closure will either be clearly defined on the shore or by a notice in the local paper. By-law 10 concerns winkles, which have to be over 16mm before they can be taken. By-law 11 sets out a minimum landing size for crabs – a size confined to Devon and Cornwall and bigger than elsewhere in Britain (*see* table overleaf).

Another order, which divers will be pleased to see, prohibits the landing in the United Kingdom of claws detached from edible crabs. Hopefully this will put an end to divers finding small crabs with both claws missing. Other by-laws of the Devon Sea Fisheries District ban trawling in Start Bay and in all estuaries in

Cod	35cm
Conger	58cm
Haddock	30cm
Hake	30cm
Plaice	25cm
Pollack	30cm
Witches	28cm
Lemon soles	25cm
Soles	24cm
Turbot	30cm
Brill	30cm
Megrims	25cm
Whiting	27cm
Dabs	15cm
Bass	36cm
Saithe	35cm
Herrings	20cm
Mackerel	20cm

Minimum sizes for fish.

Scallops (across flatshell)	100mm
Edible cock crabs (across back)	160mm
Edible hen crabs (across back)	140mm
Lobsters (across carapace – base of rostrum spines to rear of body shell)	85mm
Spider crabs (across carapace – base of rostrum spines to rear of body shell)	120mm

Minimum sizes for shellfish.

the area, and concern minimum sizes, which at the time of writing were as shown in the tables.

Devon Sea Fisheries District is based on the first floor of the Fish Market and Jetty, The Quay, Brixham (tel. 01803 854648). From this office they can talk by radio to their patrol vessel, the 72-foot *Drumbeat of Devon* whose skipper is John Friend. The Fisheries Officers welcome visiting divers at their office and are pleased to pass on any local knowledge that would help.

Divers and pot fishermen The Devon fishing industry is enormous. A year's catch brings in £30 million, of which £6 million is shellfish from south Devon boats (1994 estimates). The south Devon fishing effort is spread over trawling, netting and potting. Brixham is the principal British port for sole and Dartmouth and Salcombe are the prime British ports for crab. Much of the fishing is done by small boats from small havens or launched directly off the beach.

With all this fishing gear in daily use, divers will not be able to avoid diving or surfacing near pots at times. They should, of course, try to avoid doing so, but it will happen and divers will be seen to do so by fishermen. Even so, relations with most fishermen are reasonable and divers should go out of their way to assist the fishermen whenever possible with recovery of pots or other gear.

Annual catch It is impossible to produce exact statistics to show how valuable pot fishing is to each area, as boats based in south Devon ports fish in other parts of the UK are land at ports outside the county. Some south Devon boats land their catch directly in France and these landings are estimated as worth £1.4 million per year. To be added to these figures are the catches of many part-time fishermen and an unknown number of amateurs using a pot or two to catch their supper. There are no exact statistics.

However, the best calculations of fisheries officers produce these figures: pot fishing from Seaton to Exmouth in a year accounts for 156 tons of crab and 2 tons of lobster; Kingswear and Dartmouth bring in 1,000 tons of crab and 2 tons of lobster worth over £1 million; Salcombe lands at least 800 tons of crab and 2 tons of lobster valued at over £800,000; and Plymouth lands about 300 tons of crab and 5 tons of lobster. Though those figures, which are 1994 estimates, are by no means complete, they do show how valuable and important pot fishing is to local fishermen and how important it is for divers to ensure that good relations continue.

White phosphorus

Divers exploring the wrecks of World War One vintage in this area should be aware that wedges of phosphorus are being found in increasing numbers on these ships. One very good description of them is that they look like "wedges of Danish blue cheese – just like you see in a supermarket". Divers should avoid handling these wedges, which ignite spontaneously when exposed to air. One diver was burned after bringing up a stick of this white waxy substance and putting it in her pocket.

This white phosphorus (commonly known as "White P") was produced for the Allies in the First World War by a Midlands firm, whose output for the whole war was 6083 tons. It was used in a wide variety of munitions: incendiary shells, thermalite and phosphorus grenades, trench mortar bombs, a whole range of shells, 12-pounder aircraft bombs, and 6-inch, 4-inch and 3-inch naval shells, both incendiary and shrapnel.

White phosphorus can look yellow and almost veined like cheese and comes in various shapes. Those seen so far are either wedges or little sticks. But whether it is cheese shaped or looks like a fish finger, divers should treat it all the same way – do not touch it, do not bring it up. It not only burns, it is also deadly poisonous.

Nets

Divers in Devon waters have been trapped in tangle nets and these present a real hazard. Where nets are known to be present on wrecks this has been noted in the text on each site, though the absence of a net warning should not be taken to mean that there are no nets there.

The tangle and gill nets are made of a monofilament material that is extremely difficult to see. These nets are different from those from trawlers, which often become draped on wrecks: it is only in very recent years that nets have been deliberately placed on wrecks.

These tangle nets are often known to fishermen as "wreck nets" and their use has grown swiftly. The nets used are usually about 53m long and have floats at one-metre intervals. The bottom of the net is attached to a foot-rope weighted with galvanised steel rings. The foot-rope is designed to break so that the net can be torn free if totally snagged on the wreck.

In Devon the netting of wrecks is for pollack and ling. Wrecks are fished on Neap tides only and are left netted for 24 hours before being hauled. Nets are usually fished in a fleet of three to five nets. Nets are 50m long by 30 meshes of 127 to 152mm deep, and they are used all the year round.

Divers should not, however, think that the only danger from nets is on wrecks. Nets are often set for bass, which as long as they are set more than 3m below the surface do not conflict with the salmon netting legislation.

Tangle nets are set all the year round too, on sandy beds for sole, turbot and monkfish. These nets are 3.5m high and 110m long, but to ensure plenty of folds of the tangling material they are often set on a head-rope of only 55m. Inshore boats can work between 140 and 180 nets each, but larger vessel can lay down

Fishing boats on the beach at Beer.

30 fleets of ten nets – a total length of about 16 kilometres or 10 miles! These nets are left down for three or four days at a time. Peak catches are made between June and August, though the nets are fished almost all year round.

There is some tangle netting for crawfish, which are a rare sight for divers, in Bigbury Bay. It is the impression of Devon fishing experts that the increased use of wreck nets, a technique that had the most rapid growth of any form of fishing several years ago, has now stabilised, though this will be of little comfort to any diver caught in these invisible killers. Every diver must be on guard at all times – the tangle nets are so portable that even a small dinghy can carry an enormous length.

Worried about this threat to divers' safety, the BSAC carried out special experiments, entangling divers deliberately in this type of monofilament net. Their advice is to carry a small special knife, as the average diver's knife is ineffective. They suggest that a "dinghy" knife with a curved blade and blunt end is probably the most effective type and should be worn on the arm (the blunt end is to avoid stabbing yourself when slashing at the net close to your body). Small shears or scissors are recommended by some divers and a special net knife with replaceable "hook" blades is on the market.

If a diver becomes caught in netting, the BSAC advise partial inflation of the lifejacket making the diver rise inside the net putting it under tension and making it easier to cut. They say that the positive buoyancy will also help to tear the diver free. If your buddy is clear of the netting the best technique is to cut you out still enmeshed and finish the clearance on the surface.

Decompression accidents

The procedure to be followed if these occur is laid down in the booklet *Safe Diving Practices* compiled by the National Diving Committee of the BSAC:

Decompression sickness symptoms vary between those so sudden that immediate air evacuation to a chamber is vital, to those which may not become apparent for some hours. Some of these less dramatic symptoms, which may well be delayed, can be more serious and produce greater disability than the excruciating pain associated with a joint bend. Tingling and numbness are included in this category.

At sea Air embolism or severe Decompression Sickness symptoms, occurring at sea, require rapid transfer of the subject to a recompression chamber, laid flat on their back and, if possible, the administration of 100 per cent oxygen. Being bounced, rapidly, in a small boat is almost certainly going to worsen the symptoms rather than help the situation. RAF Search and Rescue helicopters will almost certainly be involved and the use of VHF radio is essential.

HM Coastguard, although co-ordinating all rescues at sea, are not medically qualified to diagnose diving-related medical disorders and have to seek advice before activating a "Medivac" air evacuation. The Department of Transport and British Telecom International operate a Radio Medical Advisory Service through the BTI Coast Radio Stations.

Diver on the steps of the Princess Pier, Torquay.

If your radio has a "Duplex" operating system, with Coast Radio Station working frequencies, it is advisable to contact the nearest Coast Radio Station where you will be put in direct contact with a doctor, via a telephone link. There is no charge for this service. Once the doctor has given his advice, the Coastguard is in a position to follow up without delay.

If your radio does not have Coast Radio Station frequencies, or has a "Simplex" operating system, it is advisable to contact the Coastguard on Channel 16.

This may take more time, as the Coastguard will have to contact the doctor on your behalf. If the situation is serious enough a "Pan-Pan" call would be necessary.

On land If decompression sickness symptoms arise on land and they are serious, you are advised to dial 999 and ask for an ambulance, explaining the symptoms on the phone. If a helicopter is needed, the doctor will contact the Coastguard (if you are on the coast) who will co-ordinate the rescue. Inland, rapid transport with police escort, can be arranged by the medical emergency services.

With less dramatic symptoms, contact with a GP or hospital casualty department is advisable. Ensure you carry the HMS Vernon phone number – 01705 818888 and ask for the Duty Diving Medical Specialist or Duty Lieutenant Commander – to enable the doctor concerned to get specialist medical advice. Transfer to the nearest available recompression chamber, where necessary, will be arranged.

The Military Remains Act

The Military Remains Act 1986 may in the future affect the wreck diver much more than it does at present. Its main drive is to preserve the sanctity of "war graves" – the wreckage of military ships and aircraft known to contain remains of service personnel.

The wreckage of all military aircraft of any nation is automatically protected, but ships will have to be designated by the Secretary of State and will need a statutory instrument to do so. This means that ships to be named as "war graves" will have to be named and approved by Parliament in the same way that ships to be protected as historic wrecks need a statutory instrument passed through Parliament.

There seems no doubt that those who passed the Act had little idea of the number of ships that could fall under its terms, such as a merchant ship with a Navy gunner aboard – was he among the survivors? – and as a result no ships have yet been named under the Act. This does not mean that ships are not covered by the general thrust of the Act and divers should therefore treat all possible "war graves" with total respect.

However, once these ships have been named, the diver commits an offence only by tampering with, damaging, moving, removing or unearthing remains, or by entering an enclosed interior space in the wreckage. The punishment on conviction of an offence is a fine. Nothing in the Act prevents the wreck diver from visiting the site, examining the exterior or even settling on the wreckage. An offence is only committed if the diver disturbs remains or enters a proper compartment of the wreck. The punishment on conviction is a fine.

This is of course only a brief description, and serious wreck divers should study the Act itself. Your library or H.M. Stationery Office should be able to supply a copy.

The Merchant Shipping Acts

The Receiver of Wreck is responsible for the administration of the Merchant Shipping Act 1894 and the Merchant Shipping Act 1906, which deal with wreck and salvage. It is a legal requirement that all recovered wreck (flotsam, jetsam, derelict or lagan – whether recovered within or outside United Kingdom territorial waters) is reported to the Receiver of Wreck.

Finders who conceal items are liable to prosecution, so any object – even if it appears to have no monetary value – should be declared as soon as possible. The Receiver of Wreck can then make a decision as to the future ownership of the property.

Wreck recovered from within United Kingdom territorial waters that remains unclaimed at the end of a statutory one-year period becomes the property of the Crown, and the Receiver of Wreck is required to dispose of it. This may be through sale at auction, although in many instances the finder will be allowed to keep unclaimed items of wreck in lieu of a salvage award. This, however, is at the discretion of the Receiver of Wreck, and each case is judged on its merits.

For further information contact: The Receiver of Wreck, The Coastguard Agency, Spring Place, 105 Commercial Road, Southampton SO15 1EG (tel. 01703 329474; fax 01703 329477).

The Protection of Wrecks Act

Divers who find a site that might be of historical, archaeological or artistic importance should leave everything as it is and report their findings, in confidence and as soon as possible, to the Department of National Heritage (or its equivalent in Northern Ireland, Scotland or Wales). If appropriate, the wreck can then be designated under the Protection of Wrecks Act 1973, in order to control activities on the site.

Designated sites may only be dived or items recovered if a licence for that purpose has been granted; failure to comply with this is an offence and can result in a fine. All recoveries from designated sites must be reported to the Receiver of Wreck. For further information contact: The Secretariat of the Advisory Committee on Historic Wreck Sites, 3rd Floor, Department of National Heritage, 2/4 Cockspur Street, London SW1Y 5DH (tel. 0171 211 6367/8).

The entrance to the inner harbour at Exmouth.

AREA 1:

Lyme Bay

This area runs from Poker's Pool (02 57 00W) round the coast to Dawlish (50 33 30N) and includes Axmouth, Seaton, Beer, Branscombe, Sidmouth, Budleigh Salterton and Exmouth. All face onto Lyme Bay and are exposed to southerly and south-easterly winds. This is a great trawling area; though generally shallow with the 30m depth line often miles offshore it is largely unexplored by divers. This is partly due to the underwater visibility, which can be cut to nothing by onshore winds. But there are a number of interesting wrecks and many reefs not far offshore. Tidal streams are generally weak, except off headlands and at the entrances to estuaries, where they can be violent. Divers should remember that because of the shallow sea bed there can be a large swell after only a short period of wind.

The area starts at the Devon–Dorset border, which comes to the sea almost opposite Virtle Rock, just to the west of Poker's Pool, a mile west of Lyme Regis. The best approach to the coast here is by the A3052, which continues to Exeter with side roads off it down to the sea. It is best, particularly for divers towing boats in the tourist season, to avoid the narrow streets, traffic lights and sharp turns through Lyme Regis itself, even if it means a longer journey by side roads.

Most of the shoreline to Seaton is steep cliffs, much of it the national nature reserve of Downlands Cliffs, where eight million tons of waterlogged chalk crashed down in the Great Landslide of Christmas Day 1839. Though no lives were lost, the chalk fall at first created an island offshore, but this was later washed away by storms. There is no way down to the sea from the cliff path for divers.

A mile up the river from Seaton is AXMOUTH, a thatched village on the banks of tidal salt flats, much liked by seabirds. Large ships, some of over 100 tons, once used the Axe but the broad estuary and Roman port became a narrow river when part of the eastern hills slid down into it hundreds of years ago. No ship of any size could get up the river now, even if she could negotiate the narrow entrance, because of the road bridge across the river a quarter of a mile from its

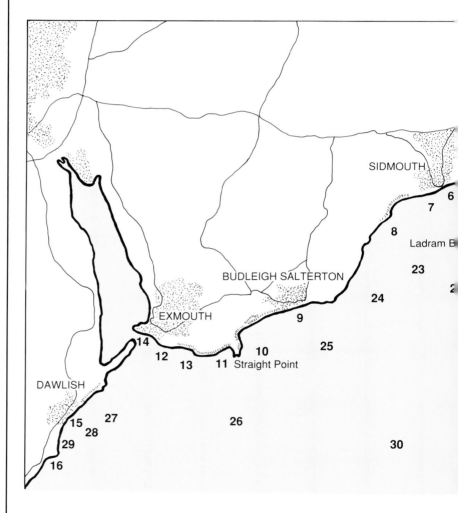

Dive Sites in Area 1: Lyme Bay. This area is covered by Admiralty Charts 3315 (Berry Head to Bill of Portland), 2990 (Exmouth) and 26 (Teignmouth and Tor Bay); Ordnance Survey maps 192 and 193.

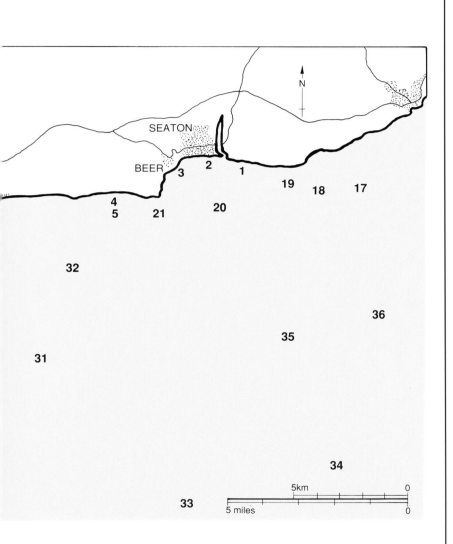

N

SEATON

BEER

3

2

1

19

18

17

4
5

21

20

32

36

35

31

34

33

5km

0

5 miles

0

mouth. The bridge has a vertical clearance of 2m and was one of the first in the world to be built of concrete, in 1877.

The narrow (7m) entrance to the River Axe and its small harbour at the eastern end of Seaton are very tricky, especially during onshore winds, and the sand and shingle banks at the entrance are often on the move. Local knowledge and advice are essential (*see* below). Bigger boats should only attempt the entrance 2¹/₂ hours either side of high water and it is best to come in right on high water. Inflatables can come in any time, but near low tide you must be prepared to get out and pull. Once in the river between the pier and the great shingle bank on the western side, there is a sharp bend to the west into completely sheltered water, though tides can run at 7 to 8 knots at spring tides. The starboard side (heading up the river) is where the channel is deepest.

The small resort of Seaton hosts a holiday camp and a chalet park, and is fronted by a long pebble beach with access down steps. Parking near the seafront is confined to car parks, particularly during the tourist season. Launching is into the river at the resort's eastern end, either from the Axe Yacht Club, via a gate just on the west side of the bridge, or from the premises of Seaton Marine Services opposite. Both launch sites are available for seven days a week.

At the Axe Yacht Club site you should ask at the low club building to get the gate unlocked. There are weekly, weekend and daily charges for boat launching and car and trailer parking. Launching at Seaton Marine Services is down an

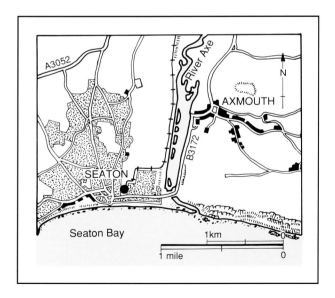

Seaton and the River Axe.

The concrete bridge over the River Axe, north of Seaton.

easy slipway behind the shop and near the compressor (*see* Air Supplies, page 202). This puts your boat in the river on the northern side of the bridge. There is a charge for launching and parking for car and trailer. Ray Kirkland and John Ledger, who own the firm, are professional divers and will be happy to advise you about local diving and boating. Seaton Marine Services is on the right as you come over the bridge from Axmouth.

Most diving is done by boat, but local divers list these shore diving sites as interesting:

1 Finger and Thumb These rocks are under Haven Cliff some 200yds to the east of the River Axe entrance. There are deep gullies running out to sea in 15m. This rough ground can harbour crabs, lobsters and sometimes flatfish in the silted bottoms of the gullies.

2 Esplanade Reef Off the long shingle beach in front of the Esplanade, the diver who is prepared to swim 150yds straight out will find several small reefs with plenty of marine life in 10 to 15m. SMBs must be used.

The small town of BEER shelters from the prevailing westerlies in the lee of Beer Head, the western limit of the chalk cliffs in the South. Access to the beach is down a steep hill, but there is very limited parking close to the beach itself. There are a number of fishing boats – whose owners pot for crabs and lobsters – that are pulled up the beach by motor winches. They are launched stern first with the engine running.

There is said to be the wreck of a Spanish galleon of 1588 at Beer. The crew made the shore, which some say accounts for the dark hair of the "Beer Spaniards" among the residents. A large Spanish anchor was reportedly found in Beer Cove in 1871.

*In Devon there are many good country pubs where you can relax
after a day's diving; this is the Mason's Arms at Branscombe.*

The only launching is across the beach, and only then with the permission of the
Beach Superintendent. It does not take many to cause diver saturation and this
has caused friction in the past. There is one shore diving site:

3 Beer Roads There are some reefs 100yds offshore in 8 to 10m with some
marine life. They are not recommended because of heavy boat traffic. An SMB is
obligatory and close boat cover is essential in summer.

There's a long, long road a-winding down to the sea from the A3052, which is the
only way to get to BRANSCOMBE. The village is not actually on the shore but
straggles down the valley, stopping well short of the beach. Much dates from
the 12th century, complete with an old forge, and is said to be inundated with
badgers at times. The rest of the time it is inundated with "grockles" (which is
what local people call the tourists), but they cope very well and both the Mason's
Arms and the Fountain Head supply good pub food.
   The launch site is right down at the foot of the valley where the tea rooms and
beach shop face the beach, beside a car park. Diver coxswains wishing to launch
at Branscombe must pluck up courage and drive through the ford – despite the "no
entry" signs. Once through, drive to the front of the shop where you pay the
modest parking fee.
   On your left you will find a short concrete ramp. The diving crew will wait until
the tide comes in or face a long haul over the soft shingle to a steep bank of the
same down to the water. The trailer must be towed round the back of the shop,

where there are toilets, down to the car park. It is a neat one-way system to be used only by boat-trailers and delivery vehicles. There are two shore diving sites:

4 Branscombe Mouth This is the official name of the end of the valley where it splays out to the sea. It has a beach of pebbles that runs half a mile east and west and there is good sole and plaice ground just offshore. Since the late 1980s though, flatfish have been in short supply, due, say locals, to dredging work in Exmouth Harbour, which has reduced the visibility.

5 Branscombe Reefs These are very low, not rising more than a metre off the sea bed in 15 to 20m. They run parallel to the beach but are some way out – 500yds for the best of them – and except for the strong diver would be best approached by boat. Good for crabs, and for scallops in sand and mud patches.

Divers' families waiting for the heroes to return can sometimes find chalcedonies among the pebbles here. These transparent crystals are two to three inches long, faceted like diamonds, and are pretty but not valuable.

One of the larger towns in the area, SIDMOUTH is a favourite for retirement as you will see if you walk along the Esplanade on any sunny day – just try to find a seat! Rosy red is the colour of the cliffs on either side of the resort. Their presence means that the only access to the sea is across the main beach. The River Sid is small and percolates through the shingle to the sea.

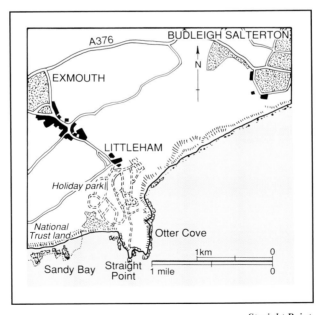

Straight Point.

29

Launching is possible at several points along the Esplanade over the sea wall and across the long pebble beach, but it is easiest at the western end, down Jacob's Ladder steps. At the other end of the beach there is another good access across the beach next to the mouth of the River Sid. No fee is charged for launching, but a permit is needed if you want to leave your boat on the beach overnight or longer. Parking on the Esplanade is difficult, but you might have a better chance in Ham Lane, behind Sidmouth Sailing and Sea Angling Club and close to the beach.

Divers should note that the town's sewer outfall is at the far eastern end of the seafront and is buoyed about a quarter of a mile south-east of the mouth of the Sid. The two shore diving sites are:

6 Sidmouth Reefs These are just offshore and extend seawards under the cliffs. They support a reasonable amount of marine life.

7 Chit Rocks At the western end of the beach, these rocks provide shallow diving without much interest but all the sort of marine life that is found close inshore. Depths up to 10m.

The approach to LADRAM BAY is another run down from the A3052, following signposts to Otterton. From Otterton, the road to Ladram Bay is signposted via Bell Street opposite the Cross Tree Service Station.

Ladram Bay is a small, privately owned, grey shingle beach, behind which is a large caravan site and a complex that includes a café, fish and chip shop, other shops and a pub. There are toilet and shower blocks and laundry facilities. The beach backs onto sheer red sandstone cliffs and is flanked by similar rock stacks. It gets very crowded in summer.

Access for launching is down a steep, narrow road to a concrete slipway. Boats of non-residents can be launched down this by arrangement with the beach operator or the site office. There is a charge, detailed on the noticeboard at the slipway. Parking at the site is good. There is one shore diving site:

8 Ladram Reefs These extend seaward to 16m, but visibility tends to be poor, 3 to 7m, except after long periods of calm. As you swim out, the sea bed of shingle and small stones gives way to sand. There is plenty of fish life, particularly wrasse on the reef and scallops on the sand and mud in deeper water. Shore divers should beware of surf in onshore winds. An Italian barque was wrecked here in a gale in the 1800s. The local fishermen take out fishing parties for mackerel. Divers should ask about diving trips at the fishermen's headquarters, a cave in the cliffs.

The quiet, mainly residential resort of BUDLEIGH SALTERTON has an air of Victorian gentility. Sir John Everett Millais painted his famous picture *The Boyhood of Raleigh* here – Sir Walter Raleigh was born nearby in 1552, and in his day he could run his ships right up to Otterton on the River Otter. It is impossible for any boat now and divers' only interest in the river is that after heavy rainfall it ruins the local visibility.

Opposite: Exmouth and Dawlish Warren.

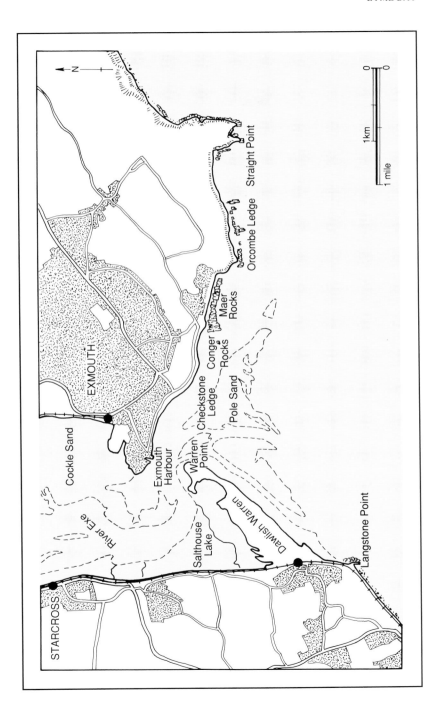

STARCROSS

River Exe

Cockle Sand

EXMOUTH

Exmouth
Harbour

Salthouse
Lake

Warren
Point

Dawlish Warren

Checkstone
Ledge

Conger
Rocks

Pole Sand

Maer
Rocks

Orcombe Ledge

Straight Point

Langstone Point

N

0

1km

1 mile

The town is fronted by a long, pinkish shingle beach that shelves steeply and runs to the west under cliffs called The Floors. There is a large car park with toilets at the eastern end of the town, close to the marshy land and shingle at the mouth of the River Otter. Launching is over the sea defence bank and across the shingle. There are no slipways. Launching at the western end of Marine Parade is not recommended, as the limited parking time is strictly enforced.

9 Eastern End Car Park Dive straight out, which means that you do not have to carry equipment very far. There are three reefs in line behind each other, with the first only 500yds off and consisting of low rocks. The reefs run parallel to the shore and are in line with Straight Point. They are of red sandstone and get bigger the further you go out. The third reef is, for example, nearly 4m high in places in 16m and can be good for shellfish. Some distance out, it is more appropriately a boat dive.

At one time Budleigh Salterton was a good place for crabs and spider crabs, but after fishermen found a French market for the spider crabs they declined rapidly. They are starting to return, however, after over-fishing made professionals abandon this market.

This is a good area for flatfish and scallops. There is more good diving to the east on reefs off Black Head and Brandy Head, but a boat is needed.

A great promontory of red sandstone 2½ miles to the west of Budleigh Salterton, STRAIGHT POINT is notorious for what has been described as the worst-sited rifle range in the world. As Royal Marine recruits fire out to sea right across the eastward approach to the River Exe, its presence is a matter of concern to divers. Rockets are used to stop firing when boats stray into the danger area, and there is a high-speed launch to warn off boats.

Despite this, the area is dominated by the 150-acre Sandy Bay Devon Cliffs Holiday Park, a massive caravan and chalet holiday complex in a superb setting overlooking the Exe Estuary. To the east of Straight Point is Otter Cove and to the west Sandy Bay.

Access to Otter Cove and Littleham Cove, to the east again and favoured by nudists, is by steep paths from the cliff top. Sandy Bay has a car park on top of the cliff. No launching is possible to the east of Straight Point, but at Sandy Bay on the west there is a steep slipway down which inflatables and small boats can be launched. Recovery is by tractor for which there is a charge.

10 Otter Cove Diving is across a pebble beach with the cliffs and rock outcrops on the southern end being part of Straight Point. Two reefs run out in line with the two small headlands of Straight Point for over a mile and are of the same red sandstone as the cliffs. They have peaks of over 5m in places. They eventually peter out into sand. Much of this is boat diving. Divers should keep their eyes open for traces of our ancient past when diving here. For it was here in only 6m that Pete Lord of Exeter Branch sighted an ancient stone anchor on Two Stone Ledge. Unfortunately he lost it in poor visibility.

11 Sandy Bay This is on similar ground to that on the other side of Straight Point, except that entry is across a sandy beach at the eastern end to pick up the reef running seawards. Depths reach 14 to 16m over low-lying rocks. This is a very

*The steep slipway at Sandy Bay Caravan Park is suitable for
inflatables and small boats.*

suitable area for training dives and has a plentiful supply of marine life with
flatfish in the gullies and lobsters and crabs among the rocks.

The cheerful and busy small port and resort of EXMOUTH lies on the eastern side
of the estuary of the River Exe. The river is navigable, by means of the Exeter
Canal, right up to Exeter for ships of up to 350 tons. Exmouth Harbour was used
by Sir Walter Raleigh as his base in the 16th century and today handles about 600
ships a year bringing in timber, cement, fertilisers, oilcake, grain, coal, wood
pulp and pebble and exporting waste paper, milk powder and scrap metal.

The main channel up to the harbour is close to the Exmouth side and is marked
by light-buoys and buoys. These are numbered from seaward with the odds to the
north-east and the evens to the south-west. There is a 10-knot speed limit.

Dive boats, pleasure craft and ferries pick up in Exmouth Harbour, at the west
end of the town near The Point. There is a canal-like entrance about 75m long with
a swing bridge at the far end giving passage to the inner dock and tidal basin. The
tide sets across the entrance, so take care coming in, and remember that the
harbour is used by ships of up to 2000 tons.

A wide road fronts the whole sandy beach of the town. This is the Esplanade,
which becomes Queen's Drive at its eastern end, where it terminates in a
roundabout. Close by there is a concrete launching slipway just before Orcombe
Rocks, with good parking. There is another slipway a short distance to the west.
At the western end of the Esplanade is the Mamhead slipway by Exmouth Pier.

This provides easy launching and there is a small pay car park beside the old café. Other parking in the area is difficult. Close by is the Diver Training School.

Shore diving sites are limited because of the fierce tides that run up and down the river. However, local divers enjoy the following:

12 The River Run This dive should be undertaken on the ebb from Mamhead slipway. Keeping close inshore the diver is carried down as far as the eastern end of Queen's Drive where the sensible diver has a car waiting for him! This 1½-mile run is not for the inexperienced. An SMB is essential. Divers see plaice, brill, turbot, thornbacks and congers on the run.

13 Orcombe Point From the end of Queen's Drive to the east around Orcombe Rocks there are flat rocks all the way to Sandy Bay. Tidal streams may make it impossible to return to the starting point, so boat cover is advisable. Divers see flatfish on this dive, and there are crabs and some scallops.

14 Mamhead This is a dive near the dock and must not be undertaken without checking first with the Harbour Master. Dive by the slipway to avoid shipping. There used to be a gun emplacement and a pier here. Judging by the number of discarded rings found by divers, it was the place to throw away the ring of a faithless fiancé. There have been finds of old coins and there is plenty of small marine life. The recommended technique is to go in at high water by walking down the slipway, swim straight across to a pole sticking up from the water and descend by that. There is nearly an hour of slack to use.

View of Dawlish, with Boat Cove in the foreground.

Across the estuary of the River Exe from Exmouth is DAWLISH WARREN, just a mile by passenger ferry from Exmouth to Starcross, but 18 miles by road as you have to go via Exeter to cross the river. Dawlish Warren is a 500-acre nature reserve, but there are chalets and amusement arcades at the landward end of the sand dunes. Do not believe the graphic local stories about a whole community living on the Warren who were swept away in a giant storm in the 1920s. In fact, there was no loss of life when the holiday homes were removed as part of coastal defence works in World War Two!

Just off the Warren is Pole Sands, blocking the entrance to the estuary from the west. Diver coxswains should use the normal approach to Exmouth from the east and should not be tempted to find a way through Pole Sands. There is a way through called the "Western Way", which can be used at high water – in the past some large sailing ships used to come in this way. It needs local knowledge and if you think it is easy just take a look at the wreck of the small steamer inside the estuary at 50 36 51N; 03 26 28W, which shows at low water. This is the *South Coaster*, which tried to take a short cut across Pole Sands on 13 December, 1943. Admiralty tugs finally got her off, but beached her where she is today.

Dawlish itself boasts four miles of red sand. Access is somewhat marred by having to go under the main railway line to the west, running right along the Dawlish seafront. Launching is possible at Boat Cove at the southern end of Dawlish. This is where fishing boats are pulled up under the high cliffs. It is exposed to onshore winds. An alternative is the Station Slipway, probably the best place for the visitor to launch inflatables and small boats. It is a public slipway right by the railway station.

15 Dawlish Beach A long swim in shallow water over an uninteresting sand bottom with only the occasional flatfish to be seen.

16 Smugglers Cove Approach by a path to this tiny cove south of Dawlish near the Parson and Clerk Rocks, whose weird shapes are said to depict a parson thundering out his sermon over the clerk. Here you walk beneath the railway line – or at high water swim under it. There are multiple arches and a cave you can swim through. A pleasant dive around rocks with flatfish common on the sea bed outside them.

Boat diving sites

Lyme Bay has mostly a flat bottom of sand and shingle with rocky outcrops. To the west are larger areas of mud or mud–sand mixture, particularly off the estuaries of the Exe and Teign. Tidal streams are weak, so silt from the rivers has dispersed and settled over a wide area. It is easily disturbed and slow to clear. This affects wreck diving in the area and, if the first pair are careless, only they get a decent dive!

Close inshore there are numerous reefs where drift diving can be rewarding. The best are listed here.

17 Hunter Widely spread around 50 42 00N; 02 59 00W are the pieces of an RAF Hunter T.7 jet aircraft, which was working for the Ministry of Technology at Farnborough. On 15 July, 1968, the Hunter was very high to the west of Lyme Regis when something went wrong. The pilot ejected safely and the aircraft crashed into the sea in Charton Bay. The wreckage is close inshore in an area of strong tides. Local fishermen have been told by the Ministry that they do not want any pieces that are brought up in nets.

18 Berar This Italian barque of 954 tons from Genoa went ashore at 10.25am on 7 October, 1896, near Culverhole Point to the east of Seaton in thick fog. The crew of 16 were all saved, but the barque was in a hopeless position and broke in two the next day. Much of her cargo of timber floated onto local beaches. The wreck and the rest of the cargo was sold by auction on 21 October.

The *Berar* was located by divers in 1972, who reported the remains of a steel sailing vessel with iron ore ballast just 100yds offshore at 50 41 52N; 03 00 12W. In 1985 the stern was still visible with a small propeller shaft nearby, but this must belong to the *Fairway*.

19 Fairway A British MFV, the 100-foot-long *Fairway* broke down off Beer Head on 13 December, 1978, and reported taking water. She later went aground at Culverhole Point and was badly holed. She is at 50 41 51N; 03 01 10W and much broken up.

20 Nine Fathom Rock This patch of rough ground lies about 1½ miles from the mouth of the River Axe. Bearings are Beer Head due west with the eastern end of the road along Seaton seafront due north. Depths are up to 14m.

21 Beer Head This is a good site for a second dive and for working the gullies and rough under the cliffs, and good ground for shellfish and flatfish.

WARNING Do not dive more than 100yds off Beer Head. Further out at 150yds a strong tide sweeps around the point and is at times quite irresistible.

22 Sidmouth Grounds These good flatfish grounds cover a quite extensive area about three miles offshore. Transit bearings are Bulverton Hill in line with the mouth of the River Sid; Haven Cliff at Axmouth just open of Beer Head; 2½ miles offshore with solitary white house at Weston Mouth straight in and out.

23 Ladram Bay Dive about three miles offshore. Transit bearings are Jacob's Ladder at Sidmouth in line with the inland end of Core Hill behind the town; Budleigh Salterton just appearing beyond Otterton Point. A drift dive to the west covers a low-lying reef with much marine life.

24 Brandy Head Straight off the head, look for 15m depth where a low reef runs parallel to the shore.

25 Otterton Three reefs run parallel to the shore here. The first is only 500yds off, the second runs in a line with Straight Point and the third is a mile out in 15m. Here the red sandstone rises some 4m off the sea bed – good for shellfish.

26 Straight Point Two reefs run out from the two small headlands. They run with breaks for about 1¹/₂ miles and are full of concealed holes where there are faults in the sandstone. There are peaks up to 5m. Do not dive too close in or you will find yourself near the sewer discharge; too far and you will be on a sand plain. Beware of the rifle range on Straight Point.

27 Dawlish Rock Wreck Though this rock usually has at least 2m over it, it was the scene of a wreck in the 19th century judging by the wooden wreckage and pottery in the mud around it. One of the most interesting finds is a soldier's boot-blacking pot – a predecessor of today's boot polish tins! Dawlish Rock is half a mile straight off the Coastguard lookout station in the town. Another way of finding it is to go 800yds east of the groyne with the beacon on it at the northern end of the town.

28 Obstruction This is a sewage diffuser – a sort of spray affair – at 50 34 45N; 03 26 44W; not really the sort of thing you want to find diving, even at 6m, though it is not connected!

29 Mysterytu At 50 34 00N; 03 28 00W this is the grave of a 29ft yacht that went aground on 3 October, 1976. The crew of two abandoned her and were picked up off Orcombe Rocks almost inside the mouth of the River Exe. The wreck is now very broken in 5m.

30 The Woodberries At 50 33 48N; 03 15 48W, you will not miss it because of the pots. In fact, on some days it is difficult to dive here without diving near pots. Named after one of the fishermen's marks using the village of Woodbury behind Budleigh Salterton, the Woodberries are two areas of raised ground at 19m with the smaller slightly lower patch to the south. Outside the ground drops down to 25m.

A drift across this ground should produce shellfish, particularly crabs, with scallops, sole and plaice in the sand and mud patches in the rough ground, which does not rise much off the sea bed although there are some pinnacles. The scallops survive here because much of the area is too rough for trawling.

31 The Sidmouth Submarine There are persistent stories among fishermen of a submarine sunk between Sidmouth and Beer Head, and it is possible that a German submarine could have been lost in this area in either of the World Wars. However, it seems almost impossible to pin down any hard facts about this submarine except for the two imaginary lines out to sea from Sidmouth and Beer Head, beyond which the submarine stories do not pass. The tales are very similar to those circulating in Dartmouth (Site **145**).

32 Christmas The wreck of this MFV is at 50 39 21N; 03 09 28W and parts of her stand 2m proud of the sandy sea bed at 23m. She was 57ft long with a beam of 18ft, but is now very broken. Local trawlers seem to make a speciality of towing into her. Quite recently the engine, shaft, propeller and all the mechanical parts were trawled out of her and divers had to cut the gear clear. As if that was not enough, another trawler fouled the bow section and the wheelhouse and towed them in the opposite direction. She sank while under tow on 9 June, 1981. The wreck is used as a second dive by Seaton boats.

33 Radaas At 50 34 13N; 03 04 50W. A victim of Oberleutnant Howaldt and *UB-40*, the *Radaas* was torpedoed on 21 September, 1917, when laden with 3400 tons of coal from the Tyne for Bordeaux. This 2524-ton Danish steamer, owned by Dampskib Selsk Primula, was built in 1890 by J. Readhead and Company. She was just over 290ft long with a beam of 40ft and was driven by 234hp engines. The torpedo struck her in the port side between No. 1 hold and the forecastle, some six feet below the waterline. One man was killed. She now lies north-north-east to south-south-west on a sandy sea bed at 30m. She is heavily broken with the boiler the highest point at 21m at the west end of the area of debris, which is now some 230ft long by 80ft wide. There is a 1m scour around the boiler.

WARNING Due to the amount of marine life around her, the *Radaas* is often heavily netted and divers should take special care when diving her. The *Radaas* is often called "Harold's wreck" by the locals in honour of the man who trawled into her twice in one week!

34 Marguerite At 50 36 06N; 02 58 39W and sometimes called "Benny's wreck" by local fishermen, the *Marguerite*, a 1544-ton French ship, was torpedoed by Oberleutnant Howaldt in *UB-40* during his mission from Zeebrugge from 25 June to 3 July, 1917. He torpedoed the *Marguerite* from a hull-down periscope position on 28 June when she was travelling from Rouen to Swansea in ballast. The torpedo hit her in No. 4 hold, badly damaging her aft. Howaldt had been told to confine his main activity to the area between Portland and Dartmouth and later the same day hit the 2099-ton *Northfield* (which managed to reach Dartmouth safely). The crew of the *Marguerite* were all picked up and landed later at Falmouth.

The *Marguerite*, owned by F. Bouet, had been built in 1912 by Osbourne, Graham and Company. She was 260ft long with a beam of 37ft and 189hp triple-expansion steam engines. The wreck is very flattened with her bows to the west on a sea bed of fine sand on top of chalk. Her highest point is 7.6m off the sea bed, but there has been a dramatic deterioration in her condition. When she was dived in 1972 she was described as almost intact with her bridge still standing aft. Now she is widely scattered and the only thing showing above the sea bed are steel plates. There is much shellfish life in and around her.

35 Landing Craft Lying with her bows partly blown off is this American landing craft at 50 38 05N; 03 02 57W. She is intact except for the bow damage, where a shell hole can still be seen, and is 36ft long with a beam of 15ft. She was powered by twin straight-eight engines – one of the engine boxes is off and divers can see all of it. There is no scour and she lies south-south-east to north-north-west in 24m with the highest part 4m proud of the sea bed. Divers should keep their eyes open for the number C23569 anywhere on her. If this is found it would prove that she was one of the landing craft carried by the American Navy's *LCT 289* and which, when damaged, was abandoned during a battle with E-boats on 28 April, 1944.

The American tank landing ship LST 507 (see Site 35).

In the darkness of the early hours the E-boats took an American convoy of tank landing ships by surprise, sank two of them and damaged others. By dawn the Americans had lost 638 men. They were practising for the Normandy Invasion at the time and Slapton Sands was standing in for Utah Beach. By contrast, on 6 June, 1944, when the Americans stormed ashore on Utah for real, 12 men were killed and 100 wounded.

Though outside the boundaries of this guide, the wrecks of the two tank landing craft *LST 531* and *LST 507* – sunk by E-boats on 28 April, 1944 – have been found by divers. *LST 531* is in two parts. Her bow is at 50 27 07N; 02 43 35W in 50m and is well broken with her bow door or ramp lying open and out to the west. About 250yds away, at 50 27 04N; 02 43 30W, is the stern, which is intact and 6m proud, but completely upside down and showing her two long skeg keels and the guards around her two four-bladed propellers, each about three feet in diameter. At the stern, the propeller and stern of an infantry landing craft poke out from under the bulwarks of the mother ship, which is crushing it into the sandy sea bed. *LST 507* is some distance away at 50 26 03N; 02 44 42W, possibly because she drifted for some time before sinking. In fact, her bow was still just showing some hours after the American convoy was attacked and a Royal Navy destroyer finished her off with gunfire. She is in 51m and lies mostly on her side with her stern to the north-west. She is well broken and though her hull plating has holes in it, most is still sound. Her stern is the most intact part, as she was torpedoed in the starboard side towards the bow.

36 Tina Anne Divers using old reference sources can stop looking for this 26ft fishing boat at 50 38 24N; 02 57 24W. She has been raised intact with lifting bags by Seaton Marine Services.

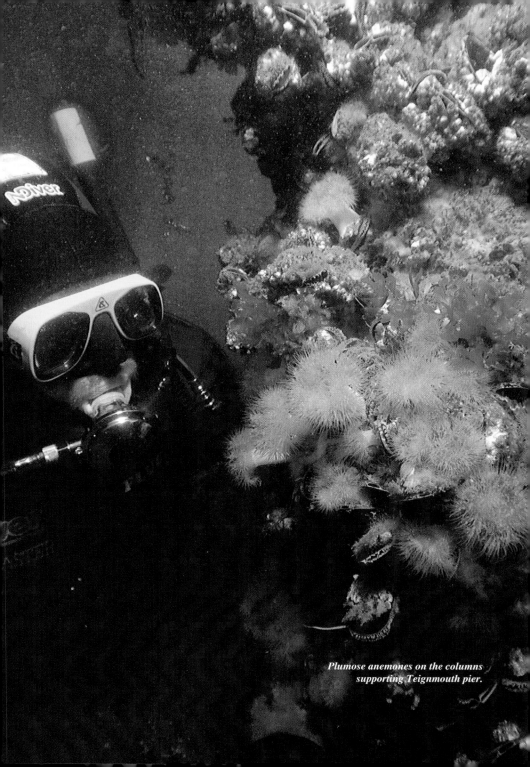

*Plumose anemones on the columns
supporting Teignmouth pier.*

AREA 2:

Babbacombe Bay

This area starts just south of the Parson and Clerk Rocks at 50 33 30N and takes in Teignmouth, Shaldon, Maidencombe, Watcombe, Oddicombe, Babbacombe and Anstey's Cove; it ends at Black Head (50 28 00N). Access to the sea is difficult along much of this stretch, with huge cliffs dominating the scenery. Although there are a number of very interesting wrecks offshore, most of the boat traffic visits them from Exmouth and Brixham.

A late developer in the tourist and shipping trade, TEIGNMOUTH has evidence of very early shipwrecks and the town dates back to Saxon times. The harbour is tucked into the land and faces up the River Teign. This is just as well, for in south and south-east gales the port is almost inaccessible. Some 500 ships a year use the harbour for the import of timber and the export of clay, and some of these are over 200ft. There is a fishing fleet. The harbour entrance is tricky to use, with shifting sand bars and strong tidal streams. Hundreds of small boat moorings are on the Salty, a hard bank of gravel that dries and juts out from Shaldon on the south side of the river. The River Teign is pronounced "Teen" and Teignmouth is pronounced "Tinmouth".

There is a large car park at The Point at the southern end of the promenade and it is possible to launch into the estuary. The launch is made across the landward beach as the deep channel curls round behind the town before extending four miles west to Newton Abbot. There is also a slipway at Polly Steps at the western end of Western Quay, which launches into the harbour and is usable at all states of the tide. There is adequate car parking.

The Teignmouth Harbour Master can be contacted at his office at New Quay Road, Teignmouth (tel. 01626 773165). Diving within the harbour limits is not allowed without his permission.

Shore diving is easy from the long promenade and pier, which allows access to a coarse sand beach, but there is little of interest close inshore except for flounders and the occasional plaice. However, in 1977 13-year-old Simon Burton

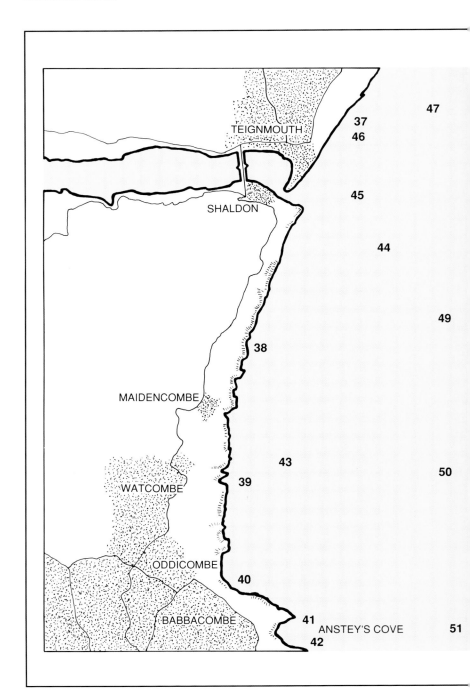

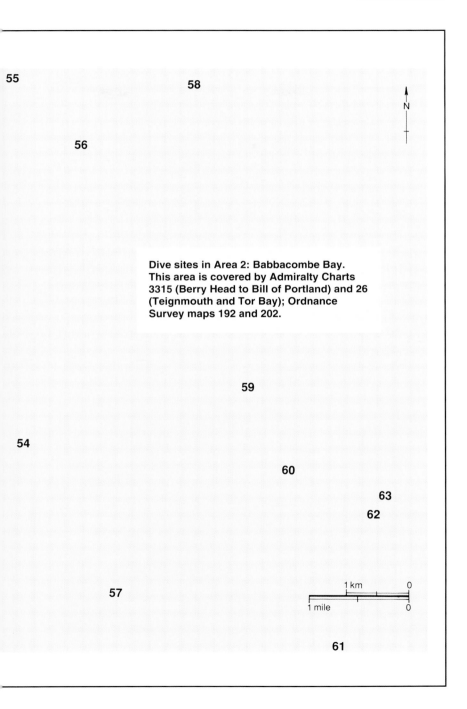

55

58

56

N

Dive sites in Area 2: Babbacombe Bay.
This area is covered by Admiralty Charts
3315 (Berry Head to Bill of Portland) and 26
(Teignmouth and Tor Bay); Ordnance
Survey maps 192 and 202.

59

54

60

63

62

57

1 km   0

1 mile   0

61

was snorkelling 50yds off the beach when he saw something almost buried in the sand – a large bronze cannon that led to the discovery of the following site.

37 The Church Rocks Historic Wreck This is an area off the Teignmouth foreshore in which you must not dive as it is designated under a Protection of Wrecks Order made in August 1977. You can see the notice of this at the northern end of the promenade.

The wreck site is buoyed off the northern groyne and is defined by the Order as "the sea bed between the four points grid reference 9465 7330, 9480 7330, 9465 7312 and 9480 7312 on the National Grid Plan SX 9473-9573. Scale 1:2500."

Since Simon Burton's first discovery the site has yielded a number of bronze cannon, swivel guns, pewter, anchors, cannonballs and copper cooking pots, but nothing that will positively identify her. Some seals found recently suggest that the wreck might be that of a Venetian ship of the 16th century.

The small town of SHALDON on the south side of the river is approached from Teignmouth by a long bridge. The town shelters behind the headland called The Ness, a red rock promontory that guards the river entrance. Although its rocky outcrops extend seaward underwater and The Ness looks as though it would give good diving, heavy boat traffic, strong tides and poor visibility make it not worth while.

Below: The pier at Teignmouth is a major tourist attraction, but also gives good access for divers.

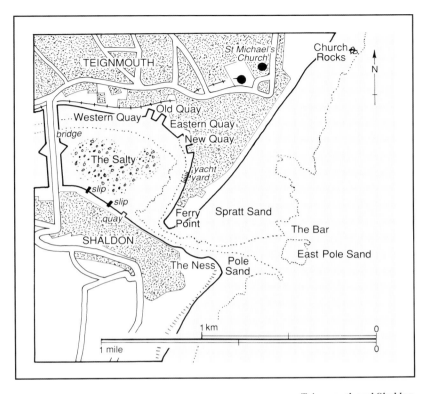

Teignmouth and Shaldon.

There is undoubtedly a very old wreck under the cliffs near MACKEREL COVE, as a shore fisherman recently found that he was standing on an ancient swivel gun as he cast his line from the beach!

The small village of MAIDENCOMBE off the A379 is reached by turning off the main road at Maidencombe Cross and going down Steep or Brim Hill to the village, where there is a small car park with toilets.

38 Maidencombe Beach The only way to reach this is to lug your gear down a path and then take a long, winding flight of steps to the small beach of coarse reddish sand. The beach is backed by a sheer 100ft cliff. Before tackling this marathon – many divers prefer to take just snorkelling gear – you must get permission, as the land is private. The flat rock slabs that flank the beach make good sunbathing spots and underwater offer interesting gullies to a sandy bottom at 7m. Small pollack, wrasse and mullet may be seen. The occasional large bass visits the small reefs just off the beach and flounders can be seen on the sand. The beach all but covers at high water.

A mile further along the A379 from Maidencombe towards Torquay is the turning for WATCOMBE BEACH. This narrow lane leading down to a car park is just inside the built-up area of Torquay.

39 Watcombe Beach Diving means a 350-yard walk to the beach, which has a café and toilets. The beach is similar to Maidencombe, with rocks at each end. Further out is sand on which the occasional plaice or flounder can be found in about 8m. Divers here suspect the presence of a wreck further out as they find pottery fragments in great quantities, both in the sand and on the beach. The beach is nearly covered at high water.

The winding and very steep hill to ODDICOMBE can be used only for loading and unloading. There is a cliff railway. This very popular beach of white rounded stones has concrete walkways along the high tide mark. Pedalos and speedboats are available for hire and a 5-knot speed limit is in force.

40 Petit Tor Point This rocky outcrop at the northern end of the beach offers safe and interesting snorkel-depth diving in the gullies. The kelp covered rocks provide cover for small pollack, wrasse and spider crabs. Plaice are a rare sight on the sand outside the rocks.

Rocks separate BABBACOMBE beach from Oddicombe. It is accessible from the southern end of Babbacombe Downs via another very steep, winding road, which leads to a small car park with toilets and a pub.

41 Long Quarry Point Avoid the small stone jetty to the right-hand end of the beach, which is very popular with anglers. Prospects to the south and under the steep cliffs of Long Quarry Point are much better and there is a good deal for the diver and snorkeller to see here in fairly shallow water. Marine life includes school mullet and black bream.
   A council by-law forbids the launching of boats from Babbacombe beach without the consent of the beach inspector. Those operating boats there have special beach rights. There is a five-knot speed limit.

There is a signposted turn for ANSTEY'S COVE from Babbacombe Road alongside the five-star Palace Hotel, and it leads to a large car park. Then it is 400yds by path to the beach, which has toilets and a café. This is the last accessible beach before Hope's Nose, the northern promontory of Tor Bay that signals the end of Babbacombe Bay.

42 The Three Brothers These rocks are at the southern end of Anstey's Cove, from which rocky outcrops lead to a sandy bottom at 7m. Similar outcrops are to be found at the other end of the beach. Pollack, wrasse and spider crabs in season are to be found in the gullies.

Boat diving sites

Most of the inshore boat diving sites at the foot of the giant red cliffs must be listed as unexplored. It seems likely that many more wrecks will be found in these waters, of ships that died in the night, unknown and unrecorded except for fragments of wreckage cast up in accessible coves elsewhere along the coastline. Further out are many wrecks, most of them victims of U-boats in World War One.

43 Watcombe Head Caves "Big enough to drive double-decker buses in" is one diver's description of these giant underwater caves at 15m just to the north of Watcombe Head. Such caves are perhaps not so surprising – not far away on land is Kent's Cavern, which was inhabited in prehistoric times. Divers should keep their eyes open for flint implements.

44 Junkers Ju 88 This World War Two German bomber is believed to have been shot down by ground fire after it bombed the gas works in Exeter in 1940.

Watcombe beach (Site 39), a mile south of Maidencombe.

There are no details of what happened to the crew of four, but the remains of their radial-engined aircraft lie at 50 31 20N; 03 27 38W.

Not all of the aircraft, which had a wing span of 60ft and a length of 47ft, is there. One engine has been raised by an aircraft recovery group. The other engine is untouched as it is said to have a 1000lb bomb under it! This is quite possible as the Ju 88 carried a 2000lb bomb load on external bomb racks between the engines and the fuselage. Originally charted as a "foul" and at one time known locally as "the stone boat", there is some fuselage left at 19m, standing 1m proud.

45 Unknown obstruction Further out to sea and south of the old boiler (Site **46**) at 50 32 23N; 03 28 40W is another obstruction in 9m of water. This one stands 3m proud; diving information is needed.

46 Boiler The boiler of an old wreck is at 50 32 36N; 03 29 13W in the approaches to Teignmouth, sticking up 30cm in the 1m of water over the sea bed. It is charted as an obstruction.

47 Galicia This 5922-ton British ship was built of steel by Wigham Richardson and Company of Newcastle in 1901, with nothing but the finest materials going into her. Just over 400ft long with a beam of 50ft, this three-decker with bronze twin screws was owned by the Pacific Steam Navigation Company of Liverpool. She seems to have had a great attraction for mines. On 31 July, 1915, when heading for Liverpool with general cargo, she struck a mine two miles from the North Goodwins Lightship. Though her forepeak and forehold were full of water the crew managed to beach her at Deal and she was later repaired.

The second time she struck a mine – on 12 May, 1917 – she was not so lucky. She was going from London to Valparaiso with a cargo of cloth and cement, plus some ammunition to be delivered to Jamaica on the way, when she hit a mine laid by one of the German UC class submarines (probably *UC-17*) off Teignmouth. Though described once again as beached, with the crew landed safely at Torquay, there was no second chance for her this time, and she was soon completely underwater. In 1923 she was dispersed to 12m and in 1950 was reported clear to 11.5m. She was much salvaged between the wars – both bronze propellers are gone, and so are most of the 12- and 14-pound shells she was carrying in her bow hold.

She is now at 50 33 16N; 03 26 17W on a sandy sea bed at 20m and is very broken. The wreck site of this big ship spreads over a large area, in which rolls of cloth and barrels of solid cement are to be found. The highest point is 15m from the surface. It is an interesting rummage dive and Maurice Webb, diver skipper of the *Grace* of Exmouth, once put his grapnel right through a fine brass porthole. Other brass continues to be found. There are many congers on her.

Transit marks are shown in the diagram opposite.

48 The Algiers Similar to the Exeters (Site **49**) but muddier, these reefs have the same marine life. Some fishermen regard them all as the same ground. They are probably named after a fisherman of long ago, but might be named after a wreck of ancient times. They are slightly shallower on average than the Exeters at 20m, and around a chart position of 50 33 24N; 03 22 54W. On the eastern

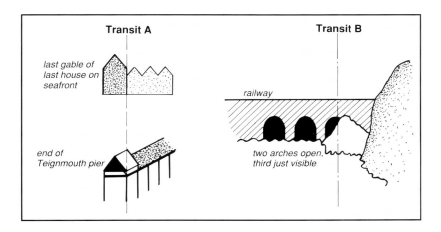

Transit marks for the Galicia (Site 47).

edge of this ground divers found the Merlin engine of a Spitfire fighter, but no sign of the fuselage.

49 The Exeters A large area of reefs covering two or three miles. There are gullies, dips, plateaux and pinnacles. Most rock formations stand 2m proud off rough ground and it is all good diving with some areas of large pebbles, some with sand and mud floors to large gullies. There are sea-fans and rose-coral, and it is a great place for crabs and lobsters. The area is always heavily potted. The average depth is 24m.

Because much of the area cannot be trawled the diver will find quite large collections of scallops in the muddy patches as well as skate, dogfish, dabs, plaice, sole and conger. The Exeters, in the area around 50 31 00N; 03 22 54W are sandier than the Algiers (Site **48**).

50 Bretagne On 10 August, 1918, the *Bretagne*, a schooner-rigged single-screw steel steamer of 1439 tons, had been in thick fog since dawn. In her holds were 1888 tons of coal from Barry for Rouen and the ship was moving slowly eastward in the swept mine-free channel. At 10.30am out of the fog came a French steamer, the *Renée Marthe*, which struck the *Bretagne* such a blow on her starboard side near the stern that the French steamer's bows crumpled. Even so, the *Bretagne* was more severely damaged − her steering gear was jammed, her stern was stove in and she was taking water fast.

Fortunately the fog thinned and a fishing trawler was able to come alongside the *Bretagne*, take off most of the crew and take her in tow. The *Renée Marthe* managed to reach Dartmouth safely, despite her bow damage. Three men were left on the *Bretagne*: the captain, J.W. Johannesson, first mate Harry Watterson and Dick Pym, one of two Naval gunners aboard, in charge of the 12-pounder stern gun. They struggled to free the steering gear to make towing easier, but had to abandon ship when the water lapped over the deck. But the first mate decided to get his money from his cabin. As he went below, a wave slammed the outer door shut and the *Bretagne* nose-dived to the bottom with him still inside.

The *Bretagne* is now owned by Bristol Aerospace BSAC branch divers. She is at 50 29 27N; 03 22 37W and is upright on an even keel, 232ft long with a beam of 35ft. She has a 106hp engine, but could put up 2000 square feet of sail when required. Registered in Norway, she was requisitioned in 1916 by the Ministry of War Transport, who fitted the gun to her stern. This gun and the bell have since been raised by Bristol Aerospace divers.

The ship has two or three feet of silt inside, so watch out for stirred-up mud. She is a small ship but when visibility is good – and it can be superb – she is a first class dive. There are handrails still in position around the deck. In places she is rusted through and the holes have razor-sharp edges. The best dive time is slack water, but the wreck can be dived at most states of the tide. Bristol divers report fishing line on the wreck – she is often visited by large parties of anglers. They warn too, of wedges of phosphorus found amidships. The depth to her deck is 18m and it is 25m to the shingle sea bed. Her bow points to south-west.

The Polly Steps slipway at Teignmouth.

51 Perrone Built in 1882 in Sunderland for the Compagnie Française Marine et Commerce of Paris as a cable-layer, this 3342-ton steamer was 320ft long with a beam of 42ft. She was heading for Barry Road from Le Havre in ballast on 1 September, 1917, when she was torpedoed by U-boat ace Kapitänleutnant Viebeg of the Flanders Flotilla in *UC-65*. All 36 crew managed to take to the boats before she went down.

The *Perrone* is now at 50 28 14N; 03 22 47W, 8m proud of a 29m sea bed. Diving reports describe her stern section as lying alongside her starboard side, which makes the wreck difficult to take in on a single dive. She is badly broken elsewhere, particularly amidships. A small piece of her is now 80m south-west of the main wreckage and another piece lies just to the north of the bows. Local divers know her as the "rocks-in-one" wreck because one bearing for her lines up the Ore Stone with Thatcher Rock.

52 Marie des Isles This is a British trawler despite the French name – she was registered in Guernsey. At 50 28 04N; 03 16 38W, she sank after taking in water while under tow by the MFV *Big Cat* on 14 November, 1980. The crew were taken off by the Torbay lifeboat.

She lies north-east to south-west, is 64ft long and looks as if she had her trawl out at the time of sinking, even though she is festooned with other nets. She shows an echo, which suggests that she is over 10m high off the sea bed, but experienced skippers say that this echo is probably from the top of the nets and the buoys on them. Certainly it is 36m to the sea bed on which the blue-hulled *Marie* rests.

53 Lord Stewart An armed merchantman of 1445 tons, the *Lord Stewart* is completely upright on the sea bed and you can see the damage on the starboard where Oberleutnant Bieber's torpedo from *UB-104* struck her amidships on 16 September, 1918. The *Lord Stewart* was the U-boat captain's last kill. Going back home by the round-Britain route to avoid the dense defences of the Dover Straits, Bieber ran into the mines of the Northern Barrage near the Orkneys and was lost with his boat.

The *Lord Stewart* was on her way from Cherbourg for the Barry Roads in ballast at the time of her sinking and the torpedo explosion killed her crew outright. The 248ft ship is at 50 29 35N; 03 16 55W. She lies east–west at 32m and stands 9m proud. Her propeller is iron and there was a small gun on the stern. Locally known as the "19" because she was charted as 19 fathoms, the wreck is owned by a syndicate headed by Ken Breeze of the dive-boat *Paulanda*.

WARNING Wedges of phosphorus have been found on this ship. They will ignite when exposed to air (*see* page 17).

54 Gefion There is some argument over whether this ship was Norwegian or British, but none at all over what happened to her. On 25 October, 1917, Oberleutnant Howaldt in *UB-40* torpedoed her and hit her slightly more towards the bow than amidships. She is now at 50 30 04N; 03 15 12W. The 1123-ton steamer was built in Bergen in 1914 and was sailing from Penarth to Rouen. The torpedo killed the master and a seaman and in their wartime confidential log Lloyds claimed her as British.

The wreck belongs to Exedive, BSAC 1049, and has been positively identified by her engine number. Exedive do not mind you diving her, but please take nothing. She lies almost due east–west with her bows to the east. The depth to the sea bed is 32m and it is 25m to the highest point of the wreckage. The wreck is "dog-legged", and broken amidships. The bow lies on its port side and in the main part of the wreckage one side has collapsed outward and the other inward. As a result the engines are all visible and so are the boilers. She cost Exedive £101 in the late 1970s.

55 Tarthouse Reef Probably named after a fisherman, this is a low reef in a fold of the 20m line on the chart. It provides good shellfish country and the many sand and mud patches in the gullies are good for scallops. In the area around 50 33 20N; 03 16 46W.

56 Boma A 2694-ton British ship heading for St Helens on the Isle of Wight from Belfast with a cargo of potatoes, hay and straw, the *Boma* was torpedoed by Kapitänleutnant Viebeg in *UB-80* on 11 June, 1918. The crew took to the boats and landed at Torquay. The *Boma* sank to a hard fine sand sea bed at 32m. Her bows still point to the north-east and are intact, but her 312ft hull is badly broken.

Salvage took place in 1970. The *Boma* has still some portholes on her, probably because the visibility on her is usually poor! Divers can enter some sections, which appear solid, but should take great care. The wreck is rated a good dive by local divers, and is at 50 32 09N; 03 14 14W. There is a 1m scour and the highest point, at the south-west end of the wreckage, is at 19m.

57 City of Swansea At 50 28 50N; 03 11 21W, this 1375-ton British steamer was carrying a cargo of coal from the Tyne to Boucau, when Oberleutnant Howaldt in *UB-40* sank her with a bow shot while submerged to periscope depth on 24 September, 1917, some 15 miles east-north-east of Berry Head. Two of her crew died in the explosion.

The 260ft ship, with a beam of 35ft, lies in 39m of water with her highest point her starboard side at 29m. She is lying on her port side and her stern section is almost completely broken away from the main part of the wreck, which lies with the bows to the south-east. One mast lies straight out from the wreck across the sea bed and there is a 2m scour. Her cargo of 1682 tons of coal has spilled out in places. This earned her the local name of "the coal boat". Unfortunately this large wreck is plagued by poor visibility and local divers go down to her prepared to abort when they encounter the nil-visibility that sometimes prevails.

58 Ursa This unarmed schooner-rigged 1740-ton Swedish steamer was loaded with 2432 tons of coal and travelling from Cardiff towards Rouen when she was torpedoed in No. 1 hold at 5.15am on 17 September, 1918, at 50 33 10N; 03 07 50W. She started to sink by the bow almost immediately and in ten minutes was gone. The second mate was made to board the submarine and answer questions about his ship, but was later allowed to return to his boat. Both boats with all 19 crew reached the shore at Beer at 8.30 am. Today she lies in a depth of 30m and is fairly intact.

59 The Corvette This wreck is said to be outside the *Radaas* (Site **33**) and highly dangerous as she was an ammunition ship and is full of mines, depth charges and shells of all kinds. The ship was discovered by accident in 1979; one position given for her is 50 30 30N; 03 04 30W, but other positions put her much closer to the *Radaas*.

60 Crane and hoses This site is charted as "foul" at 50 30 12N; 03 02 06W in 38m is the result of an accident between two oil tankers. On 4 December, 1982, one tanker, too heavily laden for the shallow run up the Channel, was transferring part of her cargo to another smaller vessel when the two pulled apart. Over the side went a crane and the hoses parted, falling into the water and sinking swiftly. The tankers were the *Naticina* and the *Berge Duke*.

61 W.H. Dwyer This 1770-ton Canadian steamer was heading down Channel, from Rouen for Newport in ballast on August, 26, 1917, when she met Oberleutnant Umberger in *UB-38* after he sank the *Claverley* off Plymouth (Site **349**). It is doubtful that Umberger saw more than an outline of his victim; in his log he notes the sinking as being in the pitch dark of early morning. The full crew of the *W.H. Dwyer* took to the boats safely. She was 250ft long with a beam of 43ft and sank swiftly, reaching the sandy sea bed at 45m.

Today she is at 50 28 09N; 03 00 35W and stands 10m proud. Her bows are badly damaged – "blown apart" is one description – but the hull and stern are fairly intact with the galley on the starboard side aft. What is left of her bows faces to the south, but the bow section has almost torn free from the main section and is to the east of the wreck. It has a scour of over 1m beside it. Divers who want to dive her should ask local boatmen for the "Portland" as that is the name many of them use for her, though the reason for this is unknown. Her bell was recovered by Teignmouth divers in 1985.

Nick Chipchase and Wellington BSAC divers have found another steamer wreck very close to this position. This appears to be a bigger ship, judging by the size of her engines, of the "three island" type. Whereas the *W.H. Dwyer* was in ballast, this one's holds are full, probably with coal though deep silt covers it. Her decks were made of teak. Her bows are badly damaged. It is possible that this is the *Tandil*, a 2897-ton collier sunk by *U-85* on 12 March, 1917, while carrying coal from Barry to Portland. Four of her crew were lost.

62 Chateau Yquem Previously thought to be the 958-ton British steamer *Bamse*, which was torpedoed on 17 April, 1918, this is an earlier victim of a U-boat, the French steamer *Chateau Yquem* of 1913 tons. Travelling from Dunkirk for Barry in ballast, she was torpedoed by Oberleutnant Howaldt in *UB-40* on 30 June, 1917, firing from a hull-down position. The crew were all saved.

Their ship today is at 50 29 05N; 02 58 53W and her hull is intact. The bridge area was demolished by a wire drift sweep in 1952. She sits totally upright on a sand sea bed at 44m from which she is 16m proud. Her bow and stern are in very good condition and much of the wooden decking can still be seen. She has been positively identified by the clearly marked bell, which was raised by Ken Breeze. The position of the *Chateau Yquem* may well give wreck divers a clue

The massive battleship Empress of India, the largest ship that can be dived in Devon waters (Site 63).

to another nearby "unknown" wreck, for earlier the same day Howaldt recorded sinking the 764-ton Norwegian steamer *Borgund I.*

63 HMS Empress of India At 15,585 tons this is the largest ship that can at present be dived in south Devon waters. Located at 50 29 43N; 02 57 53W, this battleship, one of the Royal Sovereign class built in 1893, is rated a "fabulous" dive. There is no doubt that she is big – 380ft long with a beam of 75ft.

The *Empress of India* was sunk by her own shells, fired at her from guns of similar calibre in other Dreadnoughts, during gunnery tests on 4 November, 1913. She had her propellers removed before the shoot, which was expected to take some hours, as she was protected by a belt of mild steel armour plate that varied in thickness from 5 to 17 inches. However, she did not last long, the armour plate apparently not extending down to her waterline. After a shell from one of the smaller ships had set her on fire, one of the first salvoes from the larger ships knocked a hole in her below the waterline and she turned over and sank. She is now upside down on a sandy sea bed and the hole in her side is where a condenser was blown out during salvage, rights to which are owned by a Jersey company.

The old battleship is dived regularly by groups from Devon and Dorset. The depth to the keel is just under 30m and it is 44m to the sea bed, deeper if you land in the 3m scour. Diving her needs great care and can, if you are unlucky, consist of a long fin over a solid hull with no entry point visible. Luckier divers rave about this massive wreck, saying that there are masses of huge portholes "like bay windows" and that there are two openings around the centre of the ship worth careful exploration where some of the accommodation or mess area seems to have spilled out onto the sea bed.

The wreck is surrounded by schools of huge pollack. The scour comes and goes and silt builds up on the opposite side when the scour does appear. Some divers try to make entry via the scour, going in underneath her. This is extremely dangerous, as most of the ship elsewhere is tight on the sea bed.

This Victorian print is a good guide to the location of the Duke of Marlborough.

AREA 3:

Tor Bay

This area runs south from where the previous area ended at 50 28 00W, and takes in Torquay, Paignton and Brixham. Tor Bay is bounded in the north by the headland of Hope's Nose and 4$^1/_2$ miles further south by the massive shape of Berry Head (50 22 36N). This sand-fringed bite into the Devon coastline extends 3$^1/_2$ miles inland, has an average depth of 11m and provides a safe anchorage from all but easterly and south-easterly winds, which send a heavy swell into the bay. The bottom is mostly fine sand and shingle, though there are areas of mud around 14m, which will swiftly reduce visibility in and after an easterly blow. Such disturbance takes two or three days to clear.

Tor Bay offers good protection from all other winds and it is usually possible to find a sheltered dive somewhere. This makes it popular with divers during the winter and over the early Bank Holiday weekends when trainees have their first sea dives. So divers do tend to descend on the area in large numbers at these times.

It is important to know that the overall harbour authority is Torbay Borough Council (tel. 01803 296244). Their authority extends well beyond Tor Bay itself, to Maidencombe in the north and Sharkham Point in the south. There are some by-laws that affect launching and diving:

38(1): No person shall launch a vessel without the consent of the beach inspector from Babbacombe Beach, Meadfoot Beach (both ends), Preston Beach (opposite Seaway Road, Paignton), Goodrington South Sands, Broadsands (Northern end).

(2): This by-law shall not apply to any persons to whom beach rights have been granted by the Council provided that such persons in exercising these rights comply with the conditions as to launching attached to their grants.

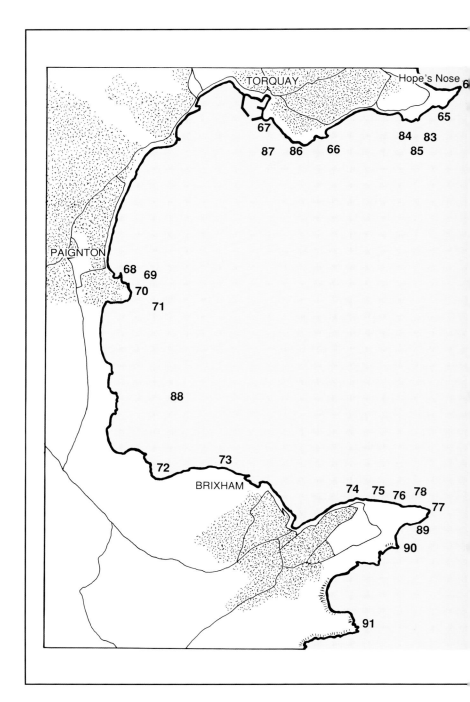

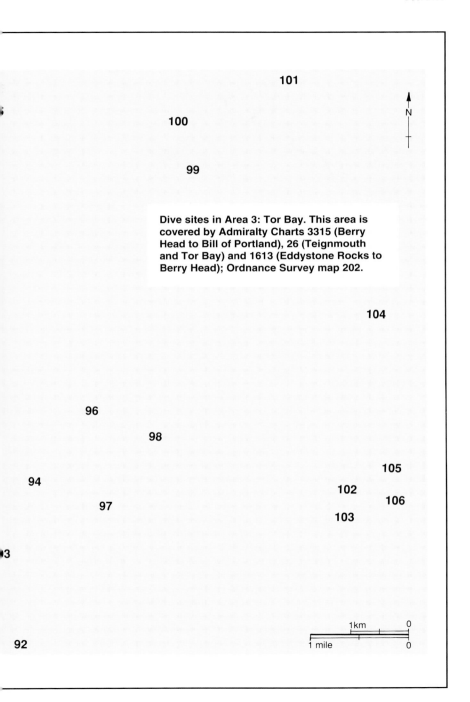

101

100

99

N

Dive sites in Area 3: Tor Bay. This area is
covered by Admiralty Charts 3315 (Berry
Head to Bill of Portland), 26 (Teignmouth
and Tor Bay) and 1613 (Eddystone Rocks to
Berry Head); Ordnance Survey map 202.

104

96

98

105

94

102

106

97

103

93

92

1km   0

1 mile   0

Above: Meadfoot Beach (Site 65) and East Shag Rock.

39: No sub-aqua swimming shall take place from the beaches known as Beacon Cove, Livermead, Elberry and Hollicombe between 15th March and 31st October nor in an Enclosed Harbour without the consent of the Harbour Master.

40(1): No person shall dive from a vessel within the harbour unless there is a lookout in the vessel at all times whilst such person is in the water.

(2): Whilst any person is diving from a vessel the lookout remaining shall ensure that there is exhibited on the vessel a rigid replica of the International Code flag "A" not less than one metre in height. Measures shall be taken to ensure all-round visibility.

(3): In this by-law "diving" means that form of diving known as sub-aqua diving and "dive" shall be construed accordingly.

If you want to water-ski after diving, there are strict rules about lanes and speed limits. A full copy of the by-laws can be obtained from the Council or harbour offices.

64 Hope's Nose This should be called Hold Your Nose, for the half-mile track to the sea leads to the site of the main Torbay sewer outfall. Though discharge is usually confined to the ebb after high water, there is a tendency for the sewage to hang around in certain tide and weather conditions. If you fancy finding out what

60

it would be like to dive in effluent this is the place, though the anglers who crowd here to fish may not welcome you before or after your dive!

65 Meadfoot Beach This is a popular beach as Meadfoot Sea Road runs along its length to join Marine Drive and Ilsham Road at the eastern end, where there is a small car park.

66 East Shag Rock Though this entails a 350-yard swim, it is well worth it, for the dive is rated by locals as the most interesting shore dive in the area. There are gullies and peaks in 9m on the landward side, with crabs in the rocks and flatfish on the surrounding sand. Cuttlefish are often seen here in the summer. The 11m high rock is also rated as a very pretty night dive.

67 Beacon Cove This small cove to the east of Torquay Harbour provides the only access to the sea along this stretch of coast. However, as diving is banned between March and October (*see* above) and as at other times there are more interesting places to go, little diving takes place here at all!

With an inner and outer basin, TORQUAY has the finest artificial harbour in the South West. When filled with yachts in the summer, and the sun shines, it looks like Monte Carlo, Positano or even St Tropez. Seeing it today, it seems impossible that this was a little village in 1800 with a small stone breakwater. Tor Bay was the favourite anchorage for the British Fleet in the Napoleonic Wars (Napoleon saw it only as a prisoner on board HMS *Bellerephon*), but even the Navy were sometimes caught by easterly gales, in one of which HMS *Venerable* came to grief (Site **71**).
    The outer harbour is formed by Haldon Pier, which comes from the south-east side, and Princess Pier from the north-west. The entrance is 53yds wide and the depth along the piers is just under 4m. The inner harbour is entered between South Pier and Old Fish Quay and most of this basin dries, though there is over 3m of water at high tide. The speed limit in both parts is 5 knots.
    There are two slipways at Beacon Quay of concrete with wood at the ends. There is a charge. They launch into the outer harbour and can be used at all states of the tide, but the wooden ends are slippery and can be difficult an hour either side of low water. A cobbled slipway launches into the inner harbour. Torquay Harbour Master's office is on Beacon Quay (tel. 01803 22429).
    There is no diving without the Harbour Master's permission and this will only be given for special works such as moorings. Diving is not banned along the outer walls of either Haldon Pier or Princess Pier, but is not recommended because these are very popular spots for anglers.
    The beaches running anticlockwise around Tor Bay on the seafront road are Tor Abbey Sands, Livermead Beach, Hollicombe Beach, Preston Beach and Paignton Beach. Livermead and Hollicombe are banned to divers from March to October, but all of them are best avoided. They have little to offer and in summer are heavily congested both on shore and off.

A small, busy harbour used by pleasure boats, PAIGNTON harbour is formed by two jetties on the north side of Roundham Head and it dries at low tide. There is 3m at high spring tides. There is a concrete slipway to sand on the south side

Above: The two slipways at Beacon Quay, Torquay.
Below: Paignton Pier.

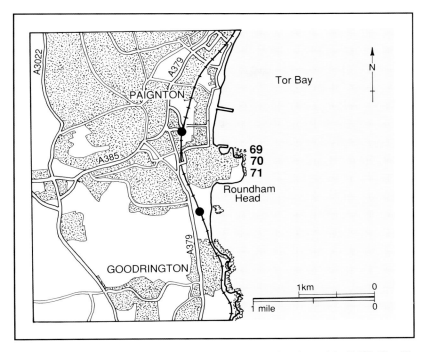

Roundham Head, showing the locations of the T-189 (Site 69),
HMS Savage (Site 70) and HMS Venerable (Site 71).

usable up to two hours either side of low water. The speed limit is 5 knots. There is a charge for launching. There is a part-time Harbour Master and the harbour office is staffed only during the summer (tel. 01803 557812). There is a trailer and car park for which a charge is made. There are toilets nearby.

Roundham Head is made of red sandstone and protects Paignton Harbour from the south. Approach is made by Roundham Road, passing Paignton Harbour, then into Cliff Road. There is a two storey car park 100yds along, and out-of-season parking in adjoining roads. Access to the shore at Fairy Cove is through the top car park and down a short flight of steps.

68 Fairy Cove It is amazing that the wrecks of three large warships can be reached by shore divers from this cove (Sites **69**, **70** and **71**). Fairy Cove has a shallow reef just off the shore. This is often used by Totnes Branch for early sea dive training for novices.

WARNING Beware of water-ski traffic near Roundham Head.

Fairy Cove (Site 68).

69 T-189 This German torpedo boat destroyer survived World War One and was under tow together with the *S-24*, another German destroyer, by the London tug *Warrior* from Cherbourg to Teignmouth for scrapping on 12 December, 1920. A strong wind from the east turned into a gale and at 11pm the tow line to the *T-189* snapped. She drove onto the rocks near Roundham Head and broke her back. The three-man running crew aboard were saved by rocket apparatus.

At 3am the next morning the *S-24* broke free and, although she went aground on Preston Beach, her three-man towing crew were also rescued by rocket line. She was not so badly damaged as her sister ship, and was got off and towed away the next day. The Torbay lifeboat was launched on each occasion and capsized on the starboard quarter of the *S-24*. Fortunately no lives were lost and the self-righting lifeboat was undamaged.

Pieces of the *T-189* can still be seen in less than 9m of water and though the ship is completely broken, some sheets of metal are clearly from her. The wreckage is about 200yds south of the beach.

70 HMS Savage A sloop-of-war of 144 tons, this Navy ship was driven ashore in an easterly gale in February 1762 and soon became a total loss, though it is believed that all her guns were salvaged. Surprisingly, quite a lot of odds and ends are found at this site – 250yds south of the beach in under 9m of water. Local divers rate it quite a good "litter" dive. Torbay Branch BSAC recently found the flintlock firing system for one of her guns on the sandy sea bed.

71 HMS Venerable This is the only British man-of-war known to have been lost because a man fell overboard! On Saturday 24 November, 1804, the Channel Fleet was at anchor in Tor Bay. One ship was the third-rate 74-gun HMS *Venerable*, under the command of Captain John Hunter. At 3pm the wind suddenly shifted wildly from west to north-east. With the wind came rain, blotting out most shore marks. At 4.30pm as the wind increased the admiral decided his ships would be safer out at sea and made the order to sail. The Navy crews raised their anchors and were lashing them to the catheads as they fought their way out of Tor Bay against the wind. In *Venerable* all was going well, but just as the men were "in the act of hooking the cat" a seaman fell overboard from his perch on the anchor itself.

The cry of "man overboard" sent crews rushing to launch a boat. In the dark and rush one of the falls was let go too soon, the boat tipped and Midshipman J. Deas and two seaman were thrown out and drowned. The boat lowered on the other side of the ship managed to pick up the man who had fallen overboard from the anchor. While this rescue was being carried out the foresails and topgallants were set, but all the time the ship had been falling back and was now unable to weather Berry Head. They tacked and headed north but found themselves nearly running down other ships of the Fleet.

In avoiding collisions they lost more ground and suddenly, on tacking, found themselves near the lights of Paignton Hospital. They tried once more to round Berry Head, but could not make it and north they went again. Another ship loomed ahead of them and in avoiding her they lost more ground. At 8.30pm the wind died and as it did so the big warship touched bottom and then grounded hard. The rain stopped and they could see that they were "under Paignton cliffs". The *Venerable* was held by rocks fore and aft.

The lull did not last. The wind came back full from the east and the sea came up with it. The crew tried to cut the masts away so that they would fall between the ship and the shore, but failed. Distress signals were fired as the ship seemed likely to capsize. By 10pm the water was up to the lower gun deck inside and huge waves were breaking right over the ship. HMS *Impetueux* anchored close by and lowered herself back on her cable until she was within 600yds. HMS *Goliath* did the same and both sent their boats out to the stricken ship. The men on the *Venerable* dropped into them from the stern ladders in a wild rescue relay among the enormous surf.

At midnight, the *Venerable* was almost right over and soon after the last man was taken off she broke in two amidships. Shortly after that Captain Hunter saw his ship "break into a hundred thousand pieces" but the loss of men, thanks to *Impetueux* and *Goliath*, which took off 547, was only eight, including the midshipman and two sailors who drowned trying to rescue the man overboard.

Captain Hunter told his court-martial – at which he was acquitted – that his crew were so brave that he would be glad to have all the men but one with him in any other ship. The one he rejected was a private of the Marines, David Evans, who during that dreadful night was dragged on deck drunk and still clutching "a tin kettle of port wine". His pockets were stuffed with articles of officers' apparel that he had stolen from the wardroom. It is doubtful if Evans was able to serve in any other ship anyway – he was given 200 lashes of the cat-o'-nine-tails on his bare back during a beating round the Fleet some weeks later.

The guns of the *Venerable* were salvaged. However, divers on the site have found cannonballs and quite a lot of small lead shot. The wreckage is 350yds to the south-east of the southern end of the beach. The *Venerable* belongs to local diver Stephen George, who is the licensee of the salvage rights and is carrying out an archaeological survey. He has discovered many items, including 3ft bronze "horseshoes" used to strengthen the bows of men-of-war of the period.

Further south, Goodrington Sands and Broad Sands have nothing to offer the diver. The little Saltern Cove between the two is a conservation area.

72 Elberry Cove Approach by a coastal path from the southern end of Broad Sands car park. Diving is not permitted between March and October, when the cove is reserved and buoyed exclusively for water-skiing.

73 Freshwater Springs These are to be found 100yds off the beach at Elberry Cove and about 400yds west of Churston Point. The springs bubble up through the sandy bottom and can be spotted by the saucer-shaped indentations in the sand. The freshwater mixing with sea water produces a shimmering optical effect.

Brixham Harbour.

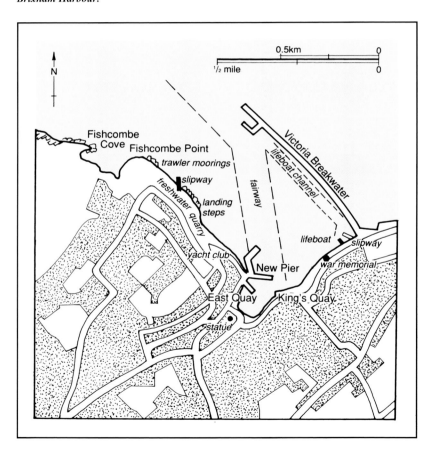

The inner harbour at Brixham.

While the rest of the sea bed in the area is almost all flat sand and not very interesting, it is in this stretch of Torbay that over twenty ships were lost during the hurricane from the east on the night of 10 January, 1866. Losses and strandings totalled 41, though some were refloated later (80 ships were sheltering in the bay when the winds struck). As most of the ships wrecked were wooden and broke up, their timbers were salvaged and used again in some of the houses roundabout. But items do turn up on the sea bed from time to time, especially after gales.

The town of BRIXHAM was Britain's top fishing port for hundreds of years and today the narrow streets run down to the harbour that is still the central point of life here. It was Brixham that produced the finest and most powerful fishing sailing vessel ever built – the Brixham trawler – but the last one was built in 1927. Today the trawlers have engines of over 500hp and some work Lyme Bay. One skipper has a chart marked with 380 "fasteners", many of which may well be wrecks, between Start Point and Portland. (Divers know who to stand a drink!) Thousands of people in Brixham are involved in fishing and diver coxswains must remember that this is a fishing port.

Brixham has an outer and inner harbour. The outer basin is protected by the Victoria Breakwater, which runs half a mile north-west from the shore, one mile to the west of Berry Head. Anchoring is prohibited within 65yds of the inner side of the breakwater so that the lifeboat has a clear run out to sea. The inner harbour is behind New Pier, which runs east from the southern end of the fish market, and mostly dries.

There are two launch sites. The concrete Breakwater Slip is usable at all states of the tide and is on the eastern side of the outer harbour. The hard is big – it was built by the Americans during World War Two to drive their tanks down to landing craft. Freshwater Quarry has a narrow slipway that will take one boat at a time, but usable at all states of the tide.

Brixham Harbour Master's office (tel. 01804 53321) is at the landward end of New Pier. There is no diving in the harbour without the Harbour Master's permission. The speed limit is 5 knots.

74 Breakwater Beach This is a small but popular diving centre. Approach from Brixham Harbour, past the memorial to the landing of William of Orange on 5 November, 1688, then first left into King Street for a quarter of a mile into Berry Head Road. Continue for another quarter of a mile, then turn left down into the Breakwater Beach car park. Parking is limited. Breakwater Beach is on the right of the Breakwater, over which boats must not be launched.

75 The Breakwater Diving from the beach along the outer wall of the breakwater reveals plenty of holes for crabs and the occasional lobster. This is rated by local divers as a super night dive. The only problem is the anglers, with whom it is very popular both night and day.

76 Shoalstone The rocky shoreline from the beach towards Berry Head seems to support many species not found in other parts of the bay, with conger, angler fish, octopus and the common pollack and wrasse. Diving is not advisable beyond Shoalstone Point without boat cover as the tidal streams strengthen towards Berry Head. Another hazard is the broken lines with hooks attached left by anglers who fish this shallow area in great numbers.

77 Shoalstone Beach There is a car park just past the Coastguard cottages. The beach is shingle. There is an open-air swimming pool at the eastern end of the beach. Go straight down here and out over the rocks into the water. A reef runs out and deepens swiftly to 20m. About 100m off the pool in 20m is the three-bladed propeller of an aircraft. There is no sign of any fuselage so it may have been dumped by a homeward-bound trawler. Take care on the ebb, which runs strongly to Berry Head.

78 Scrap Alley This is the local name for the area between Berry Head and the Breakwater. Some of the junk trawled up by Brixham vessels is dumped here on their way home.

WARNING There is very heavy boat traffic in the whole of Tor Bay, but nowhere is this so evident as around Brixham, an extremely busy fishing and commercial port. It is essential that all divers and diver coxswains are aware of this at all times. It is vitally important that all shore diving is carried out with clear SMBs and out of the obvious traffic lanes. It is just as important to see that all offshore diving is carried out with adequate boat cover, SMBs and out of obvious danger areas. At least one unmarked diver has been killed here by surfacing directly in the path of a fishing boat.

Boat diving sites

79 Ore Stone The Ore Stone stands 32m high and is just over half a mile south-east of Hope's Nose. The Sunker Rock lies just 2m under the surface 100yds south-west. These rocks are far enough away from the sewer outfall to give reasonable visibility. There is a hole right through the Ore Stone from north to south just below the surface. There is a dog-leg in it, but once in you can see the light at the other end. It is wide enough for even the area's largest diver and the current tends to carry you through. At the northern end there are two exits.

Around the Ore Stone itself, kelp-covered rock inshore descends across rocky ledges with gullies and small caves to a mixed bottom of mud and sand among slate outruns. Plenty of life here includes large wrasse, pollack, dogfish, conger and lobsters. Flatfish are found on the surrounding sandy bottom, which reaches a depth of 20m. There are strong tidal flows and much boat traffic in season, so slack water is essential. Slack is about two hours before and four hours after high water.

From the Ore Stone a low reef of rubble runs right across Tor Bay to The Ridge (Site **88**), disappearing under the sand and emerging as isolated low rocks in places.

80 The Ammunition Dump Really the wreckage of a landing craft, which seems to have been transporting ammunition during World War Two. It ran onto the back or inside of the Ore Stone and there is very little left of her. But the cargo of rifle ammunition, in clips of five, is still to be found in quantity, though the days of lifting boxes of it are over.

81 Lead Stone or Flat Rock This lies 400yds south-east of Hope's Nose, in the full tidal flow around the point. It is close to the sewer, so is not recommended. Even so, from 200yds to the north-east of the rock, divers have recovered a 10ft diameter three-bladed aluminium propeller, which is riddled with bullet holes. It comes from a Focke-Wulf Fw 200 Condor reconnaissance bomber, of the type renowned for its attacks on Allied convoys and guidance of U-boat packs in World War Two.

82 Tucker Rock At 650yds north-east of the Ore Stone, with at least 6m of water over it at all times, Tucker Rock is regarded as a beautiful scenic dive along a ridge, with rocky gullies festooned with sponges and other growths. There is a good drop-off on the north face, which is also highly decorated down to 25m with a mud and sand bottom. High water slack on neap tides is when to dive this one, because of strong currents at other times. The transit marks shown in the diagram on page 70 will put you 200yds south of the rock. Then head slight west of north (355° magnetic) and the rock will show on the echo sounder or connect with a dragged anchor.

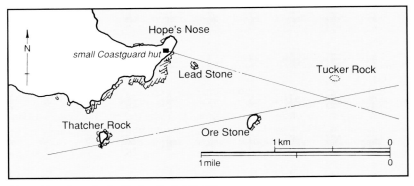

Above: Transit marks for Tucker Rock (Site 82).
Below: Transit marks for the Morris Rogue (Site 85).

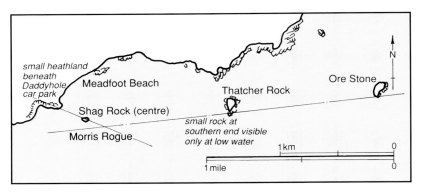

83 Thatcher Rock Situated three-quarters of a mile west of the Ore Stone, standing 41m high with a small islet close to the south, the Thatcher Rock is only 300yds from the shore and is sometimes linked to it by a ropeway by climbers, who seem to regard it as some sort of challenge.

Tidal streams here are less severe than on the Ore Stone or Tucker Rock, but slack water (about two hours before and four hours after high water) is best, giving a pleasant dive in Thatcher Gut between the rock and the shore in 10m. Around the rock is terrain similar to that of the Ore Stone, with kelp giving way to sand at about 12m. Inside the rock the bottom is sand, to seaward it is muddy. Watch out for pleasure and angling boats in season.

84 HMS Vigilant A single cannon, made of iron and very worn, at the southern end of Thatcher Rock might possibly be from this Revenue cutter, commanded by Lieutenant H. Nazer, which sank "near Torbay" on 5 December, 1819. It could be from many another armed ship. The cannon is close in to the end of the rock and the area must be worth a proper search.

85 Morris Rogue This is a completely submerged rocky outcrop lying half a mile west-south-west of Thatcher Rock with a depth of 8m to the top and 14m to the sandy sea bed. There is much life, particularly plaice, crabs and starfish of many colours. There are masses of plumose anemones. An interesting reef runs away from the main rock in the direction of Thatcher. Tides are not usually a problem, except on spring tides.

Transit marks are shown in the diagram opposite.

86 Duke of Marlborough This well-armed brig was lost close to London Bridge on 11 October, 1836, in a storm that tore her from her moorings in Torbay and drove her into a rocky inlet surrounded by sheer rock walls. In an attempt to save themselves, the crew cut the port shrouds of the mainmast, which allowed it to fall against the cliff, and made a ladder to the top. The mate and a seaman were the first to climb, but the ship shifted on a wave and threw the two men to the deck. The seaman was killed but the mate tried again and finally reached the

Torquay Harbour and London Bridge, showing the locations of the Duke of Marlborough (Site 86) and the Dutch Barge (Site 87).

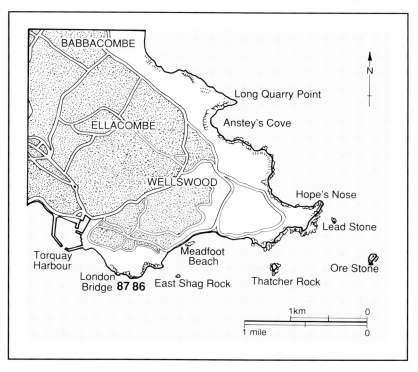

top of the cliff in safety. None of the other seven men would try the climb and they all drowned when the ship sank.

Salvage work began quickly on this former Post Office packet vessel, which had been anchored in Torbay while her captain underwent some hospital treatment, and had been fitted out for a trading expedition to West Africa. The Deane brothers were engaged to raise the ship, but managed only to lift six cannon and some fittings. Later work by other divers from the smack *Mary Ann* in 1851 is reported to have raised valuables. So far as is known she has not been relocated this century, though the Victorian print reproduced on page 56 should give divers a good idea of her position. All diving for her recently has been on the other side of London Bridge. Rocks in the area descend vertically to a rocky sea bed, then to sand at 8m.

87 Dutch Barge Her cargo of 20ft iron pipes lies under London Bridge on the sea bed at 8m. Divers have failed to find any sign of the barge itself, and believe that she may have tipped off her cargo here, either without sinking or later sinking elsewhere.

88 The Ridge The Ridge is the only piece of rough ground right within the Bay that is worth a dive to itself. In 7 to 10m of water, this 3m high reef is excellent for flatfish. Lying in a line roughly east–west, The Ridge is about three-quarters of a mile directly north-east of the Broad Sands end of Churston Point and is at approximately 50 25 00N; 03 32 00W. Tidal streams are virtually non-existent at all states and the site is usually calm and accessible, except in north-easterlies and easterlies of Force 4 and above. It is an angling mark for dabs and plaice. When you are over the middle of The Ridge, the tip of Brixham breakwater will be lined up with the west end of Shoalstone Point Coastguard station.

East of Brixham, BERRY HEAD is a sheer 200ft headland, designated as an area of outstanding natural beauty – which it certainly is. The waves have carved out huge caverns. These and the cliff ledges provide nesting sites for kittewakes, guillemots, shags and fulmars. As a result, the southern cliffs are now officially declared an area of special protection. No one is allowed into the area between 15 March and 31 July. Divers and pleasure craft are requested not to come in too close and to refrain from sudden noise. The nesting birds take flight at such noise and eggs and young get knocked off the ledges.

Berry Head lighthouse is at the end of the headland, beyond the Coastguard station. It became known as the smallest, highest and deepest light in the British Isles after its establishment in 1906 – because the tower is all of 5m high, the light is 58m above the water on top of a headland from which you can see 800 square miles of sea, and the optic used to be turned by a weight falling down a 150ft deep shaft (a motor now does the job). The light has a range of 18 miles – white group flashing twice every 15 seconds.

The fortifications on Berry Head were erected in 1793 against a possible invasion by the French. The waters below do not provide very interesting diving as the bottom is mainly mud.

89 The Trawler Dump The divers who found charred woodwork and steel wreckage at 50 23 41N; 03 29 10W a few years ago got quite excited about it.

They should not have done – the whole of this area just to the south of Berry Head has been used as a dump for old trawlers and other old boats for years. It is sometimes used to dump objects trawled up by local fishermen. At least two aircraft engines were dropped in there and smartly pulled out again by aircraft recovery groups. Certainly there is a steel barge in 12m with a lot of steel hawser around it, and some other wooden wreckage that looks distinctly charred.

90 Cod Rock These rocks offer sheltered diving but little of interest. They are heavily potted by local fishermen, though for no obvious reason. There has been some friction here, particularly during Bank Holiday weekends when the whole diving world seems to come to Brixham. Diver saturation results and great care is needed to avoid upsets.

To the south, SHARKHAM POINT is best avoided. This is where the main sewer serving Brixham and district exits.

91 Bretton Hall This British steamer was bound for Cardiff from Antwerp when she ran ashore in St Mary's Bay near Sharkham Point at 6pm on 6 December, 1885, in an easterly gale. The crew were all saved. Her cargo was sand and 450 tons of Belgian malleable iron ingots. The ingots were later salvaged. At 5am the next day, the seas were washing right over her. The captain then left her.

The *Bretton Hall* is now very broken, but a large part of her keel and many plates can be seen in 7m at 50 23 03N; 03 29 52W. This is rated a good novice shore dive, but with a long snorkel from the beach to save air. Kelp covers the wreck remains and there are plaice to be seen on sand patches.

92 Bleamoor A 3755-ton steamer of the Moor Line (W. Runciman and Company), the *Bleamoor* was built in 1902 by W. Doxford and Sons. She was armed, 342ft long with a beam of 46ft and her 300hp engines could produce 9 knots. She was travelling at less than her full speed on 27 November, 1917, when she was torpedoed from a hull-down position by *UB-80* commanded by Kapitänleutnant Viebeg.

The *Bleamoor* sank swiftly and though at first seven men were reported missing, the final death toll was eight. She had been bound for Falmouth from Hull with a cargo of coal and is now at 50 22 43N; 03 25 14W. She is 12m proud of the sea bed at 43m and lies east–west, with her bows to the east. She is in a poor state and divers should take great care in exploring the wreckage, which is badly broken and completely separated in places. A scour of 3m is on the south side.

This wreck is owned by a syndicate of divers headed by Ken Breeze, who believe it to be not the *Bleamoor* but the *Kendal Castle* (Site **180**). They base their identification on shipping line pottery found on her.

93 Dudley Rose Straddled by a stick of bombs from a lone Heinkel He 111K on 9 April, 1941, this 1600-ton Admiralty collier was hit close to the bridge and sank soon afterwards, though all her crew of 16 were saved. She was built in 1929 by Hendersons of Partick for Richard Hughes and Company of Liverpool. She was powered by triple-expansion engines made by McKie and Baxter of Glasgow sited aft, and was carrying 2200 tons of coal from Plymouth for Portsmouth, though she had called at Dartmouth on the way.

The Red Rose, sister ship of the Dudley Rose (Site 93), which was bombed and sunk four miles off Berry Head in 1941.

This 250ft ship was 4 miles from Berry Head lighthouse on a bearing of 150° when attacked. She now lies on the sea bed in 35m at 50 23 38N; 03 26 20W. She stands 6m proud and is upright and complete, though some of her coal has spilled out on the sea bed on either side of her. She has been trawled into many times and divers say there is net all over her, so great care must be taken.

The binnacle is still in place on the centre of the bridge, though the compass has been gone for some time. A feature of the bridge of the *Dudley Rose* is the large concrete blocks lying there. These were originally bolted to the wooden walls of the wheelhouse to protect against shellfire or bomb splinters, and the fixing bolts can still be seen.

WARNING In addition to the net hazard, divers should look out for any unexploded bombs. When first dived by amateurs in 1964, one diver reported a cylindrical metal object under the bridge area. The wreck is best dived on slacks at four hours after or two hours before high water.

94 Northville Packed full of 3400 tons of good Welsh coal, this British steamship with a length of 304ft and a beam of 44ft was on her way from Newport to Dieppe on 17 February, 1918, when a torpedo from *UB-33* sent her to the bottom. Though the attack had come without warning the 2472-ton *Northville* stayed afloat long enough for all the crew to take to the boats.

Oberleutnant Gregor noted in his log that he was at periscope depth when he fired and that the *Northville* was "in the service of the Navy" (though how he decided this no one knows). He and all his crew were lost on 11 April the same year, when they dived amid the nets of the Dover Barrage and set off one of the mines. Weeks later, Royal Navy divers got down to the wreck and recovered a steel chest containing the submarine's signal books, log and confidential code books.

The *Northville* today is at 50 24 25N; 03 24 33W and is upright on a soft sea bed at 39m with her bows to the east-south-east. The sea floor rises in the east and the bows are the highest point of her at 30m. There is some silting of the wreck, which has a 2m scour on each side. The coal is still in the four holds and the hatch covers, some 20ft square, are off. She has two spare anchors on her deck amidships. Another anchor of a modern pattern is hooked into one of the holds and looks like an accidental loss.

The stern gun is lying off its pedestal and the ship seems to stop short at the stern. This mystery was solved by diver Ken Breeze when, in poor visibility, he launched himself off the end and a few fin strokes further on found himself on the complete stern of the ship, which had broken right away from the main wreckage.

95 The Trawler Local divers have always regarded this wreck charted at 20m on early copies of Admiralty charts 3315 and 1613 with deep suspicion, though some were prepared to believe it was there somewhere and was the wreck of a small steel trawler. It was charted at 50 27 33N; 03 27 03W. Their suspicions about it were proved right when the Navy survey ships "disproved" it, and it does not appear on new editions of Admiralty charts!

96 Stryn A 2143-ton British ship, the *Stryn* was 281ft long and her 214hp engines could push her along at 9 knots. She was built in 1901 by Bonn and Mees and was requisitioned from her owners Constantine and Donking by the Government Shipping Controller soon after the outbreak of war in 1914.

She nearly made it through the whole war but was torpedoed by Kapitänleutnant Viebeg when hull-down in *UB-80* on 10 June, 1918. The *Stryn* was then on her way from Rouen in ballast to pick up a cargo in Barry Roads. Eight men died in her and the remainder of her crew and captain were picked up five miles east of Berry Head in their boats and landed at Plymouth. She is lying on her port side in a depth of 40m at approximately 50 25 00N; 03 23 00W and the depth to her top rail is 30m.

97 Sevilla This Norwegian steamer, owned by the Thoresen company and built in 1913 by Wood, Skinner and Company, was carrying a cargo of wine and fruit from Valencia to Bergen on 25 April, 1918, when she was torpedoed at 50 24 18N; 03 22 51W by *UB-80*, commanded by Kapitänleutnant Viebeg. The *Sevilla* was sunk by a torpedo aimed from periscope depth and one man on board died instantly. After she sank much of her cargo of oranges, from the groves around Valencia, floated free and covered the sea. The wreck is still known locally as the "orangeman". The ship's last port of call before her sinking was Cadiz, where the wine was loaded.

The 1318-ton 260ft ship lies the right way up, with a list of 20° to port and it is exactly 30m to her deck and 41m to the sea bed. The *Sevilla* is in a good state and divers have found bottles of sparkling white and red wine aboard. The Chief Engineer's cabin has a great number of bottles in it, giving rise to the suggestion that he was having a party when she sank! Some of the crockery found on her is marked Kristiania (a former name for Oslo). She lies almost north–south.

98 Rota At 50 24 57N; 03 18 50W. There is no doubt about the identity of this one. The bell of this British, formerly Danish, 2171-ton armed merchantman built in 1915 by Dunlop, Bremner and Company, was raised by Devon divers Ken Breeze and Dave Baker in 1981. The 310ft ship was heading from Beni Saf in Algeria with a cargo of iron ore for Middlesbrough on 22 July, 1917, when she was torpedoed by *UB-40*, commanded by Oberleutnant Howaldt. On this mission from Zeebrugge (14 to 25 July), Howaldt had already sunk the liner *Salsette* in Dorset waters on 20 July and had been heavily depth charged on several occasions. When his torpedo struck the *Rota*, the captain and four men died.

Today the ship is upright and the torpedo damage can be clearly seen between bows and bridge on the starboard side. She lies almost east–west, in 28m to her deck and 44m to the sea bed. There is a 2m scour on her port side. Until recently her gun was still on the stern.

99 Glocliffe Despite positive identification by local divers of this wreck at 50 27 05N; 03 17 17W as the *Glocliffe*, some fishermen insist on calling her the *Irex* (Site **100**), which has caused much confusion. The *Glocliffe*, a 2211-ton, 287ft British steamer had a hard war. On 2 January, 1916, she hit a mine in the North Sea and was beached. After repairs, she went to war again and was loaded with 3281 tons of Welsh coal at Barry and headed for Southampton.

U-boat ace Oberleutnant Howaldt in *UB-40* was patrolling his favourite killing ground in Lyme Bay and spotted the *Glocliffe* as she came up to Berry Head on 19 August, 1917. Howaldt was near to the end of his mission – he was due back in Zeebrugge on August 23 – and fired one of his remaining torpedoes from a hull-down position. It struck her amidships, killing two men. The *Glocliffe* had no chance to use her stern gun, indeed it is doubtful if the gunners even saw *UB-40* with just her periscope showing among the waves.

The gun on her stern is still in position and divers sit on it looking down her decking. The *Glocliffe* is now completely on her port side on a sea bed of fine sand at 38m. The wreck's highest point is on her starboard side towards the stern and over 12m proud. She lies north-west to south-east and is in a reasonable state of preservation.

100 Irex This 16-ton fishing smack was sunk less than a mile from the *Glocliffe*, which accounts for the confusion between the two ships. The *Irex* was sunk by Oberleutnant Gregor in *UB-33*. On the morning of 21 February, 1918, he surfaced in the midst of a small fishing fleet that included the *Irex* of Brixham, the *Leonora*, another sailing fishing boat of 26 tons from Ramsgate, the *Rosebud* of 44 tons, the *Idalia* of 23 tons and the *Onyx* of 38 tons. After warning the crews to take to their boats, Gregor sank the lot just before midday with the 8cm gun on his casing. It is doubtful if there is much left of such a small boat as the *Irex* but one position given for her was 50 26 55N; 03 14 33W.

101 Greleen This was not the name on the bell when divers brought it up. It read "Ballater", but the name under which the ship was launched in 1894 after her building by Harland and Wolff was *Blairmore*. She appears to have changed her name twice before World War One, but was definitely called *Greleen* by her owners, the Haenton Shipping Company, when torpedoed on 22 September, 1917.

She was laden with iron ore from Bilbao and heading for Middlesbrough. A 2286-ton ship of 313ft, she was given no warning and was caught completely by surprise by the attack of Oberleutnant Howaldt in *UB-40* just 7¹/₂ miles east of Berry Head. Only eight men got clear when she sank suddenly after the torpedo opened a huge hole in her port side. Nineteen men including her captain died.

Known locally as the "22 fathom", the *Greleen* is at 50 27 38N; 03 13 47W and is intact apart from a few holes. Even her stern gun is still there, broken off the mounting pedestal. The midships bell is the one raised by Exedive, who describe her as a good dive, "light and airy". It is 30m to her highest point and 40m to the sea bed where there is 1m scour.

102 Lord Hailsham This Admiralty trawler of 891 tons was built in 1934 and bought by the Navy in August 1939. She was 156ft long with a beam of 26ft and was torpedoed by E-boats on 27 February, 1943, on the same sweep that sank the *Harstad* (Site **103**). The position for the *Lord Hailsham* is the same and is also approximate.

103 Harstad This requisitioned whaler of 258 tons, formerly the *Kos XVII*, was sunk by an E-boat on 27 February, 1943. She had been taken over by the Navy in July 1940 with her Norwegian crew and was used as a minesweeper. This whaler was built in 1932 and is now at approximately 50 24 00N; 03 07 00W, but has not so far been located by divers.

104 Isbjorn The Naval Officer in Command, Dartmouth, gave the position of this wreck only hours after the 597-ton ship was sunk in December 1944. Navy surveys of the area in 1984 indicated a shipwreck on a sea bed at 48m standing 8m proud, but queried whether this could be a 597-ton vessel as they were getting echoes from an object at least 295ft long with a 39ft beam. Diving information is not available. The position is given as 50 26 07N; 03 03 26W.

105 Modavia In the same small convoy attacked by E-boats on 27 February, 1943, when the *Harstad* (Site **103**) and the *Lord Hailsham* (Site **102**) were sunk, the *Modavia* was a much bigger ship – a motor vessel of 4858 tons. She had come across the Atlantic in a large convoy to Milford Haven and was on her way to Southampton with her valuable war cargo of 5645 tons, which included 13,545 ingots of aluminium, 17,200 ingots of zinc, aluminium tubing and 300 boxes of copper wire.

She was 14 miles directly east of Berry Head when the E-boats attacked. When she sank her crew of 45 and nine gunners were all saved. She has been located and identified at 50 24 23N; 03 01 49W, and is probably the same wreck as the next one described.

106 The Bofors Wreck Said to be at 50 24 28N; 03 01 45W, this one is called the "Bofors wreck" by local divers for the simple reason that this unknown ship, lying on her starboard side in a depth of 48m, has deposited on the sea bed a huge quantity of ammunition for Bofors guns. The pile is said to be ten feet high and ten feet across. It is 31m to the highest point of the wreck, which appears to be of a vessel of over 3000 tons. It is likely that this ship is in fact the *Modavia*.

Dartmouth Castle.

AREA 4:

Start Bay

This area runs south from Dartmouth (50 22 36N) – taking in Stoke Fleming, Blackpool Sands, Slapton, Torcross, Beesands and Hallsands – to Start Point (50 12 48N). A mixture of sweeps of sand and towering cliffs with a great river estuary thrown in, this part of the Devon coastline should be all things to all divers. Only the shore diver might be a little disappointed. Divers know that when an area is described – as this is – as being of outstanding natural beauty it means that access to the sea is likely to be poor. That is certainly true in the northern section of the area.

107 Man Sands This is the only place to reach a shore dive before Dartmouth, and then only for the really fit. Approach from Torbay by the B3205 Brixham to Kingswear road. Turn left three-quarters of a mile beyond Hillhead, signposted to Kingston. Then follow signs for Woodhuish Farm. This narrow road becomes impassable for cars about half a mile from the beach and parking is extremely limited. The rest of the journey is on foot down a rough track. Carrying diving gear, it is hard going!

The beach at Man Sands is of shingle giving way to sand at low tide. However, the southern end of the beach is rocky and here CRABROCK POINT lives up to its name, with plenty of crabs and other marine life among the rocks and sand-floored gullies, which run from 3 to 15m.

The town of DARTMOUTH is on the west bank of the River Dart and the smaller town of Kingswear is opposite, on the east bank. Dartmouth is steeped in history: Richard the Lionheart and the crusaders sailed from it, Raleigh and his contemporaries used it, nine ships went out to fight the Spanish Armada from it, in 1620 the Pilgrim Fathers' ships *Mayflower* and *Speedwell* were repaired there, and on 4 June, 1944, 485 ships, mostly American, sailed to land 33,000 men on the Normandy beaches from it. Old buildings abound. Britannia Royal Naval College stands on high ground on the north of the town. Prince Charles, President of the BSAC, was a cadet there in 1971.

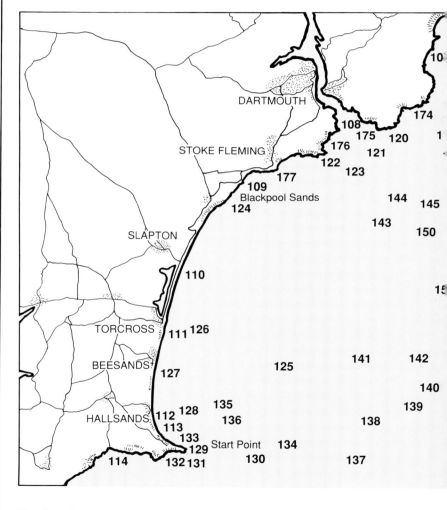

**Dive Sites in Area 4: Start Bay. This area is covered by
Admiralty Charts 1613 (Eddystone Rocks to Berry Head,
1634 (Brixham to Salcombe) and 2253 (Dartmouth Harbour);
Ordnance Survey map 202.**

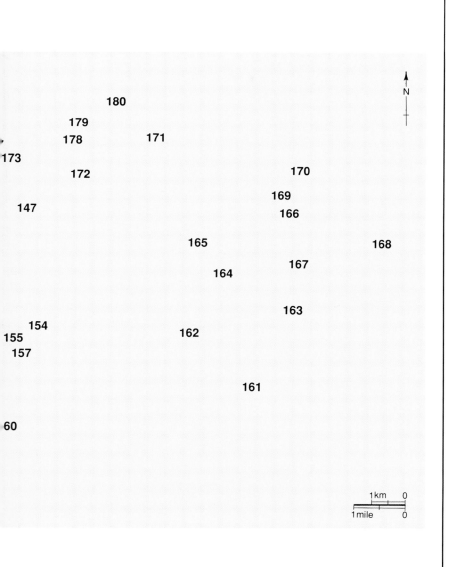

180
179
178
171
173
172
170
169
147
166
165
168
167
164
163
154
155
162
157
161
60

1 km 0
1 mile 0

N

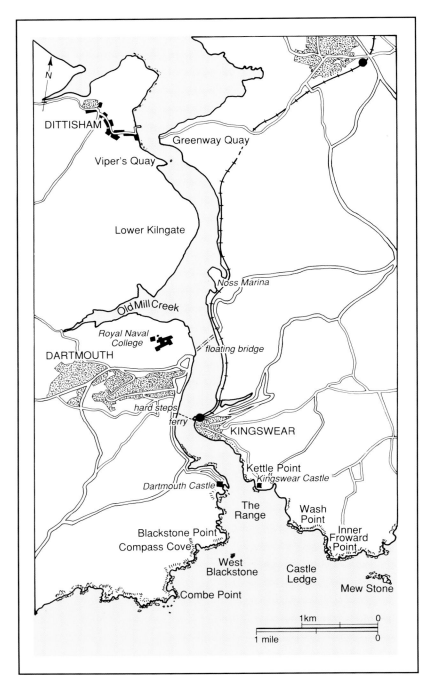

DITTISHAM

Greenway Quay

Viper's Quay

Lower Kilngate

Noss Marina

Old Mill Creek

Royal Naval College

DARTMOUTH

floating bridge

hard steps

ferry

KINGSWEAR

Kettle Point

Kingswear Castle

Dartmouth Castle

The Range

Wash Point

Inner Froward Point

Blackstone Point

Compass Cove

West Blackstone

Castle Ledge

Mew Stone

Combe Point

1km

1 mile

Above: The Lower Ferry on its way from Dartmouth across to Kingswear.
Opposite: Map of the Dartmouth area.

Dartmouth Harbour lies on the west bank of the River Dart half a mile up from the entrance and is one of the best protected on the whole of the South Coast. It has three marinas and the river is navigable as far as Totnes, some ten miles upstream. The harbour is deep, and can take big ships of up to 8.2m draught. Though the harbour is mostly used by yachts and pleasure craft, there is an expanding fleet of crabbers. Their catch is mostly exported to France by means of a ship from Guernsey with special holds full of salt water.

There is a car ferry between Dartmouth and Kingswear (the Lower Ferry) and a floating bridge paddling across on guide wires by the Dart Marina Hotel (the Higher Ferry). Both these ferries become overwhelmed by traffic in the summer and very lengthy delays are common. Approach from the A379 from Torbay and you will see signs that read "up to two hours from this point" and so on down the hill, where the queues wind down to the floating bridge ferry – they are not joking!

Strong south or south-east winds are the only ones to affect the harbour. Then a heavy swell can run in up to the Lower Ferry.

There is a free public slipway right beside the Higher Ferry – care must be taken not to obstruct the ferry as it paddles its way across on cables or delivers its load on the Dartmouth side. It is usable at all states of the tide. It is also possible to launch at the Boat Float, which leads down into the floating boat park behind the Embankment. Exit to the river is under the road; it is not usable two hours either side of low water.

Harbour dues are payable no matter where you launch, but the real difficulty in Dartmouth is not launching but parking. Parking can be extremely difficult in high season. Use the official parks if you can and, if not, think hard about the cost of fines because you might be better off launching from somewhere like the Dart Marina – where there is a charge but where car and trailer parking is much easier. There are launch facilities at all the marinas in Dartmouth and Kingswear.

The Harbour Master's office is in Dart House on the South Embankment, Dartmouth (tel. 01803 832337). Diving in the harbour or estuary is forbidden without his permission. There is a strict 6 knot speed limit in the Dart.

It is the Dart that is responsible for poor visibility in the area and the silt brought down by the river during heavy rainfall can ruin the diving close in and for some distance around. Divers should bear in mind that because of the shallow Skerries Bank (which runs north-east from Start Point up to the Bell Buoy at 50 16 30N; 03 33 50W) the tidal streams turn into a sort of giant whirlpool within Start Bay. This produces some very strong currents at spring tides, and gives very odd times for slack water at various dive sites.

108 Dartmouth Castle Built in 1481, this castle was one of the first designed to take cannon. It had seven guns that covered a 750ft chain, supported on small boats, which was fastened across the estuary in times of trouble. Kingswear Castle, on the other side, was abandoned as a fort when cannon became powerful enough to cover the entrance from one side. In the Civil War, Dartmouth supported Parliament, but fell to Prince Rupert after a short siege. The Castle was stormed in January 1646 by Roundheads, who captured it with the loss of just one man. Today it is open to the public.

Access to diving is via the car park, from which steps beside the castle lead down to the cove. There are strong tides here that race through the entrance – at 3$\frac{1}{2}$ knots after heavy rain or in northerly winds – and the shore diver must keep really tight in to avoid being swept out into the middle of the busy channel.

The steamer English Trader aground on Checkstone Rock, close to
Dartmouth Castle, in 1937.

Close in are worn iron cannon. These are probably from the castle, but may have come from a ship. The 26-gun HMS *Crown Prize* was reported lost at the harbour entrance on 9 February, 1692, with 22 men drowned (*see* Site **127**). There are other worn cannon on the other side under Kingswear Castle. On both sides the marine life is to be found close to the shores. Avoid diving up-river from the castles on the harbour side, as this area is often used by crabbers for store pots.

Close under Dartmouth Castle are a very few remains of the bow section of the steamer *English Trader*, which ran onto the Checkstone Rock while entering Dartmouth on 23 January, 1937. Her steering gear had failed and she ended up in Castle Cove. Laden with grain from Argentina, she was coming in for bunkering on her way to the Baltic. Three attempts by Dutch tugs to refloat her failed. During the night, heavy seas swung her broadside to the rocks. The Dartmouth lifeboat took off 52 men. The steamer was stuck on the rocks for weeks and finally cut in two. The undamaged stern section was towed to Southampton and then to South Shields, where a whole new bow section was fitted. Exactly 100 days later the *English Trader* was at sea again.

109 Blackpool Sands This beautiful, sheltered and pine-fringed bay is about one mile south of Stoke Fleming on the A379 Dartmouth to Kingsbridge road, and is part of the private estate of Lady Newman, who owns the charge car park and surrounds. There is a café and toilets. Ask the beach attendant if you wish to use the slipway to launch, or if you want to dive at night or barbecue. This is a place for the family diver, with a paddling pool for children, though no dogs are allowed.

The fine shingle beach slopes gradually to a clean sand bottom at about 10 to 15m, but there is little underwater life straight off the shore. Best diving is at north and south ends where it is rocky, with sand gullies in which the occasional flat fish is found in the latter part of the season. A very popular place during holiday times, Blackpool Sands is a favourite anchorage for small boats. Tidal streams are weak.

Also backed by the A379 is SLAPTON SANDS, running straight for two miles between the shore and Slapton Ley, the 270-acre freshwater lake leased to the Field Studies Council as a nature reserve. Halfway along the sands is a car park next to the Monument. This granite pillar, flanked by flagpoles, was erected by the United States Army in thanks to the local inhabitants who were evacuated from the surrounding area during World War Two to make way for a live-ammunition practice assault area, in preparation for the D-Day landings of 1944.

110 Monument Reef A dive definitely for slack tides as it involves a 500-yard swim straight out from the Monument. The reef rises from a shingle bottom in a maximum depth of 18m. To find the reef once in the water, use a transit bearing of the lifebelt post in line with the curving section of road running inland opposite the Monument to Slapton village. This is a small reef, but has plenty of fish life, crabs and the occasional lobster. There is also a much photographed and friendly conger, who poses as though he has never recovered from his experience of appearing on television in one of the superb underwater films made by local diver and naturalist Laurie Emberson.

Cannon lie underwater off Beesands (Site 127).

At the end of Slapton Sands is the small village of TORCROSS. In the car park you can see what used to be an interesting dive offshore – a Sherman tank. The tank sank during invasion exercises in 1944 and was raised by a diving team from Fort Bovisand in 1984 after local hotelier Ken Small bought it from the US Army. It is now a memorial to all the Americans lost in the exercises, including those in the convoy caught by E-boats in April 1944 (Site **35**).

111 Limpet Rocks Continue along the beach from the most southerly car park in Torcross, where it is clear that the cliffs extend into the sea. They run out for about half a mile underwater, and the reef so formed is called the Western Rough – a good spot for flat fishing (Site **126**). This may be due to the sewer outfall near Limpet Rocks, a small reef with some marine life.

112 North Hallsands Approach by the A379 to Stokenham, then take the well signposted route south. Parking is available on the foreshore and the Hallsands Hotel is run by divers. Steep cliffs and rocks extend underwater to give reefs with sand gullies in 10 to 15m. Well protected from south-west to north-west winds, there is calm shallow diving here. The interesting scenery with marine life of all kinds makes it very popular for trainee diving.

113 South Hallsands Access is only just possible here near the one remaining dwelling to survive the savage easterly gale that swept most of this village into the sea in 1917. As the underwater terrain is the same as that found at North

Hallsands, and as the entry is so difficult, divers would do better to stick to North Hallsands. Erosion of the cliffs in the area by the sea is continuing.

114 Great Mattiscombe Sand This little bay with its rock stacks is approached by a path from Start Point car park beside the gate across the road to the lighthouse. It is pronounced "Matchcombe", though locals also call it More Rope Cove and say that is because when a rope was thrown to a drowning sailor in the sea after a nearby shipwreck, it fell short. He shouted "more rope, more rope!", but there was no more and he drowned.

This may be a reference to the wreck of the 578-ton barque *Spirit of the Ocean*, lost near Peartree Point on 23 March, 1866, when Samuel Popplestone of Start Farm became the first man to win the Albert Medal when he used a rope to rescue some of her crew. Even so, there were only four survivors of the 38 aboard. Divers have found her pintles and a gudgeon, lead letters and sheeting amid the huge gullies and offshore rocks. Take care with strong tidal flows off Peartree Point.

In season you must be early to find a place in the small car park at LANNACOMBE BEACH, limited to a dozen cars at most. The last section of the road is very bad. The rocky sea bed dips swiftly to 15m and there is abundant marine life.

Boat diving sites

Most of the following sites are visited by the bigger boats from Dartmouth, Brixham and Salcombe, but inflatables are fairly easy to launch across beaches at Slapton, Torcross, Beesands and Hallsands.

115 Sharkham Point to Downend Point All along this stretch of coast (which ends just south of Scabbacombe Head) the inshore boat diver will find shallow reefs extending some 200yds seaward, and running down to a sand and mud bottom in depths of up to 16m. They have an abundant marine life and are very rewarding for photographers. Tidal streams are weak inshore. The area is good crab ground and is heavily potted, often across the tide, which makes drift diving difficult in some areas.

116 Druids Mare This rock dries to 2.8m and is a good mark for some excellent rough ground out to sea from it in 10 to 25m. The rough ground is in patches and the area makes a good drift dive with many crabs, some lobsters and plentiful other marine life.

117 The Bull At 50 20 33N; 03 29 08W this is Dartmouth's "seamount" and is rated a superb dive. Attention must be paid to correct timing. Slacks are two hours before and three hours after high water. It is 20m to the top of this undersea mountain and 30m to the sea bed on this very scenic dive. There is a great deal of fish life. Divers would be wise to stay on the Bull – the area around it is as barren as the Sahara!

WARNING Do not drop shot lines too fast here – you might score a bull in more ways than one! They say that a fisherman who netted a mine dropped it back out of harm's way (as far as trawling was concerned) on the Bull.

118 Nimble and Boatfield Rocks Charted inshore and to the west of the Bull, these rocks are about 700yds apart. It is about 6m to the top and 15m to the bottom. They are heavily potted and can often be spotted by the surface turbulence. The tides are the same here as on the Bull. There is good scenery and plenty of fish life. Large numbers of small crabs are often seen amid a maze of narrow gullies and holes.

119 Eastern Blackstone A prominent rock and an exceptional dive, this rock (marked "Eastern Black Rock" on Ordnance Survey maps) stands 16m out of the water and is 1000yds north-east of the Mew Stone at 50 20 09N; 03 31 07W. The rock lies in the main tidal stream, so must be dived at slacks two hours before or three after high water. The northern end drops off to 30m, the eastern side is shallow with rock gullies, and the inshore (western) side is 20 to 25m.

The southern end is decorated with a mass of plumose anemones in a variety of colours, and crinoids abound. The spectacular northern drop-off is covered with more plumose anemones, sagartia, brittle stars, and Devonshire cup coral,

Scabbacombe Head, showing Nimble Rock (Site 118), the Eastern Blackstone (Site 119), the Mew Stone (Site 120) and The Pin (Site 121).

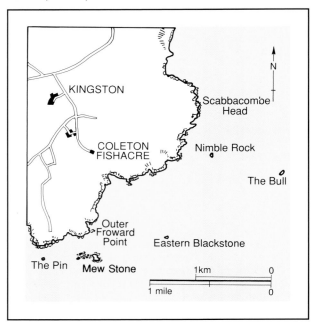

all of which make it very photogenic. There are masses of mussels too, which make a fine soup. In the deeper fissures in the rocks are large bream, wrasse and pouting. Lobsters and crabs are fairly common.

If you leave the rock and dive on the ebb towards the Mew Stone, the remains of a British Spitfire fighter aircraft may be seen as well as some iron ship wreckage of unknown date.

120 The Mew Stone At 50 20 00N; 03 32 00W the 35m high Mew Stone is surrounded by a cluster of prominent rocks with names like Shooter Rock (14m) and Cat Stone (5m). It is an excellent dive into the heart of crab country, so it is often heavily potted. At the eastern end there is an interesting reef area in about 15m. The south side slopes off dramatically as you head south reaching 30m and more. The sea is often quite choppy for dive boats off the south-east point. Seals are often seen, but are shy underwater. The western end is heavily silted by the Dart and is not worth a dive.

The 240-ton brigantine *Eureka* was off the Mew Stone on 6 February, 1870, when she missed stays, fail to go about and in foul weather was driven on shore. She was a nearly new ship and carrying coal from the Tyne, which she had left on 24 January. She was hit by a south-east gale off Portland and her cargo shifted. For a time Captain Tim Please of Guernsey rode out the storm, but then tried to make Dartmouth. Three of the crew were drowned when the ship broke up on the rocks below Brownstone Farm. Today she is at 50 20 11N; 03 32 40W. An anchor is embedded in the rocks just below the surface in the inlet formed by an island rock. Scattered remains of the hull lie 50yds around.

121 The Pin At 50 19 40N; 03 33 13W this submerged rock is charted in the entrance to the Dart in line with the Mew Stone and the red and white entrance buoy. A bearing using a line through Kingswear Castle to the house behind it will fix its position. A reef runs west from the Pin towards the buoy some 400yds from it. The bearing from the Pin to the buoy is 270° magnetic.

The depth of water over the Pin is about 6m and reaches 30m near the buoy. This can be a very scenic dive, but if there has been heavy rain two or three days before your dive, go somewhere else! Silt from the Dart quickly ruins it.

122 Combe Bay A good shallow dive for novices when westerlies make other sites too lively. The best area is right up under the Coastguard lookout and the outer ring of rocks. These are known as Old Combe Rock (Site **123**) and the Dancing Beggars. If conditions allow, the Homestone is 500yds due east of Combe Point – a small reef there provides a picturesque dive.

123 Old Combe Rock At 50 19 28N; 03 34 11W. The seaward side of this rock, which is shaped like a conning tower, is a pretty dive where the reef extends some 200yds to seaward and goes down to 20 to 25m.

124 Strete Head Reef This reef runs from Shiphill Rock, which is charted, to the eastern end of Pilchard Cove and is about 200yds offshore. The reef consists of low rocks to a depth of 18m, and has plenty of marine life. During the summer your presence will not be welcomed close in to Pilchard Cove, unless suitably unclad. It is a beach strictly reserved for nudists!

125 The Skerries Bank A famous name among flatfish sea anglers, the bank is a shoal of pulverised shell, sand, fine gravel and shingle. It extends 3¹/₂ miles north-east from a point about 1200yds north-east of Start Point up to the Bell Buoy at 50 16 30N; 03 33 50W, which marks the northern end.

The shallowest parts of the bank are at the south-west and north-east ends, where there can be depths of only 2m. Yet the bank plunges steeply on the south-east side and can reach over 30m depth in just 300yds. In bad weather the sea breaks heavily on all parts of the bank, and this rough water comes right in to shore in easterlies.

The bank itself is a desert as far as diving is concerned. There is nothing to see except unending, undulating sandbanks. However, inside the bank the water deepens to a maximum of 16m, with reefs and rocky outcrops. These reefs and gullies are good for plaice, sole and the occasional crab, lobster and scallop.

126 The Western Rough Noted under Site **111** as part of a possible shore dive, this reef off Torcross and behind the Torcross Hotel is much more interesting. It gradually deepens to 15m but is narrow. A drift dive, with the tide running parallel to the shore, quickly carries the diver across the reef onto the flat shingle bottom on either side of it. So slack water is the best time to explore, on an east–west bearing. It is good for plaice, sole and sometimes lobsters.

127 Beesands At sea, off the village green, which older divers will remember used to be a large and handy caravan site, is the next patch of rough ground. One set of bearings to locate it are: the string of telegraph poles down the hill behind the Crabpot Inn at the southern end of the caravan site should all be in line; then the Black Stone, 300yds south-south-east of Start Point, should be showing just clear of the point. A drift dive using these marks will take the diver across low rocky outcrops in 16m with sand and mud gullies in between.

At one time these gullies sheltered an abundance of scallops, plaice and sole. Sadly – due to gross over-fishing by divers – the scallops are now almost non-existent. This area of rough ground extends eastward for about 200yds and southward to a line opposite the White House, the last building at the south end of Beesands. Beyond this point the rock grows less and less and gives way to flat sand and shingle, which extend to Hallsands.

There have been two recent discoveries of cannon at Beesands. Most of the iron six-pounders are Swedish, cast near Uppsala between 1670 and 1690. This does not make the wrecks Swedish, nor does it give an accurate dating, for during that period the Swedes supplied guns to most of Europe and they were carried in ships for several decades afterwards. One group of cannon is a few hundred yards off the Cricket Inn, the others are off the extreme east end of the beach at the Cellars, where fish were once salted. Some pewter has been found by divers on the sites.

The cannon at the Cellars might be from the *Crown Prize* (*see* Site **108**), a 26-gun English warship captured from the French in 1691 and wrecked on 9 February, 1692. Some reports put her wrecking at Dartmouth, others as "near", which might mean Beesands. Twenty-one men and Captain William Tichborn were lost when the 223-ton 6th-rate ship was driven ashore. Four cannon have been recovered by divers, one of which bore the broad arrow Navy mark.

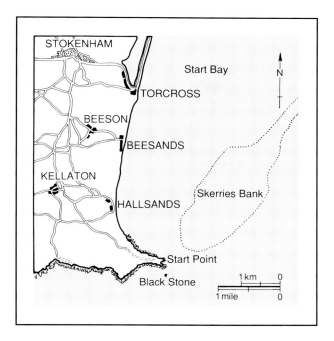

Start Bay and Skerries Bank.

Little is known about the *Janus* – or even if this was her name when she was wrecked at Beesands – but divers recently found a bell marked "Janus 1813" not far off the shore. She could have been one of the three unknown ships lost in the area in the Great Blizzard of 1891.

128 Hallsands This is another area of mussel-covered rocks, with sand gullies extending close to Start Point in the lee of the cliffs south of Hallsands. Aligning the two radio masts on the cliffs with a reddish landslip in the cliff face between them provides a rough east–west line. A drift dive southwards about 500yds offshore towards Start Point is pleasant. The depth is about 14 to 20m. This area is sheltered in strong westerlies.

The area from Beesands to Start Point has involved divers in some confrontations with fishermen, who rightly blame divers for the removal of most of the scallops. The area is a breeding ground for flatfish, and trawling is prohibited within the line from Start Point to the Bell Buoy to Torcross Hotel. So now you know that those fishermen you thought were trawling were – as they will tell you – just scallop dredging!

129 Start Point One of the most exposed peninsulas on the English coast, Start Point – often referred to as "the Start" – is a sharp headland running almost

Start Point lighthouse sits on the headland where a pirate was hung in chains in 1581. A mystery wreck (see Site 129) lies in the sea immediately below the lighthouse.

a mile into the sea. It takes its name from the Anglo-Saxon "steort" meaning a tail. When passing, divers might spare a thought for Henri Muge, a pirate, who was hanged here in chains on 28 September, 1581, as a warning to other seafarers! The lighthouse, which is now fully automatic, is right at the tip and is approached by a narrow road cut out of the rock – just wide enough for one car. There are some rough steps at the very tip, which lead down to a little cove with a tiny shingle beach, useless for divers.

Diving the cove by boat puts you into a weeded area with heavily undercut rocks and good marine life down to about 15m. The lighthouse keepers sometimes used small pots here for prawns, which are prolific in the area. The very rough ground gives way to a shingle bottom at 35 to 40m some 500yds to the south and east.

There is a mystery wreck 10 to 25 yards – certainly no further than the average sea angler can cast – from the cove in front of the lighthouse. The boiler and engine block of a steamer are here, and there is some connection with Rotherham, the place name found on a piece of the wreckage. The remains are in very shallow water and the first divers to find her found nine brass portholes – not to mention the bronze deadlights!

Start Point lighthouse is 62m above sea level and the height of the tower is 28m. It has a range of 25 miles for its 800,000 candle power light, which is white, group flashing 3 times every 10 seconds. In fog the siren sounds once every 60 seconds.

130 Start Race In strong winds the Race (riptide) may extend up to one mile south-east from Start Point. In calm weather the Race is still a daunting sight from a small boat. The tidal streams here are very strong – nearly 4 knots off the point – and this is not an area for the inexperienced. Slack water is short at about three hours after high water, though this varies according to the height of the tide and the position relative to Start Point. The Race is sometimes dived during the period two hours after high neap tides and is said to be a very exciting drift dive with alternate sand and deep-gullied rough ground, "boulders as big as bungalows" and rocks at 24 to 27m. There are large numbers of large flatfish and lobsters.

WARNING Diving the Race is only for the very experienced and skilled diver after careful planning. Inflatables have been overturned in the Race, as has the Salcombe lifeboat when coming to rescue them! And there is potting across the Race, with the risk of entanglement.

131 The Black Stone This rock is divided in two and lies 300yds south-south-east of Start Point. It is really the northern end of the Cherrick Rocks, which dry and extend 200yds further south. One peak of the Black Stone is nearest to the lighthouse, then there is a gap and the other two small peaks lie directly out to sea. The rocks are surrounded by kelp in less than 10m and are often heavily potted. Divers should take care not to come into conflict with these crabbers, particularly when diving the *Marana*.

132 Marana An auxiliary schooner-rigged steamer, this was yet another ship to be wrecked in the easterly hurricane and great blizzard of 1891 near Start Point. Built of iron in Glasgow in 1880 and of 1692 tons, she sailed from Victoria Docks, London on the morning of Sunday 8 March with a full crew of 28, bound for Colombo with a cargo of railway sleepers.

When the *Marana* was off St Catherine's Point the blizzard overtook her, and from then on she steamed at half speed with all her sails furled, the crew not really knowing where they were in the blinding snow. She was next seen – on the Monday – by the Coastguard at Hallsands. She was behaving in a strange manner in the tremendous seas, inside the Skerries Bank, as though her steering gear was out of action. When the Coastguard lost her in the white-out she was heading out to sea towards Start Point.

At 6pm that day she ran straight onto the Black Stone. The captain and crew had no idea where they were, Start Point and the lighthouse were quite invisible, so great was the snowfall. The *Marana* slewed broadside on to the seas and quickly began to break up under the battering from the east. Twenty-two of the crew took to one of the boats; the captain, chief engineer, three mates and the cabin boy went in another smaller boat. The bigger boat pulled to the west, capsized close in, and only four men survived to scramble ashore. The men in the smaller boat were never seen again. During a break in the storm, the 286-foot long *Marana* was seen by the lighthouse keepers to break in two.

Today she is at 50 13 13N; 03 38 32W and well broken amid kelp in 7m. The bow section is on the north-west side of the Black Stone, a little over 200yds from Start Point. Some years ago a small brass plate bearing her name, probably from one of the lifeboats, was found by divers.

A much more exciting find was made by Exeter BSAC in March 1984. They found a thick brass plate in the form of a decorated scroll about 15 inches square, bearing her name. This is the builder's plate put on her by Aitken and Mansel of

Tom Brooks of Kingston BSAC looks happy as he holds a deadeye from the Dryad, which he found in 1977 (Site 133).

Glasgow in 1880. It was found amid the rocks on the side nearest to Start Point, presumably where she struck.

133 Dryad The Great Blizzard of 1891 struck the West Country on Monday 9 March and lasted for four days. During that period of howling winds and snow in sheets, four ships were lost in the immediate area of Start Point. One of these was the *Dryad*, but no one saw her going and no one will ever be able to tell why Captain William Thomas of Pembrokeshire, her master, was so close in on his way down Channel.

The 1035-ton, fully-rigged iron sailing ship of Liverpool had left the Tyne on 3 March, bound for Valparaiso with general cargo. It is known that her wreck, close to Start Point lighthouse, must have been after midnight on 9 March – but not much else is known. Perhaps she had lost her compasses in huge seas when pooped, perhaps she was in distress and running for port, but no one can say for all her crew of 21 died in the wreck. One man survived longer than the others. The Coastguards had found the wreck about 2am, her masts and yards dragging in the water, but there was little to be seen of her hull. At daybreak a sailor was seen on a rock, just clear of the swirling surf, about 100yds from the wreck. A cliff-ladder was unrolled and lowered. Reaching for it, the sailor slipped, fell into the icy sea and disappeared. The wreck broke up and wreckage was washed all along the coast.

Tom Brooks of Kingston BSAC found her in 1977 while helping a local fisherman to recover his pots. He first discovered timbers in a "cave" in a small cove near Start Point lighthouse. He probed further, and amid the kelp and under sand, found rigging and deadeyes. She is at 50 13 24N; 03 38 24W and very broken though it is thought that there is much more to be found there under the sand. Divers may have found the bell of one of the other ships sunk that night (*see* Site **127**).

134 Colorado This British steamer of 7165 tons was carrying 8000 tons of coal when she was sunk on 20 October, 1917, by *UB-31*, commanded by Oberleutnant Bieber. She was on her way from Hull to Alexandria. Though her captain reported two explosions, one in the port side of the engine room and another further aft, Bieber logs firing only one torpedo at her when she was 1¹/₂ miles off Start Point. Four men were killed.

This Ellerman Wilson Line steamer was armed with a 4-inch gun. She now lies at 50 13 30N; 03 34 00W and is well broken. This is mainly due to patrol vessels locating the wreck during World War Two and depth-charging her thinking she was a submarine. The wreck lies at 40m.

135 Bidart This French steamer's claim to fame is that she put a Q-ship out of the war by colliding with her on 31 August, 1918, in the dark before dawn south-east of Start Point. As a result of that collision the *Bidart* of 1737 tons drifted a very long way until she grounded on the Skerries and capsized.

The *Wexford Coast* had set out from Plymouth as "Storecarrier No. 80", an innocent looking small steamer of 423 tons, three masts, and engines placed aft. Though this was hidden until the screens fell away, the *Wexford Coast* was well armed, hoping to lure a U-boat within range. These plans were spoiled by the collision at 4am in a strong north-west wind. The *Wexford Coast* was so badly damaged that she put back into Devonport for repairs; the damage was so severe that the war was over before the repairs could be completed.

The *Bidart*, 260ft long with a beam of 38ft, was laden with coal from Newport and heading for Le Havre at the time of the collision. She is somewhere on the Skerries, possibly at 50 14 09N; 03 37 42W, and since her sinking has sunk another ship – the British motor yacht *Osprey*. On 24 September, 1919, the

Osprey hit an underwater obstruction at that position. With a magnetometer the *Bidart* should not be difficult to pin-point.

136 Apotek At 50 14 00N; 03 32 09W is the very broken up wreck of this 36ft British motor ketch. She sank on the Skerries on 16 June, 1981, and her wreckage is now to be found in less than 2m of water.

137 Jean Frederic This wreck is known locally for some reason as the "Skerries coal boat", possibly due to a mix-up with the *Bidart*. A former French trawler, built in 1919, she was requisitioned for service with the Royal Navy after the fall of France. This 329-tonner served until 1 May, 1941, when she was strafed and bombed by German aircraft. She sank at 50 13 24N; 03 33 50W and stands 14m proud in 60m, lying north-east to south-west. She is 130ft long.

138 Waikawa Another of Oberleutnant Bieber's victims, this armed merchantman of 5666 tons was torpedoed from periscope depth by *UB-31* on 19 October, 1917, when returning from Rouen to Barry in ballast. The crew of the steamer, which was built in Flensburg in 1907, were saved when she sank 4 miles east-north-east of Start Point, an area that Bieber had orders to patrol. Today she is at 50 14 06N; 03 32 58W on the sea bed at 55m from which parts of her are 13m proud.

This big ship is about 400ft long and her bows point north, though they are over on her starboard side. Her centre castle is over even more. The port side has collapsed inwards and there is a proper jumble, with decks and hull reversed in places.

WARNING This is a deep and sometimes confusing dive with poor visibility, as the many reel lines left on the wreck bear witness.

139 Wreck, name unknown At 50 14 00N; 03 32 09W, in 46m, is a wreck about which very little is known and which shows very little on the echo sounder. Diving information is needed.

140 Eveline A 2605-ton British steamer carrying coal from Barry to Rouen, the *Eveline* was another victim of *UB-31* and Oberleutnant Bieber on 20 December, 1917, the same day as he sank the *Warsaw* (Site **192**). Bieber was certainly busy that December. On the 18th he had sunk the *Riversdale* (Site **217**), on the 19th the *Alice Marie* (Site **142**), and now two ships in one day.

The *Eveline* was torpedoed 9¹/₂ miles south-south-west of Berry Head and her approximate position is 50 14 30N; 03 30 40W. Diving details are needed.

141 Livonia There were only two survivors from the torpedoing of this armed merchantman on 3 December, 1917, and they were picked up after clinging to wreckage. All the rest of her crew of 25, including her master, Captain H.G. Orchard, died when a torpedo from Oberleutnant Stöter in *UB-35* hit her in the port side amidships. The explosion nearly cut her in half and she sank in seconds.

The *Livonia* was carrying 3000 tons of iron ore from Bilbao for Jarrow. She was of 1879 tons and 285ft long, with a beam of 42ft, built in 1904 at the

Howaldtswerke in Kiel. The gun on her stern is a 12-pounder. She now lies at 50 15 30N; 03 33 15W in 40m.

142 Alice Marie This is probably the wreck at 50 15 29N; 03 30 58W, though there is a bit of a mystery about this site. The *Alice Marie* was an armed steamer of 2210 tons that was carrying 3000 tons of coal from the Tyne to Rochefort when Oberleutnant Bieber in *UB-31* caught her just after midnight on 19 December, 1917. He torpedoed her while he was surfaced and she sank swiftly, but the crew all had time to reach the boats safely.

In 1969, the position of the *Alice Marie* was suddenly declared to be that of HMS *Formidable* by salvage boat skipper Silas Oates. A look at scanner film appeared to bear him out – it showed an enormous wreck sitting on the bottom with a slight starboard list, turret guns and torpedo net booms seemed to be clear. The superstructure had all the appearance of the old battle cruiser, with a hull well over 300ft long lying south-east to north-west – there certainly was something big down there, though the *Formidable* was 430ft overall and this was apparently the wrong area.

Another diver reported diving the position and said it certainly was not HMS *Formidable*. It was a steamer lying east–west, on her port side, there were no guns anywhere in sight and she only had one propeller, while *Formidable* had two! That seemed to be that.

Then, in 1980, a Plymouth man dived in the same position and found, in bad visibility, something enormous "standing 40 to 50ft proud of the sea bed" and so big that the top of one bollard measured three feet across. Back went the diver who had reported it was not *Formidable*. He surfaced to declare that it was the same single-screw steamer that he had dived the previous year, with its cargo holds and winches. He reported that several cargo booms lie outward from the wreck to the sea bed. He added "there is no other 400ft wreck in the close vicinity".

Divers on the position given will find the steamer still on her port side and very well over. The depth to the sea bed is 55m and she is 15m proud. If you find yourself on something much bigger, please let the author know!

143 Picton Castle This Admiralty-hired trawler of 245 tons was sunk by a mine off Dartmouth on 19 February, 1917, at 50 18 20N; 03 32 11W. She is now upright in a deep scour, with the bow section separated from the main hull. The depth is 37m to the sea bed and 33m to the top of her. A great deal of fish life is both around and in her, but conditions are usually dark. She is listed by the Admiralty as an "unknown" and is best dived on slacks two hours before or three hours after high water.

144 Benton Castle Though charted by the Admiralty as an "unknown" at 50 18 29N; 03 31 38W, this is the *Benton Castle*, an Admiralty-hired trawler of 283 tons. She was off Dartmouth on 10 November, 1916, when she ran straight onto one of the mines laid by UC class German submarines to catch traffic in and out of Dartmouth.

The *Benton Castle* is an excellent wreck dive at a depth of 40 or 44m depending on the huge scour on the western side of the wreck. Diver skipper Tony Aylmer says that if the shot line is put on the wrong side it can be quite off-putting for any divers going down the line as they end up in the great black hole of the scour. It is not advisable to try to locate the *Benton Castle* by the big yellow buoy put out in summer by yachtsmen, which is sometimes within 200yds of the wreck and sometimes well off it. This trawler is a substantial wreck, lying on her port side with a gaping hole in her bow where she was mined. It is 35m to the top of her deck. She is well silted at times and home to large conger.

145 The Dartmouth U-boat A team from Totnes BSAC suddenly found themselves on the conning tower of an World War One U-boat in appalling visibility at 50m. This was in July 1981 and the dive was not to find U-boats, but to help a local crabber salvage his gear. They had no time to explore fully, but merely noted that all hatches appeared closed and the submarine was cocooned in fishing nets. Totnes divers did not revisit her until the summer of 1989, when they were able to look again and note that she had no mine chutes and had a single stern tube.

In fact there are five U-boats of World War One lost somewhere in the Channel but their positions are unknown to this day. They are the *U-37*, lost in April 1915 with Kapitänleutnant E. Wilcke in command; the *UB-36* missing in June 1917 (Oberleutnant von Keyserlinck); *UB-113*, September or October 1918 (Oberleutnant U. Pilzecker); *UB-108*, July 1918 (Kapitänleutnant W. Amberger); and *UC-18*, February or March 1917 (Oberleutnant W. Kiel).

The single stern tube of the Dartmouth U-boat and lack of mine chutes would suggest that this is probably the *UB-113*. The last message from *UB-113* was received on 28 September, 1918, saying that she had just torpedoed the steamer *Aldershot* (Site **155**). The same day a De Havilland D.H.6 seaplane reported dropping a 65lb bomb on the periscope of a submarine in the same area. However, only more diving will give us the final proof. She rests on a silty bed at 51m, from which she stands 4m proud and upright. She lies north-east to south-west at 50 19 57N; 03 29 54W.

146 Elsa A Norwegian steamer of 3581 tons, 335ft long with a beam of 48ft, the *Elsa* was torpedoed from periscope depth by Oberleutnant Bieber in *UB-31* on 24 January, 1918. She was sunk while travelling from Calcutta to Kristiania (now Oslo) with 2000 tons of coal, 200 tons of coke and 600 tons of general cargo. She called at Falmouth and Plymouth before heading up Channel. The torpedo hit her in the starboard side, 35 feet aft of the engine room; No. 5 hold was completely destroyed. The *Elsa* settled by the stern and sank 20 minutes later after her crew of 28 had all got clear. They landed at Dartmouth.

Built in 1904 by the Tyne Iron Shipbuilding Company, she now lies at 50 19 55N; 03 29 54W, 4m proud of the sea bed at 48m. She is very broken. The area is heavily potted, and the wreck provides excellent hiding places for shellfish.

147 UC-49 Commanded by Oberleutnant H. Kukenthal, this mine-laying U-boat left Zeebrugge in the early morning of 1 August, 1918, with enough hours of darkness ahead of her to get through the Dover Barrage before daybreak. She was lucky, and two days later was well down Channel.

On 3 August the *UC-49* torpedoed and sank the *Warilda*, a 7713-ton steamer, 32 miles south-south-west of the Owers Light Vessel and correctly reported this sinking as that of a hospital ship – 113 wounded soldiers, a nurse, 2 medical staff and 7 crew died in the sinking. On 5 August she torpedoed the *Tuscan Prince* (5275 tons) but though the explosion killed two men on board the steamer she managed to reach port safely.

On 8 August Kukenthal was detected by the Torbay Hydrophone Division, which consisted of the old torpedo boat destroyer HMS *Opossum* and 13 motor launches. They pinpointed him four miles south-east of Berry Head. *UC-49*, one of the older minelayers, had come into service in November 1916. By now she had laid the 18 mines she carried, and tried to escape at her full underwater speed of 7 knots, before lying doggo on the bottom. Unfortunately for the Oberleutnant and his crew of 25, the listening devices worked well and the destroyer and launches had no shortage of depth charges. They plastered the sea bed in the area where the *UC-49* was lying and finished her off.

She is now at 50 19 45N; 03 26 45W. The 511-ton, 173ft submarine is lying well over on her side, with her rudder blown away at the stern. Her highest point is her periscope and her outside shell plating is "well rotted". The depth to sea bed is 51m and she lies east–west.

148 Greatham This 2338-ton British steamer was in a convoy on 22 January, 1918, steaming from Grimsby with a cargo of coal for Blaye, near Bordeaux. Oberleutnant Bieber in *UB-31* fired both his bow torpedoes from periscope depth at the group of ships. One missed, but the second hit the *Greatham* and seven men died when she sank. Bieber saw the sinking, but only later was his victim identified.

This ship was built by W. Gray and Company of Hartlepool and launched in April 1890 under the name of *Bussorah*, but later that same year she was renamed *Greatham*. Just 290ft long with a beam of 38ft, she was owned by the Middlesbrough shipping firm of Coombes, Marshall and Company. Her triple-expansion engines gave her nine knots and her wartime signal letters were LQRP.

She now lies almost east–west and is 10m proud of the sea bed at 44m though there is a huge 8m scour beside her as she stems the tide. Her shallowest point is amidships at 34m where the bridge is still in place. The section from the bridge forward is the best of her, the stern section being the most broken. This is a regular dive from Dartmouth, though conditions on her can often be dark and silty. A sextant was recently recovered from the bridge area. Loading derricks are still in position over the forward hold.

149 Emma This small British fishing vessel capsized and sank on 12 April, 1985. She is at 50 18 18N; 03 29 19W and when found by divers was lying on her port side, 5m proud of the sea bed at 40m.

150 The diver trainer wreck So called because the Navy has it listed as "much swum over by sub-aqua enthusiasts" and notes that she was used to train divers. Despite all this activity she is still an "unknown" and lies upright north-north-west to south-south-east in 43m from which she is 8m proud. There is an 8m scour around her. She is in good condition at 50 17 58N; 03 30 30W.

One report says that she is a coastal-type ship of about 300 tons, but other divers say she is much bigger. She is probably a World War One wreck. There are a lot of shell cases around her stern. Identification is made difficult by the generally very poor visibility. Local divers say she is rarely dived, despite the Navy's note. However, it is possible that there are two wrecks here within yards of one another, as one estimation of her length gave her as 440ft and another as barely half that.

151 Coaster, name unknown She is upright with her bows to the north-east at 50 17 49N; 03 29 02W. A steamer some 300ft long, this wreck is festooned with nets, and divers should therefore take great care. She has a 2m scour and is a three-hold ship with an iron screw and an iron spare. The holds are empty and the ship seems very old, being heavily encrusted with marine growth and rusting badly. The depth is 46m and the wreck stands 9m proud.

152 Wreck, name unknown A ship of 115ft standing 4m proud of the sea bed at 52m, this unknown has apparently not been dived, though many dive boats have had a look at her on their echo sounders. She lies north–south and there appears to be a shallow scour to the west of her. She is at 50 17 01N; 03 29 15W.

153 Shirley Betty This 23-ton fishing vessel sank on 22 August, 1981, and now lies at 50 16 48N; 03 29 12W, 7m proud of the 53m sea bed. The wreck is south-east to north-west and is just 38ft long.

154 Wreck, name unknown At 50 16 51N; 03 26 15W lies the wreck of a 197ft ship. She lies in 53m and stands 7m proud. To the north of her lies some debris, which could be her superstructure.

155 Aldershot The last torpedo Oberleutnant Pilzecker ever ordered to be fired from *UB-113* sank the British steamer *Aldershot* at 50 16 29N; 03 28 02W. The 280ft merchantman was from the Clyde and heading for Nantes. She was four miles off Dartmouth on 23 September, 1918, when the U-boat attacked, killing one man in the crew. What happened to *UB-113* after that is not known and she could be the "Dartmouth U-boat" (Site **145**).

The *UB-113* went into service on 25 April, 1918, and after working-up trials joined the Flanders Flotilla at Zeebrugge on 24 July. Her first mission was against Allied shipping between Flamborough Head and Sunderland. Her second and last mission started on 14 September, when she went to sea with *UB-111* under orders to join the "commercial war" – sinking merchantmen in the western approaches to the Channel. She was not to try to slip through the Dover Barrage, but to get to her targets by going through the North Sea and circumnavigating Britain. Apart from her sinking the *Aldershot* (and possibly the *Aldebaran* in Cornish waters, though that was claimed by *UB-112*), nothing more was heard of *UB-113* and there were no survivors or bodies.

The *Aldershot*, built in 1897, is upright and on an even keel at a depth of 55m from which she is 15m proud. Her bows, one of the best preserved parts of the wreck, point to the south-west. Her bridge is her highest point and she is 15m proud in a depth of 55m.

WARNING There are many fishing nets on the wreck.

156 Garm One man died when a torpedo from *UC-65* slammed into the 725-ton Norwegian collier *Garm* on 25 August, 1917. Kapitänleutnant Viebeg spotted the *Garm* when she was eight miles off Start Point, bound for Rouen from Liverpool with 880 tons of coal. Viebeg fired from a hull-down position and the collier sank swiftly at 50 16 33N; 03 28 21W. She is now upright, intact and 11m proud of the sea bed at 55m.

157 Wreck, name unknown A 260ft ship is at 50 16 13N; 03 27 29W. She lies north–south, at 54m from which she is 10m proud. Not reported as dived.

158 Farn This 4393-ton British steamer was 370ft with a beam of 50ft. She was built in 1910 and torpedoed on 19 November, 1917, by Oberleutnant Bieber in *UB-31* from a hull-down position. The *Farn* was on her way from London to Thessaloniki (Salonica). All 34 of her crew were saved and landed at Dartmouth. Today she is complete and upright in 55m at 50 15 42N; 03 29 23W. Her bows are almost due south and she stands 15m proud. She has been identified by her bell.

159 Antonio Built in 1905 by J. Blumer and Company, this British steamer of 2652 tons worked for the Egypt and Levant Steamship Company. She was bound for Cherbourg from Barry when she struck a mine on 7 March, 1917, and sank so swiftly that eleven of her crew, including the master, died.

She is 314ft long, with a beam of 46ft, and now lies at 50 15 27N; 03 29 05W in 54m from which she stands 15m proud. She is badly broken, lying on her starboard side from north-east to south-west and is almost in two in places.

WARNING There are nets all over this wreck.

160 Brunhilda This British steamer of 2296 tons, homeward bound from Bona in Algeria with a cargo of aluminium ore, had called at Falmouth before heading on to Sunderland. She was seven miles "east-by-south of Start Point" when she was torpedoed without warning by *UB-31* on 11 July, 1917. All the crew were saved. She now lies at 50 14 34N; 03 28 29W, east–west on a sea bed at 57m from which she stands 11m proud.

161 Steamer, name unknown Lying upright with her bows to the north-north-west, this is an old 180ft coaster of about 2000 tons. She seems to be of about World War One vintage and may have been torpedoed, because she is badly damaged behind the bridge, where her central superstructure has collapsed into itself. She is at 50 15 19N; 03 19 23W, and stands 6m proud in a depth of 57m.

162 Irma Germaine This 19-ton fishing vessel was lost on 3 August, 1943, when she hit a mine some eight miles south-east of Berry Head. She was found in 1984 in 56m and standing 5m proud but broken. The 100ft boat is lying east–west at 50 16 39N; 03 22 28W.

163 Wreck, name unknown A 99ft ship with a beam of 17ft, this one is at 50 18 41N; 03 17 25W. She is 6m proud of the sea bed in a depth of 52m. She lies north-east to south-west.

164 Wreck, name unknown At 50 17 57N; 03 21 06W. This wreck is 279ft long, lying on the sea bed at 52m from which she is 4m proud. There is a small scour beside her, and she lies almost exactly due north–south. No further diving information is available.

165 Christoffel Columbus This Belgian MFV is at 50 18 49N; 03 21 58W. She sank on 5 June, 1970, after suddenly taking in water some six miles north-east of Start Point. Shortly afterwards divers found her, stern stove in, upright and covered in nets. The 70ft boat is now badly broken up, with the debris spread over a wide area. She stands 4m proud of the sea bed at 53m.

166 Concrete Blocks Why are there seven concrete blocks in a group at 50 19 05N; 03 18 02W, covering an area 36ft by 22ft on the sea bed at 51m? No one seems to know!

167 Aircraft, type unknown At 50 17 20N; 03 18 16W, this area of debris is some 120ft long at its widest, which points to the possibility of some large bomber such as a Flying Fortress with its 104ft wing-span. The debris stands only 1m high off the sand-shingle sea bed at 55m. No diving information is available.

168 Wreck, name unknown At 50 18 43N; 03 15 11W, this 75ft wreck stands 7m proud of the sea bed at 54m. She is upside down and broken in two, making a great V on the sea bed pointing due east.

169 Wreck, name unknown First found in 1939, just before the start of the Second World War, this small area of wreckage was relocated by the Navy in 1984 at 50 20 07N; 03 19 05W. The highest point is 5m proud of the sea bed at 52m. The wreck lies east–west and appears to be no more than 40ft long.

170 The Boiler Divers have found a large boiler on the sea bed at 50 20 18N; 03 18 00W in 52m. The boiler appears not to have a ship around it, but there must be a wreck very close to this point. More diving information is required.

171 Buesten This large Norwegian tanker was fully laden with 7200 tons of benzine and kerosene from Baytown, Texas, when German Heinkel He 111 bombers caught her on 9 April, 1941, some four miles off Berry Head. The 5187-ton tanker was lucky at first and the accurate fire of her anti-aircraft guns, manned by five British gunners, made the pilots shorten their bombing runs. All their bombs missed, but the Germans pressed on with their attacks with 7.92mm machine guns and 20mm cannon.

The 388ft tanker was difficult to miss and some of the German gunfire ripped into her cargo. There was an explosion, tanker erupted into flame, and was soon gone. Of the 30 Norwegian crew and five Navy gunners on board, only seven survived.

Built in 1927 by Barclay, Curle and Company, the *Buesten* now lies on the bottom at 50m on her starboard side. Her bows are to the east and she is 14m proud. Her bell was raised in 1979. Her position is 50 21 07N; 03 24 11W.

172 Steam trawler, name unknown At 50 20 14N; 03 26 11W. She is 102ft in length, with a beam of 23ft, lying east–west with her bows to the west on the sea bed at 50m. She is 5m proud, with a 1m scour on both sides. The four-bladed propeller is iron.

173 The Bull "Steamer" At 50 20 44N; 03 28 16W, this is no shipwreck. In fact the "steamer", called after the nearby Bull rock, is just another huge rock. It gives the most beautiful echo sounder trace, just like a 470ft ship on a sea bed at 49m, standing 14m proud and lying east–west.

Veteran diver skipper Tony Aylmer was one of the first to detect that this was no ship. He towed a magnetometer over it and there was not the slightest twitch! When dived it turned out to be a large rock with smooth, straight sides. It is however a very good site for crabs!

174 The Dutch Tug At 50 20 18N; 03 31 15W, this tug is upright in 15m of water, and is 5m proud. Her steam engine was made by H.J. Koopman of Dordrecht. The firm still exists, though the 75ft tug probably dates from the 1930s. Diver Tony Aylmer has contacted the firm who say that if he can find an engine number they will be able to give him the name and full details of the tug. This is a popular dive, best done on slacks at either 2 hours before or 3 hours after high water. Can any diver help with the engine number?

175 Broadmayne Outward-bound for Newport News, Virginia to pick up a cargo, the 3120-ton oil-tanker *Broadmayne* of London ran aground in Mill Bay

The tanker Broadmayne after she ran on to the rocks in Mill Bay Cove on New Year's Day, 1921. Everything except her bow was lost (Site 175).

Cove near Warren Point at the entrance to Dartmouth in the evening of 1 January, 1921. The conditions that New Year's Day were ghastly with thick fog, rain and a south-westerly gale kicking up huge seas. Sixteen of the crew scrambled ashore and up the cliffs.

The fog was so thick that the Brixham lifeboat searched for six hours before finding the wreck and taking off the 24 men left on board. Later, the tanker broke in two. The forepart was floated off and salvaged. The stern section is still on the sea bed at 50 20 15N; 03 33 02W. Her two boilers are in 10m of water in Mill Bay Cove and there are plates there and outside the cove. The bottom is large rocks and after a storm new pieces of the tanker's wreckage are sometimes to be seen.

176 No name wreck This mystery ship is at 50 19 30N; 03 34 18W and is in only 7m of water under Combe Point and not far from the quaintly named Dancing Beggars rocks. The wreck – 100ft long – is right in under the old Coastguard station and was found by Totnes BSAC. They discovered the ship's bell (with no name on it), portholes, and a large boiler bearing the name Dewrance and standing 3m high.

The makers of the boiler and engine have told the branch the kind of ship the boiler would be in, but cannot name the ship. She is thought to be a tug, about 100ft long, with a four bladed iron propeller. Another clue is that the brass top of the steam capstan says it was made in Gateshead. Can you name this ship? Totnes divers would very much like to know.

177 Compass wreck It is perhaps unfair to call this site at 50 19 06N; 03 36 18W a wreck, and better to say that it is good evidence of one. Here a diver found a large steel "baulk" some 16ft long and a brass compass, but no ship. In 1979, Totnes BSAC found a huge mast in the same area. It seems likely that these came from the mystery ship only a mile away from where the compass and mast were found (*see* Site **176**).

178 Jade Star Gypsy Originally at 50 21 18N; 03 25 35W, this 37ft fishing vessel may soon be back on the surface and taking out divers to other wrecks. At the time of writing there were plans to raise this ship, which sank due to a faulty sea-cock in 15 June, 1985. Divers reported she was intact and upright with a trawl hanging out and that she could be salvaged.

179 The "Harrow wreck" Known by this name after the first BSAC branch to dive her, this unknown is at 50 21 12N; 03 26 30W. She is difficult to find, as the whole of the main deck area is below the level of the sea bed, into which she is sinking. The only parts that stand proud are the bow and the bridge, which gives an echo sounder trace as though she is broken in two. In fact she is intact, 217ft long with a beam of 23ft on a yielding, silty sea bed at 45m. The bridge stands 5m high.

180 Kendal Castle On 15 September, 1918, the Coastguard at Berry Head reported a massive explosion some three miles east-south-east. What he saw was the end of the *Kendal Castle*, a 3885-ton British steamer of the Lancashire Shipping Company. Two torpedoes from the bow tubes of *UB-103* exploded simultaneously on her port side. The ship sank so swiftly that she took down with her the captain and 17 of the crew.

The *Kendal Castle* was built in 1910 by Short Brothers, and was over 350ft long, with a wide beam of 50ft. She was quite fast, with a top speed of 10.5 knots from her 353hp engines, but not fast enough to save her from Kapitänleutnant Paul Hundius in *UB-103*, one of the later types of submarine, which could do 14 knots on the surface, had four bow tubes and one stern tube, and carried 10 torpedoes.

It is possible that Hundius used two torpedoes on the *Kendal Castle* because he wanted to make sure of sinking her, and because his mission was over and he was heading for home. He was not to make his home port. The next day he was spotted as he tried to run through the Dover Barrage by the submarine-scouting *Z-1*, a small patrolling airship that reported his position to a group of drifters equipped with depth charges. Hundius was trapped and his submarine destroyed with its crew of 33. While he was on his last mission Hundius had been awarded the *Pour le Mérite*, Germany's highest decoration, but was never to know this.

The *Kendal Castle* lies upside down at 50 21 38N; 03 24 37W, on the sea bed at 48m, from which she is 12m proud. She was in ballast from Le Havre heading for Barry Roads, and today her bows point almost exactly due north. She has a 2m scour on the west side. Her bow is cracked across near heavy damage, probably from the torpedoes.

WARNING There are fishing nets caught in and on the wreck, some rising vertically from the wreck as their floats are still intact.

The beach at Lannacombe.

AREA 5:

The Bolt

This area extends from Prawle Point (03 30 00W) in the east to Bolt Tail (03 52 18W) in the west. It includes the approaches to Salcombe, Salcombe Estuary and the Bolt (the coast from Bolt Head to Bolt Tail), covering some of the most magnificent, often awe-inspiring, cliff scenery in England. The area is very short of shore diving sites – in fact only one is worth a mention – but it provides some of the best boat diving and clearest water to be found in southern England. There are many shipwreck sites, both inshore and offshore, which represent a heavy toll in lives, particularly from the crews of those sailing ships unfortunate enough to run into the Bolt in bad weather.

The key to diving in this area is SALCOMBE. Except for the far western end near Bolt Tail (which can easily be reached by boats launched from Hope Cove and Thurlestone) most of this area will be explored from boats launched at Salcombe or by the use of the bigger dive boats based there. Salcombe Estuary is a well-sheltered port much loved by the yellow-wellie brigade of yachtsmen. It is not really an estuary at all, for no great rivers feed it, and it could be better described as a drowned inlet, though a very pretty one.

The estuary is controlled by the Harbour Master, whose office is to be found on Whitestrand Quay next to the car park (tel. 01548 843791). He supervises over 1800 moorings of all kinds. There is no diving in the estuary without the Harbour Master's permission, and this includes the *Placidas Farroult* (Site **233**). There is an eight-knot speed limit, enforced by harbour patrol boats. Harbour dues are payable.

Boat traffic in and out is very heavy and the Salcombe lifeboat is moored in the centre of the harbour. Salcombe is the home of a small crabbing fleet, each boat shooting about seven strings of pots, 44 to a string. Relations with divers are generally reasonable.

Salcombe Bar is a sand bank that has built up across the mouth of the estuary and rises sharply to less than 1m below the surface at low tide. Diver coxswains should note that with such shallow water large breakers can build up. It was here in 1916 that the worst lifeboat disaster in Devon history took place when the

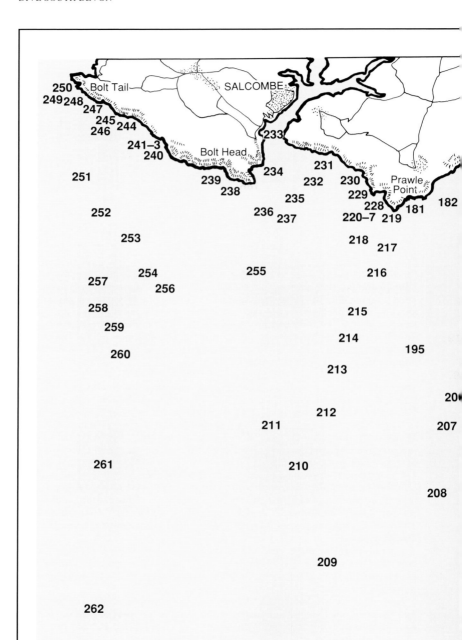

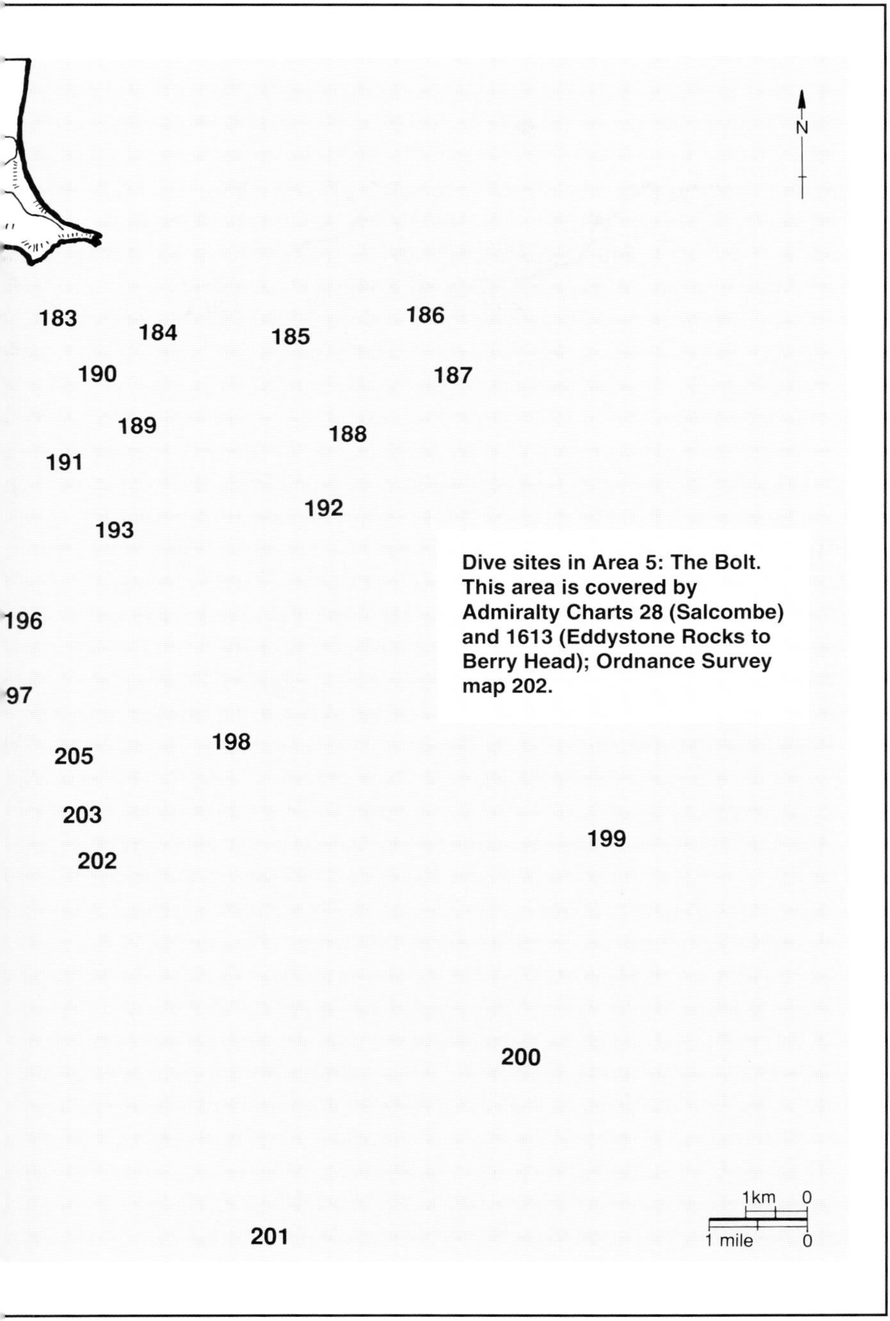

N

183

184

185

186

190

187

189

188

191

192

193

Dive sites in Area 5: The Bolt. This area is covered by Admiralty Charts 28 (Salcombe) and 1613 (Eddystone Rocks to Berry Head); Ordnance Survey map 202.

196

97

205

198

203

199

202

200

201

1km 0

1 mile 0

Salcombe lifeboat, the *William and Emma*, capsized on the Bar and 13 of her crew of 15 were drowned.

WARNING The Bar is dangerous in onshore winds between east and south, particularly during ebb tides. These conditions will cause the Bar to break and crossing it during breaking seas can be extremely dangerous. Should there be any swell running a crossing should not be attempted until the tide has risen considerably. Diver coxswains should take advice before leaving Salcombe Harbour about possible conditions on the Bar at the time of their return. They should also bear in mind that there are no other havens in the immediate vicinity. The Admiralty Pilot gives this advice:

"To cross the Bar in the deepest water keep well over to the west shore and steer with the Poundstone Beacon in line with Sandhill Point Light structure bearing 000°, and at night in the white sector of Sandhill Point Light. Pass between the Bass Rocks and Wolf Rock and then bring the leading lights near Scoble Point into line, bearing 042$\frac{1}{2}$°, which leads through the harbour to the anchorage off the town."

Salcombe provides some of the best launch sites for small boats in the whole of Devon. Approaching by the A381 from Kingsbridge, turn sharp left after passing a garage on your right before the town. The left turn is signposted for car and boat parks. Descend the steep hill; at the sharp left-hand bend turn left following signposts, then turn right to reach Shadycombe car and boat park. This is known to locals as The Dump.

The car park is on your right as you approach. For the boat park keep left around the back of the cars, which brings you directly to the boat park and launching ramp into Batson Creek. Remember that the estuary is tidal, and this creek dries out at full low water. Launching is by an excellent, wide concrete ramp down which cars can be backed. Harbour dues and parking fees must be paid. An attendant is on duty.

For other launch slipways, do not turn left for Batson Creek, but continue downhill to the centre of the town. Directly ahead of you is a narrow cul-de-sac, at the end of which is a slipway.

For another launch place, turn right and continue through a narrow shopping street to the pay-and-display car park at WHITESTRAND. There is a slipway here, though Whitestrand gets very crowded and car parking space is often filled very early. This is where diving boats operating from Salcombe sometimes pick up divers. The main pick-up point is the slipway at The Dump.

Another launching site is SOUTH SANDS. This is over a beach and at low tide it can mean a long haul. To reach it continue along the one-way road past Whitestrand and follow signposts to South Sands. There is a ramp from the road to the sand near the South Sands Hotel. An air filling station is often open at normal hours on this slipway in the old lifeboat house. The car park tends to fill up very early.

Opposite: Map of Salcombe and the Salcombe Estuary,
an area much loved by the yellow-wellie brigade.

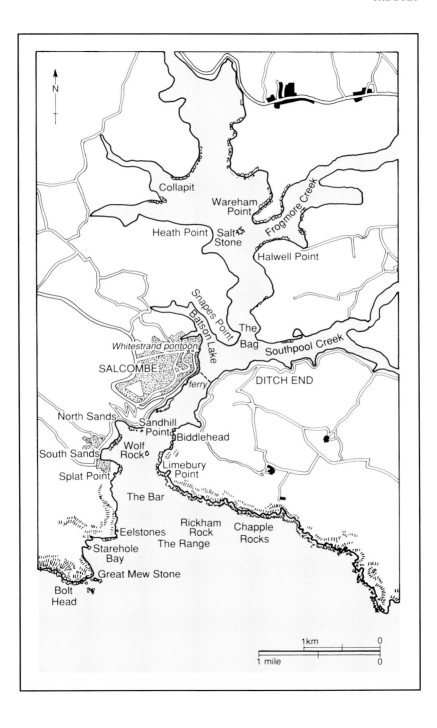

Salcombe Estuary is very sheltered and has nearly two thousand small boat moorings.

There is a good car park at North Sands. Although launching is not allowed, it is permitted to approach North Sands by boat and divers use the beach as a family base, being picked up by boat and brought back to the same spot.

It is possible to launch at Kingsbridge when the tide is in, down a good concrete ramp at the end of the car park on the quay, and bring the boat down to Salcombe this way. Stick closely to deep-channel marker posts and observe the speed limit carefully.

There is only one shore diving site in the area unless you are Superman:

181 Landing Cove The very name of this small cove tells you how difficult it is to get ashore anywhere along this stretch of coast to the east of Prawle Point. Approach is by the A379 Torcross to Kingsbridge Road, turning off at Frogmore and following signposts for East Prawle. At East Prawle keep right at the village green past the Coastguard rescue hut. This lane leads to the Coastguard station at Prawle Point.

There is a small National Trust car park on your left near the Coastguard cottages. Access to the sea is via a five-bar gate and a walk of 100yds down a path over National Trust land to the cove. At peak season go early to get into the car park.

Diving from the stony shore is into depths of 10 to 15m with a rocky bottom with gullies and a deal of kelp. Cowrie shells are common and sometimes so are edible crabs, collected by locals from the rocks at low water spring tides.

Visibility is unusually superb and attracts diver-photographers. Some strong swimmers work around Prawle Point from here, but tides are strong and great care should be taken. The wreck of the *Gossamer* (Site **219**) is here.

Boat diving sites

182 Yvette This Brixham trawler struck the rocks at Langerstone Point on 12 March, 1978, and all attempts to pull her off failed. The crew of three were taken off by line from rocket apparatus and the skipper by helicopter. She soon became a total wreck half a mile east of Landing Cove at 50 12 26N; 03 42 08W. Part of her still shows at low water.

183 Newholm Mined when on her way from Bilbao to Middlesbrough with a cargo of iron ore, this 3399-ton steamer, 330ft with a beam of 48ft, is today lying with her back broken over a large sand bank at 50 12 31N; 03 38 27W. The minefield she hit was laid by *UC-31*.

Her master, Captain Magnus Smith, and eight men were the only survivors when twenty of the crew died in the explosion and sinking on 8 September, 1917. The *Newholm* was built in 1899 by Swan Hunter of Newcastle. Her signal letters at the time of her sinking were RCPT and her 293hp triple-expansion engines could drive her along at 10 knots. At the time of her loss she belonged to the Newcastle Steamship Company.

Though she is charted as swept to 20m, divers say that the depth to her stern rails is 28m near the cast-iron propeller. Her stern is the nearest part of her to the shore, with her bows to the south-south-east. She lies down the sand slope on her starboard side. The first break in her is by a mast lying nearby at about 32m and there is another gap before the bow section starts much deeper at 43m. The deepest point is at the bow at 44m. The sand has filled her amidships. There is much marine life on the wreck.

184 Novice This British harbour tug was heading for the Isle of Man from Brixham when she struck a submerged object at 50 12 34N; 03 37 05W. She sank swiftly on 23 February, 1973, and stands 4m proud in 54m. She is in the middle of the Start Race (*see* warning under Site **130**) and is very rarely dived.

185 Wreck, name unknown At 50 12 10N; 03 33 52W, she stands 3m proud of the sea bed at 60m. The wreck has not been dived, but echo sounder traces suggest that this big ship lies north-east to south-west and is significantly sunk into the sea bed.

186 Medina This P&O liner is a massive wreck at 50 12 25N; 03 32 11W and is at the great depth of 60m to the sea bed, on which she sits upright with a 15° list to port. The 12,350-ton armed steamer was three miles east-north-east of Start Point after leaving Plymouth on 28 April, 1917, on the last leg of her voyage to London from India, when she was torpedoed at 6.30pm.

The torpedo was fired from *UB-31* at periscope depth by Oberleutnant T. Bieber and struck the *Medina* in the starboard engine room killing Mr Palmer, the Fourth Engineer, and five firemen. The engines stopped immediately and the liner started sinking. Captain Henry Sandys Bradshaw sent out distress calls while loading the 411 passengers and crew into the boats. At 7.15pm the *Medina* sank. Her boats were towed by destroyers and launches to Dartmouth, while other warships laid a pattern of depth charges over the spot where the U-boat was believed to be. They were close, but not close enough and Bieber lived to sink many more Allied ships before being killed in *UB-104* in 1918, by the mines of the Northern Barrage.

The *Medina* was 550ft long with a beam of 63ft and a draught of 35ft. She was built, starting in 1910, by J. Caird and Company of Greenock for the Peninsular and Oriental Steam Navigation Company, who expected to take delivery in 1912. However, on completion she was chartered as a royal yacht to take King George V and Queen Mary to the Coronation ceremonies in Delhi. She was handed back to P&O in June 1912 and was used on regular runs to Australia. During World War One she was armed, but relied more on her speed – her 1164hp engines gave 19 knots – to protect her on the long voyages she continued to make until she was torpedoed.

The wreck of the *Medina* is still reasonably intact despite a good deal of salvage work over recent years for her cargo of copper ingots. It is 39m to her deck. The stern has suffered the most damage, and it is here that she appears to be sinking into the sea bed. She lies north–south and her hull metal is getting very thin. Many of her bulkheads have collapsed, letting compartments fold down like stacks of cards.

In l988 there was a highly publicised treasure hunt by a professional diving team for the baggage of Lord Carmichael of Skirling, who was believed to be bringing home his priceless collection of antiques in the ship. His baggage was recovered from forward holds, together with ivory figures and Indian brasswork, by bell divers tunnelling through the mud that filled the holds. Some 6000 items were raised by the divers and 2000 were auctioned at Sotheby's, but the sums raised were disappointing.

187 Gro A torpedo fired from the German U-boat *UB-47* while surfaced sank this 2667-ton Norwegian cargo ship on 22 August, 1917, while she was steaming from the Clyde to Rouen with a cargo of coal. *UC-47* was commanded by Oberleutnant Paul Hundius, who was later to be promoted to Kapitänleutnant before being killed in the last U-boat to be destroyed in the Dover Barrage (*see* Site **180**).

Despite suffering huge damage to her port side amidships, the *Gro* did not sink at once; she was towed towards Dartmouth by Torpedo Boat 99 and Admiralty trawlers for some time before finally sinking. All the crew managed to take to the boats. Now their ship is at 50 12 12N; 03 32 04W, standing 10m proud of the 60m sea bed. She lies only 370yds from the *Medina* (Site **186**) and has been identified by divers who raised the builder's plate – she was built in 1895 by W. Hamilton and Company. She is positioned north-east to south-west and is 309ft long with a beam of 42ft.

188 Llamedos A British fishing vessel despite the Spanish name, this 36ft wooden boat sank while under tow by the Torbay lifeboat on 4 February, 1983. She is now in 60m, standing 5m proud at 50 11 30N; 03 34 30W.

189 Talvaldis This Latvian steamer from Riga was moving over a calm sea on 9 July, 1940, when a German aircraft attacked her with machine guns and bombs off Prawle Point. She sank at 50 11 19N; 03 38 27W. A motor boat from Lannacombe Bay was first on the scene and rescued six of the crew from a raft. The Salcombe lifeboat found another six in a waterlogged boat.

The *Talvaldis* was small (534 tons) and now lies at 58m from which she stands 9m proud. Her stern is intact and upright. The centre section has collapsed onto the sea bed. The area forward of the bridge, where the bombs hit, is completely broken off. The main wreckage is about 180ft long and lies east–west.

190 Neches This 5426-ton American steamer-tanker was laden with petrol when something came out of the dark and hit her on 15 May, 1918, at 50 11 54N; 03 37 48W. The *Neches* promptly sank, but no one knows what happened to the small steamer said to have collided with her. That ship, too, may well have sunk for no report of a collision was ever filed except that of the crew of the *Neches* (who were all saved).

Two reports of the time will interest divers. The first was on 18 December, 1917, six months before the *Neches* was sunk, from the steamer *Isle of Lewis*, which reported striking a submerged object at the same position. The second came from another steamer, which reported on 27 July, 1918, that there was a wreck with the mast showing above water at that same position. This second report was probably of the wreck of the *Neches*, but the first raises a question: did the *Neches* hit a steamer or that "submerged object"? Only diving will give the answer and the dive reports studied so far reveal that she is very badly broken, more like a scrap yard than a ship. The depth to the sea bed is 53m, from which she stands only 4m proud.

191 Agnete Though eight of the crew survived, twelve including the master died on 24 April, 1918, when this 1127-ton armed merchantman going from Newport to Rouen was torpedoed by *UB-40* south of Start Point at 50 11 04N; 03 39 02W. The 214ft ship now stands 9m clear of the sea bed at 58m. Her deck has collapsed inwards, and a large part of the forward section ahead of the bridge is missing. For some time this wreck was thought to be that of the steamer *Hazelpark* (Site **196**).

192 Warsaw This British steamer of 608 tons, 209ft long with a beam of 25ft, was torpedoed by Oberleutnant Bieber in *UB-31* on 20 December, 1917. She sank so swiftly that there were only 3 survivors, landed at Dartmouth. The other 17 crew including the master were lost. The *Warsaw* was on her way from St Malo for Liverpool in ballast. She now lies at 50 10 44N; 03 34 07W, deep on a rocky sea bed at 66m from which she stands, very broken, 5m proud. Her 12-pounder gun (weighing over half a ton) is still amongst the wreckage.

193 Chorley The 3828-ton *Chorley* was heading for Le Havre after a transatlantic voyage from Norfolk, Virginia. She was torpedoed by Oberleutnant Ramien in *UC-48* from a hull-down position on 22 March, 1917. The crew of the 160ft ship were all saved. Today she lies north-west to south-east at 50 10 29N; 03 37 41W, is intact and deep at 61m. She stands 9m proud.

194 Baychattan So confident was one German U-boat that on 15 May, 1917, she surfaced and attacked this 3758-ton armed merchantman with the gun on her casing. It may be that the submarine had run out of torpedoes, but the British steamer returned fire with her 13-pounder quick-fire gun and drove the U-boat away.

The *Baychattan* was less fortunate when spotted on 11 October that same year, by the mine-layer *UC-50*. Kapitänleutnant R. Seuffer did not surface and expose himself to the gunners of the *Baychattan*, but let go one torpedo from periscope depth. It struck the 361ft steamer towards the stern on the port side. All the crew including the master, Captain R. Saunders, took to the boats, were picked up and landed at Plymouth.

Seuffer got away, but was killed with his crew when *UC-50* was destroyed by depth charges in the Channel by HMS *Zubian* on 4 February, 1918. The *Zubian* was an extraordinary destroyer built out of the pieces of the *Zulu* and *Nubian*, which had both been damaged in action.

The *Baychattan* had sailed under another name: she was built as the *Kilchatten* in 1906 by Charles Conell of Glasgow. Later this two-boiler ship was bought in 1917 by the Bay Steamship Company of London, who renamed all their older ships, and others they bought around that time, with the *Bay* prefix. She now lies with her bluff bows to the east at 50 11 23N; 03 42 07W and her holds are empty, for she was travelling in ballast from Le Havre at the time of her sinking. She is upright, on an even keel, swept of her superstructure, but with the torpedo damage at her stern clear to see. The depth to her deck is 37m and it is 54m to the sea bed.

195 Laertes The crew of this 4541-ton British steamer failed to spot the periscope of *UB-31* when they were 1¼ miles south-south-west of Prawle Point, heading from Southampton to Montreal in ballast. So 14 men died on 1 August, 1917, when Oberleutnant Bieber fired a single torpedo that struck the steamer abreast of the aft hold.

The *Laertes* had been attacked before, on 10 February, 1915. Then it was her speed that took her away from the submarine that fired a torpedo and shelled the 382ft steamer. Since then the ship had been armed, but she had no chance to fire or run away this time. Built in 1904 by Hawthorne Leslie and Company, she now lies in 62m with her bow to the north-west, upright, and 13m proud of the sea bed. She has been identified by her bell, which has been recovered. Her position is 50 09 38N; 03 43 19W.

196 Hazelpark This 1964-ton steamer, with a cargo of coal, was coming from South Shields and heading for La Rochelle in the evening of 20 March, 1917, when she was torpedoed by Oberleutnant Herbert Pustkuchen in *UC-66* from a hull-down attitude south of Start Point. She sank at 50 09 43N; 03 39 28W, but all her crew were saved. She now lies north–south, upright but badly broken in 64m from which she stands 9m clear.

Pustkuchen did not leave the area. The very next night, five miles south of Start Point, he torpedoed the hospital ship *Asturias*, which had disembarked wounded from Thessaloniki (Salonica) at Avonmouth and was on passage up the Channel. She had all her lights on and the large Red Cross on each side was floodlit. The explosion killed 35 crew and medical staff, but the *Asturias* floated long enough to be beached in Starehole Bay, Salcombe, where some casualties were brought ashore and nursed at Sharpitor, near South Sands. She was later refloated.

Pustkuchen was killed in June that year, when he became the first victim of the new "hydrophones". He was detected by the Lizard Hydrophone Division, which guided warships to the scene by radio. The depth charges they dropped detonated the cargo of mines aboard the *UC-66* and one witness said "the sea boiled over".

197 Wreck, name unknown At 50 09 01N; 03 38 55W, lying north–south in 66m from which she stands 7m proud, this steamer is badly damaged at the bows, which are to the north, and is broken elsewhere. She is 115ft long.

198 Wreck, name unknown At 50 08 48N; 03 35 10W, this one is about 290ft long and is lying in a hollow between two huge sandbanks, so she is not easy to pick up on an echo sounder, though she is a large wreck. She is intact but slightly sunk into the sea bed at 66m. She stands 13m proud.

199 Bob This small Norwegian steamer of 678 tons was heading from Llanelli with 748 tons of coal for Rouen on 29 November, 1917, when she was caught by Oberleutnant Stöter in *UB-35*, who surfaced and started shelling her from a range of 1000yds when 8 miles south-south-east of Start Point. The ship was soon riddled with four-inch holes and the crew took to the boats, though three were killed before they could do so. Instead of finishing the job, the U-boat suddenly dived.

The reason was the approach of a British destroyer and patrol boats. Naval volunteers went aboard the *Bob* and got her under way while waiting for a tug. When the tug took the tow, however, it proved too much of a strain for the little steamer and she was soon listing. Shortly afterwards she rolled completely over and sank. Her present position is close to 50 08 00N; 03 30 00W and the depth is 64m.

200 Flourish This British MFV sank over 8 miles from Start Point on 17 October, 1975, after a collision with an unknown vessel at 50 06 00N; 03W 31 40. All the crew were picked up safely.

201 Eagle This small British merchant ship of 182 tons was captured by a boarding party from *UB-35*, commanded by Oberleutnant Stöter, in the moonlight of 4 December, 1917. The boarding party placed bombs aboard and she sank at 50 03 30N; 03 34 20W, some 10 miles south of Start Point. The crew in their boats were picked up safely. The *Eagle* had been bound from Guernsey for Swansea. The position is approximate, and she is estimated to be 50m deep.

202 Wreck, name unknown At 50 07 41N; 03 38 35W, lying on her port side, north-east to south-west, this wreck is intact on the sea bed at 68m. She stands 9m proud and is 180ft long.

203 Frederick Details of this one at 50 08 04N; 03 38 57W are extremely scanty. All we have is a position, a depth (66m) and a name. More details are required of the ship's history and her condition.

204 HMS Penylan This Hunt Class Type III destroyer was torpedoed by an E-boat off Start Point on 3 December, 1942. Of 1050 tons, 272ft long with a beam of 28ft, and with 19,000hp turbines that could drive her at 27.5 knots, this Navy ship today is at 50 08 16N; 03 40 05W.

Captained by Lieutenant-Commander J.H. Wallace, D.S.C., the *Penylan* was built by Vickers Armstrong at Barrow and completed on 31 August, 1942. Two officers and 34 ratings were killed in the E-boat attack on her. Today she stands 13m proud of the sea bed at 66m, lies east–west, and is in reasonably good condition.

205 Grelhame This British steamer of 3740 tons was torpedoed by *U-62* on 30 August, 1917. She was travelling from Cuba and Norfolk, Virginia for Le Havre with a cargo of sugar. Though she sank in four minutes after the torpedo struck her in the port side just under the bridge, all the crew took to the boats safely. She is now four miles south-west of Start Point at 50 08 29N; 03 39 44W. This armed ship – the 4.7-inch gun is still in place on her stern – lies east–west at 66m. To her highest point it is 56m and she is broken clean in two amidships.

206 Perm Built in 1883 by Burmeister and Wain, this 1112-ton Danish steamship was torpedoed on 28 November, 1917, and sank at 50 08 21N; 03 41 30W. She was 236ft long with a beam of 30ft and was laden with 762 tons of coke at the time of her sinking, on passage from Cardiff to St Malo. Two of the crew died when she sank in 66m. She stands 7m proud and lies north-east to south-west.

207 Wreck, name unknown At 50 08 14N; 03 40 57W, this is a merchant ship of the "three island" type of about 120ft. She lies north-east to south-west and is well sunk into the sea bed at 67m.

208 Wreck, name unknown At 50 06 35N; 03 42 28W, this unknown lies north–south, is small and well broken and stands only 4m proud of the sea bed at 69m.

209 Wreck, name unknown At 50 04 31N; 03 46 36W, she stands 15m proud of the sea bed at 68m and is believed to be considerably sunk into the sea bed.

210 Santa Godeleave A British wooden MFV that sank on 21 March, 1969, some five miles south of Bolt Head in 64m of water at approximately 50 07 00N; 03 47 00W. No further details are available.

211 Wreck, name unknown At 50 07 58N; 03 47 40W, she is 160ft long, lying east–west, on a sea bed at 65m from which she is 6m proud.

212 Amelie A Belgian steamer of 1463 tons, the *Amelie* was torpedoed on 13 November, 1917, when she was on her way to Le Havre from Cardiff. Six of the crew of this 226ft steamer with a beam of 32ft were lost and five injured.

The *Amelie* was built in 1883 at the Howaldtswerke at Kiel in Germany. Today she is at 50 08 21N; 03 46 12W. No U-boat commander claimed her as a victim and she now sits upright, largely intact on a sea bed at 64m, from which she is 7m proud.

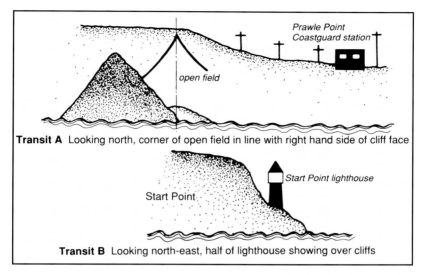

Transit A Looking north, corner of open field in line with right hand side of cliff face

Transit B Looking north-east, half of lighthouse showing over cliffs

Transit marks for the Riversdale (Site 217).

213 Wreck, name unknown At 50 08 36N; 03 45 25W, this wreck is about 290ft long, intact and upright on the sea bed at 65m. She lies north-west to south-east and is 11m proud.

214 Havbris This small Norwegian steamer of 677 tons was torpedoed by the submarine ace Oberleutnant Viebeg in command of *UB-32*. He fired at her from periscope depth as she was carrying coal from Newport to Honfleur, near Le Havre. All the crew were saved. She is now at 50 09 28N; 03 44 45W on the sea bed at 59m, from which she stands 7m proud. She is 150ft long and lies east–west.

215 North Sea This 1711-ton coastal collier gave her position as 3¹/₂ miles south-south-west of Bolt Head when she was torpedoed on 13 October, 1917, while carrying coal from Hartlepool to Pauillac. One man died and the submarine responsible was *UC-65*.

The *North Sea* is now at 50 10 32N; 03 45 04W at a depth of 54m, upright but badly damaged at the stern, which is where the torpedo struck. All her superstructure is gone, as is her decking; only her hull and the coal remain on the rippled sand sea bed. She stands 8m proud.

216 HMS Jasper This 596-ton Admiralty trawler was built in 1932, and was formerly called *Balthasar*. She was torpedoed by an E-boat on 1 December, 1942, and now sits upright in 55m at 50 10 51N; 03 44 00W. She is 8m proud of the sea bed, 145ft long with a beam of 25ft. She is listing 45° to port according to diver Tony Hilgrove.

217 Riversdale Any hopes that it was going to a quiet run-up to Christmas in 1917 were dashed by Oberleutnant Bieber in *UB-31* when he torpedoed this 2805-ton British steamer on 18 December, killing one man in the explosion. The 317ft steel single-screw ship was beached close to Prawle Point – she had been on her way from the Tyne to Savona in Italy with a cargo of 4000 tons of coal for the Italian railways. Bieber hit her with a shot from periscope depth. The gunner on duty on the *Riversdale*, Cornelius Simms, spotted the periscope and managed to get off four shots at it from the 12-pounder gun, though without apparent success. He may have frightened Bieber away, for *UB-31* did not wait around to see the steamer sink, but headed away north-east and at midnight found the *Alice Marie* (Site **142**).

Built by J. Blumer and Company of Sunderland in 1906, the *Riversdale* had been well placed ashore by her master, Captain J.T. Simpson, and salvage experts thought she could be saved. Her bulkheads were shored up and compressors installed on her decks to hold back the sea from the patched-up torpedo hole. Then the tugs pulled her off. Unfortunately, though she came off without much trouble, she sank upright before the tow had gone 1000yds at 50 11 44N; 03 44 04W. She is still upright on the sea bed; it is 30m to her deck and a further 11m to the sea bed. Her superstructure is gone, the result of a wire sweep. The bow section is largely uninteresting and has broken away from the wreck.

The *Riversdale* was first dived by Torbay BSAC, who identified her by means of the letters HGMR amateurishly centre-punched onto one of the spokes of a small bronze wheel they had raised. These turned out to be the ship's wartime signal letters. Having identified her, the Torbay divers then approached the Ministry of Transport in 1964 to see if they could buy her. War loss compensation had already been paid so the Ministry asked for an offer. Torbay offered £5 and to their amazement it was accepted.

Divers will be envious of such a bargain, but they should respect the fact that the wreck still belongs to Torbay. There has been some recent salvage on her for her coal cargo. There is a 2m scour on the west side. Do not bother checking the propeller – it is iron. Her bell has been raised by Torbay divers. Transit marks for the *Riversdale* are shown in the diagram on page 119.

WARNING This is another wreck on which phosphorus wedges have been seen (*see* page 17). Do not touch them.

218 Prawle Point The name comes from an old English word for a lookout, and that is exactly what Prawle Point provides today, with a large Coastguard station at the most southerly point in Devon. Perhaps due to the fact that the point juts out so far into the Channel, there have been more recorded shipwrecks in this vicinity than on any comparable stretch of coast in the country.

Local divers were quite upset when on 18 December, 1992, yet another wreck was added to the wrecks off Prawle Point and sprawled right across several interesting and much older sites. The newcomer was the 9700-ton cargo ship

The Demetrios on Prawle Point, 1992 (Site 219).

Demetrios, formerly the Chinese-owned *Longlin*, which was being towed from Dunkirk by the Russian tug *Nastoroh* to a Turkish breaker's yard when the tow parted 16 miles off Start Point in a Force 10 gale.

A second tug tried to get a line aboard but failed. The *Demetrios* was then blown for five hours before crashing into Prawle Point, just by Gull Island, where massive seas broke her in half. She is now spread along the cliffs around 50 12 07N; 03 43 18W. Some salvage work has been carried out, and in a flashback to the bad old days there was looting when some of the thousands who went to see her climbed aboard from the rocks.

Prawle Point is well over 300ft high and has an arch at the tip at sea level. Prawle Island is a large rock almost attached to the point and slightly to the west. North from the island is Gull Rock, which lives up to its name, being usually crowded with seagulls. Those with a good imagination will spot The Horse, a shape that can be made out of the rocks on the point from a boat at sea.

Diving around Prawle Point illustrates the old adage that the sea bed follows the shape of the land above it. Depths of 18m just off increase steeply to over 30m. This is dramatic diving, with good visibility at most times of the year. Tidal streams round the point can be strong.

219 Gossamer This 734-ton fully-rigged tea clipper was wrecked on 10 December, 1868, when she was driven onto Prawle Point by a huge gale from the south-south-west. This 181ft sailing ship, which had a beam of 30ft, was built in 1864 by Alexander Stephen and Sons at Kelvinborough, Glasgow, and was one of the few composite ships built in Britain – with an iron frame and wood planking.

The *Gossamer* was a famous clipper and had been the second ship home from China in the annual tea race from Shanghai to London only two months before she was wrecked. Outward-bound for Australia carrying 24 crew, four passengers and general cargo, she had a stormy passage down the Channel. Captain John Thomson stayed on deck for hours, and had two whole nights without sleep. When, finally, he did go down to his cabin and slept, the pilot was said to have got drunk and the watching Coastguards on Prawle Point saw the *Gossamer* attempt to tack, fail, and then reef most of her canvas before dropping anchors. This awoke Captain Thomson, but there was little he could do. The anchors held for half an hour, but then both cables snapped and she smashed ashore.

She missed Landing Cove by just 100 yards. Thirteen were drowned. The captain was seen to lash his bride of a fortnight to a spar and for a time kept her up in the water, but neither survived. A tombstone near the entrance to Chivelstone Church marks the grave of the captain and his wife, Barbara Kerr, who came from the Isle of Bute. It had been her first and last voyage. The pilot was sent for trial at Exeter charged with manslaughter.

The wreck of the *Gossamer* lies amid rock gullies in quite shallow water though the sea bed falls steeply quite close in. Local diver Stephen George (*see* Site **296**) has recovered many items: brass bolts stamped "A.S&S", blocks, inkwells (still full), cruet sets, compass bowl dolphins, door knobs, dividers and dinner plates. He believes from his hours of work on her that her stern lies to the east and her bow is nearest to Prawle Point.

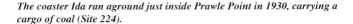

The coaster Ida ran aground just inside Prawle Point in 1930, carrying a cargo of coal (Site 224).

220 De Boot This Dutch East Indiaman, captained by Jacob van Duijnen and homeward bound from Batavia (now Jakarta), ran onto Prawle Point on 8 November, 1738. She was packed with porcelain, stowed in loose tea in the holds of the 130ft ship. She also carried boxes of uncut diamonds, and one box is known to have been stolen by one of the local people who came to help with salvage work on the wreck. Her cargo, according to the captain, was worth some £250,000.

Some of her cannon were raised at the time, though divers who have worked in the gullies on the Point and around Gull Rock will know that one six-foot cannon is still there. So are a lot of concreted cannonballs, though these may well come from HMS *Crocodile* (Site **221**). Belgian underwater archaeologist Robert Stenuit, who found the Armada ship *Girona* and has worked many other East Indiamen, trenched across the site several summers ago, and was disappointed not to find one single intact piece of porcelain. He did however find so many broken bits amid the sand that he said the sea bed at times seemed to be made of Ming, gleaming and glistening with tiny shards of the blue and white porcelain. Divers today will have no difficulty in finding small pieces of it in the gullies and on sand patches amid the kelp.

221 HMS Crocodile A 24-gun frigate, homeward bound from India, 114ft long with 170 men aboard, the *Crocodile* ran onto Prawle Point at 2.30am on 9 May, 1784, in thick fog. While everyone reached the shore unhurt, the Navy ship was a total loss. Though there was a good deal of salvage at the time, only 14 of her guns seemed to have been saved. This would account for the badly eroded specimens to be seen near The Horse.

There too, under the hatch covers of the *Heye-P* (Site **227**) is a bed of concreted cannonballs that may have come from the *Crocodile*. Her wreckage seems scattered right along a stretch from Prawle Point to the west past Gull Rock, where there have been finds of copper pins bearing the Admiralty broad-arrow mark, copper sheathing, barbed nails, a pan weight bearing the figure 14, and a sounding lead that might have come from *De Boot* (Site **220**).

222 Maria On 27 June, 1892, the Greek steamer *Maria* ran onto Langler Rocks on the west side of Prawle Point in thick fog. The Salcombe lifeboat went to help, but by the time they reached the ship the two passengers and 23 crew had rowed ashore in their own boat.

The *Maria* had a short life. She was launched in Sunderland in May, 1891 and was declared a total wreck on 19 July, 1892. Today you can see her three boilers in 20m, close to the west side of Prawle Island. One of the boilers is upright among the wreckage, the other two are lying on their sides.

223 Glad Tidings This 1292-ton sailing ship carrying a cargo of linseed oil from Calcutta and bound for Amsterdam ran onto the rocks in rough weather on 15 December, 1882. Sparks from a distress flare set the whole ship alight. A Coastguard team with rocket apparatus saved 19 of her crew, but two others drowned trying to swim ashore. She is now very broken up, a quarter of a mile north-west of Prawle Point, towards Elender Cove, in 10m.

The Louis-Yvonne was a French onion boat. She became a total wreck near Prawle Point in 1935 (Site 226).

224 Ida On passage from Cardiff to Portsmouth with a cargo of coal, this coaster ran ashore just inside Prawle Point in thick fog on 22 September, 1930. Coastguards saved the crew of 12. She remained broadside on to the cliff until early October when a gale broke her in two and she slipped into deeper water. The boiler and shaft can be seen in 10m.

225 Bona Although very broken, some remains of this 80-ton ketch from Ipswich can be found in the rock gullies to the west of Prawle Point. Her cargo was coal from South Wales and some is still there. She sank on 4 August, 1907, when she was just nine years old. The crew of four got safely to shore.

226 Louis-Yvonne This French onion boat ran aground between Prawle Island and Gull Rock on 29 September, 1935. She is very broken up in 5m and her large anchor is 18yds to the west in a gully between the point and the island.

227 Heye-P This 296-ton West German motor vessel was carrying a cargo of china clay from Par to Velsen in the Netherlands when she ran aground on Prawle Island in a Force 8 gale on 16 December, 1979. She started breaking up almost immediately and a helicopter from HMS *Culdrose* rescued the crew of three.

She now lies at 50 12 07N; 03 43 18W. Part of the wreckage dries at low water spring tides and can be seen between Gull Island and the mainland. Her wreckage lies across that of the *De Boot* (Site **220**) and at least six other vessels are close by: HMS *Crocodile* (Site **221**), the *Ida* (Site **224**), the *Bona* (Site **225**), the *Louis-Yvonne* (Site **226**), the *Maria* (Site **222**) and the *Gossamer* (Site **219**).

228 Lalla Rookh This square-rigged tea clipper was homeward bound for London from Shanghai with 1300 tons of tea and 10 tons of tobacco. Aboard were 19 crew, a passenger and a stowaway. On 3 March, 1873, she was running before a south-westerly gale in poor visibility when she struck Gammon Head, but was carried on round into Elender Cove. One of her masts collapsed and pushed out some of her bottom plates; she started to sink. By then she had four fewer crew aboard, as they had been in the bow and had jumped onto the rocks at Gammon Head when she first hit.

Another 15 people were saved by breeches buoy when a rocket line was put across her by Prawle Coastguards. The only casualties were the mate, Thomas Groves, who was drowned trying to launch a boat, and the stowaway, who it is believed was dead in his bunk from dysentery before the ship struck. Within a week the ship broke in two, but not before 100 cases of tea had been salvaged as well as many of the ship's fittings.

The ship is interesting for two other reasons. One is that her figurehead was picked up on a beach in Jersey – and can now be seen on board the *Cutty Sark* at Greenwich. The second is that this was one of the first ships to have her crew

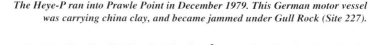

The Heye-P ran into Prawle Point in December 1979. This German motor vessel was carrying china clay, and became jammed under Gull Rock (Site 227).

rescued by breeches buoy. A description of the rescue from RNLI records shows how new this method was:

> It was just becoming light when she struck a rock and this was seen by one of the coastguards. He whistled to warn the crew of their danger, but seeing it was in vain, ran to the station for the rocket apparatus.
>
> Mr Segrue (the Chief Boatman) and his men speedily got it, brought it to the scene of the disaster, where it was worked with a will. The first line fell across the ship and was secured. The basket soon followed. One man and a boy went across singly, but the rest of the crew, who clustered on the mizzen top-mast, most of them nearly naked, hesitated to trust themselves to the basket two at a time until Captain Fullerton, the master, said that he would set an example and got in with a sailor. When they were drawn ashore there was no longer any hesitation and the men followed, the coastguards working the apparatus with such hearty good will that in 25 minutes the fifteen were rescued.

The remains of the *Lalla Rookh* are completely scattered in less than 10m, but plates and anchor chain are easy to find.

229 Reliance This 31-ton paddle-steamer tug foundered on 30 December, 1888, in a Force 6 north-easterly. The 98ft tug, built at Yarmouth on the Isle of Wight in 1874, was under tow by another tug, the *Conqueror*, and was bound from Gravesend to Troon when she sprang a leak and was abandoned by her crew of four. She is in a gully off Gammon Head at 50 12 21N; 03 44 15W at 20m.

Two large boilers and paddlewheels are to be seen as well as the engine, iron frames and wooden planking. The *Reliance* is not easy to find, as the gully in which the wreckage lies is so deep that a diver going along the edge of the reef can go right past without seeing it.

230 Bronze Age Sword Wreck This is at 50 12 42N; 03 44 20W, but you cannot dive an area within 150m of this point (just off Moor Sand, the bay to the west of the headland known as Pig's Nose) as it has been designated as a Protected Wreck site. This protection was given in 1978 after diver Phil Baker found a fine bronze sword and two other bronze weapons on the sea bed the year before.

In 1978 an archaeological survey was carried out under the direction of the late Keith Muckelroy and more 3000-year-old bronze weapons, including two axe heads, were discovered. But no other traces of a wreck were found. Today a large notice warning against diving in the area is mounted on the cliff and can clearly be seen from the sea..

231 Meirion This 1372-ton fully-rigged iron barque, only a year old, was homeward bound from Rangoon for London on 7 September, 1879, with a cargo of 2000 tons of rice, when she ran ashore below Gara Rock Coastguard station in fog and a strong south-easterly. The rocket apparatus saved her crew of 16 including her captain, William Williams. Attempts to pull her off failed and after

The Meirion, wrecked near Gara Rock in 1879 when homeward bound for London from Rangoon (Site 231).

only 120 tons of her cargo had been saved, she broke in two a fortnight later. Divers have found some of her plates and bits of her keel in less than 10m.

In June 1994, Duncan Gray of Henley BSAC, while on a drift dive near the *Meirion* site, found himself in a small gully, not far offshore, the end of which was blocked by a pile of cannon. Henley divers found 11 cannon, many of which are 7ft long and one of which is 8ft 6in. Two large anchors are nearby. The ship was at first thought to have been carrying a cargo of bricks as there are hundreds scattered close by, but these have been identified as coming from a barge that sank there in 1929. A full archaeological survey is being carried out and the cannon ship may become a protected wreck.

Though there is no definite identification, the ship may be the *Resolution*, sunk on 13 December, 1806. She was am American armed ship and two of her crew were lost in the sinking "near Salcombe".

232 Salcombe Range This is the name for the sea area immediately outside Salcombe, bounded on the north by the Bar. To the south an imaginary line from Gammon Head to Bolt Head is the limit. Depths vary from 6m to 25m and the bottom is varied too. Some areas have razor-backed ridges, some are shingle among low rocks, and some pure sand.

The marine life suits the terrain and includes gorgonia, crabs and lobsters, the hard but brittle rose coral, fan worms and flatfish. One particularly beautiful area is the Chapple Rock Plateau to the east, offshore from Rickham village. Here you will find the Handon Rocks, the Gulston Rocks, Cat Rock and Chapple Rocks, which give an immensely varied bottom with ridges and gullies and several rock pinnacles in less than 10m. This rocky area is at and around 50 13 00N; 03 45 54W.

The figurehead of the Herzogin Cecilie. This four-master was lost in 1935 after hitting the Ham Stone and being towed into Starehole Bay, near Salcombe (Site 234).

233 Placidas Farroult This 136-ton coaster lies immediately inside the Blackstone at the entrance to Salcombe in 10m at 50 13 36N; 03 46 26W. She lies parallel to the rocks, onto which she drifted in a south-westerly gale on 1 November, 1940.

The ship was built in France in 1927 and was one of about twenty small French and Belgian ships that escaped the fall of France in 1940. At this time the Admiralty ordered a boom defence to be set up across the entrance to Salcombe Harbour. The *Placidas Farroult* and a French lifeboat were used as gate vessels and all buoys and beacons marking the entrance were removed. The Wolf Buoy, together with some cable, was stored in the hold of the French coaster.

Both gate vessels were securely moored but the *Placidas Farroult* broke free and was badly holed on the Blackstone. She lay on the rocks, her sides corrugated, with her bows to seaward, but the next tide drove her off and she sank broadside on the inside of the Blackstone with her funnel showing at low water. Since then she has settled right into the sand, but for a long time her mast was used as a datum pole for minefields laid locally.

She is a good wreck dive for beginners, largely intact on an even keel with rudder, propeller and handrails in position. The conical, wooden Wolf Buoy is still in her hold. The forward section is starting to break up. Divers here must have permission from the Harbour Master at Salcombe (*see* page 107). Take great care during tide runs as vast quantities of water flow in and out past the Blackstone. Slack is at high water and low water, and lasts about 30 minutes.

234 Herzogin Cecilie Sailors all over the world called her "The Duchess". And duchess she was as she swished across the world's oceans at her top speed of 20³/₄ knots. This was not quite a world record – the Yankee clipper *James Baines* held that with 21 knots. She was called "The Duchess" because she was named after the Duchess Cecilie, daughter of the Duke of Oldenburg, and her figurehead was a romantic carving of the Duchess Cecilie herself.

Today the *Herzogin Cecilie* lies very broken in Starehole Bay, just outside the entrance to Salcombe at 50 12 49N; 03 47 01W. A 3111-ton four-master, she was launched at Bremerhaven in April 1902 and at first she was the crack cadet training ship of Norddeutscher Lloyd. In World War One she was interned in Chile.

At the end of the war she was handed over to the French, who sold her to a Finnish shipping firm. It was then that she really showed what she could do. During the great grain races she left them all standing, which is not surprising because when she had all sails spread she had an acre of canvas aloft. With all that pushing her along, her 336ft hull, with a beam of 46ft, smashed its way from Australia to England in under 90 days. In one run from Melbourne to Taltal in Chile she managed 2120 nautical miles in seven days – a record that has never been equalled.

Her last voyage was her fastest ever: Australia to Falmouth in 86 days. But at 8pm on 24 April, 1936, she left Falmouth for Ipswich. The night was dark with rain,

The Herzogin Cecilie in Starehole Bay, with the grain from her cargo staining the water around her (Site 234).

and a moderate south-westerly kept her running free. At midnight the wind dropped and the rain became fog. The *Herzogin Cecilie* moved on over the light swell and sounded her foghorn every two minutes. At 3am the night broke, but the fog remained. Suddenly Captain Sven Eriksson saw a dark line through the fog. He had no doubts, and ordered "Hard a-starboard", but it was too late, and she hit the Ham Stone off Soar Mill Cove. (Soar is pronounced "Sewer" and owes its origin to the Anglo-Saxon "sae ware" – sea dwellers – suggesting that there was an early settlement here.)

The mate, Elis Karlsson, later described it like this:

The ship lifted, then struck again with a sickening thud; then the swell lifted her again and she drifted away from the hump or rock ahead and broadside on, current or swell carried her towards a steep cliff on our port side. The Captain ordered me to let go both anchors; the ship took ground perhaps a cable-length from the cliff.

Holed in the forepeak, the *Herzogin Cecilie* settled by the head. The Salcombe lifeboat soon arrived and the captain asked them to take off a woman passenger and 21 of the crew. Eight stayed – the captain and his wife, the two mates, and four crew. By afternoon a rocket line had been fired from the cliffs and a breeches buoy was in operation. Ashore went sails and rope. Down came the topgallant and royal yards and off they went to Salcombe. Small coasters shifted 450 tons of undamaged grain. But the rest of her cargo was already swelling and pushing up the deck in places. Those left aboard were not cheered to learn that 100yds astern of them lay the bones of another clipper, the *Halloween* (Site **241**). It looked as though the *Herzogin Cecilie* was going to join her.

But then it seemed that she would be saved. A group of well-wishers put up the money to save the famous ship and to pay for towing her in to Salcombe. Once there the damaged cargo could be removed, the holes sealed and she could be fully repaired in dry dock in Plymouth. And it is likely that she would have been, except for local opposition to taking her into Salcombe itself. The stench of rotting wheat would, it seems, do nothing for the holidaymakers, so it was agreed to put her in Starehole Bay until all the wheat was taken out of her.

On 19 June, 1936, with the help of pumps and crews from Plymouth Dockyard, the *Herzogin Cecilie* came up from her rocky couch. Then with two tugs pulling and a spring tide helping, the ship was towed round to Starehole Bay and allowed to settle gently on a sandy bed. Unfortunately, no one knew how thin that sandy mattress was. Underneath it lay a very rocky base. A rope bridge was rigged from ship to shore and volunteers, largely Cambridge University students, started getting the wet mass of wheat out of her. They did well, reducing the original cargo of 4250 tons to just over 1000. But as they worked so did the ship. She worked herself down through the sand nearly 4m to the solid rock and poised herself amidships.

On 18 July a south-easterly gale sent a vicious swell surging into the bay. Elis Karlsson knew then that she was finished:

We stood listening to rivets snapping with reports like pistol shots; the ship was working heavily in the swell and had reached rock. Stanchions between the decks bent and buckled. It was the end.

The wreck was sold to Kingsbridge metal dealers Messrs Noyce for £225, but she did not go all at once. The ship stayed upright with her masts still up for months. Then the sea came back to finish the job, almost 11 months after her wrecking. This storm broke her up, her masts crashed down and overnight she was just a dark shape under the water.

She has, of course, broken even more since then, but you can still see the bow locker, mast and cleats. There are steam pipe tunnels in the wreckage that are big enough to swim down. At her deepest, the wreck is just 7m down, which makes it an ideal second dive after a deep wreck dive elsewhere. The wreck is popular with photographers as this is one of the shallowest places to find Devonshire cup coral. On a night dive some decent-sized congers appear from under the plates.

The bow of the *Herzogin Cecilie* points out to sea and there is anchor chain leading away to seaward. Visibility is usually good – from 10 to 18m – and it is often easy to pick out her shape by the standing ribs. She can usually be seen from the surface, but if that fails the best way to find her is to look at the headland at the north end of the bay. On the right are two caves. When you are looking deep into the left-hand one you are right over the bows. Take care – the bow section can dry out at extreme low water spring tides. Because of this, her bow is usually buoyed. The buoy is just to seaward of her bows. Do not moor to it as it can be dragged.

There have been other wrecks in Starehole Bay (originally Stair Hole because of the track up which seaweed was carried to manure the fields of East Soar Farm). The *Star of Belfast* was wrecked there on 18 December, 1847. She was bound for Antigua from London with general cargo. The captain was the only man saved. On 24 July, 1852, the smack *Nelly* was also wrecked there. She was attempting to land smuggled goods! Wreckage from both ships should be in the bay, but there have been no reports of divers locating either.

235 Soudan One of the most dived wrecks from Salcombe, this small French steamer of 844 tons first came to grief some distance from her present position of 50 12 29N; 03 46 31W. She hit the Ham Stone in thick fog in the morning of 27 June, 1887, when carrying a cargo of peanuts, hides and oil, together with eight passengers and 24 crew.

When the fog lifted, the passengers were taken off by a yacht, and the *Soudan* was seen to be firmly seated on the outer ledge of the Ham Stone with 12ft of water in her foreholds. At 6pm the tugs *Vixen* and *Raleigh* were standing by. As the tide rose, the *Soudan* floated free, or "glided towards the mainland" as the Lloyds agent put it. By 10pm she was well afloat, though deep by the head, and the tugs started towing her towards Salcombe. She proved very unmanageable and progress was slow. At midnight when they were a little to the west of the entrance to Salcombe, it was clear that the water was gaining fast. Suddenly the engine room bulkhead broke, and as the tugs cut their hawsers she plunged forward and sank. At 3am her main topmast was still visible above the water, but the cargo was starting to float out of her.

Not that she was abandoned – salvage steamers tried to raise her for two months by all sorts of methods, by putting chains around her, by using air bags and by blowing air into her ballast tanks. But nothing worked, and she is now in the

The steamer Liberta struck the Mew Stone at Bolt Head in 1926. When the tide went down her bow was perched on a rock. She broke in two soon after the crew were rescued (Site 236).

same place, broken, though the stern is complete in 18m and she stands 5m proud.

Twenty minutes of slack at high and low tide give enough time to have a look at her boilers and iron propeller, which has a brass boss. Some idea of how often she is dived comes from the fact that the boss is always polished – by divers' hands! The foredeck is flat on the sand, but the bows stand proud. Some large congers call her home.

WARNING Watch out for heavy boat traffic. One of the Salcombe yacht club race marks is sometimes placed close to the wreck!

236 Liberta This Italian steamer of 4073 tons went onto the Mew Stone under Bolt Head at 50 12 31N; 03 47 05W on 15 February, 1926, in the strange combination of fog and a gale that whipped up tremendous seas. The Hope Cove and Torbay lifeboats got close to her, but both coxswains agreed that it would be suicidal to go in among the rocks in the darkness and thick weather, and they waited for dawn. Even then it was impossible to get alongside, so a line-throwing gun was used to make contact. Three Italians were saved by this. The remaining 30 were hauled up by breeches buoy once the Hope Cove rocket apparatus was set up on the cliffs above. When the tide went down, the bow of the *Liberta* was poised on a rock out of the water. Soon afterwards she broke in two.

The 376ft steamer, which had a beam of 48ft, was on her way from La Spezia to Rotterdam in ballast. She had been built by Barclay Curle of Glasgow in 1900 as the *Vermont*. Her boilers are there today, as is a deal of iron plating, in very shallow water and many gullies. This is a dive only to be undertaken on days of complete calm as the flow of sea between the Mew Stone and Bolt Head can produce violent currents at other times.

237 Bolt Head This towering headland, 128m high, has meant the end for several ships. Two, well recorded but not yet found by divers, are the *Bellona* and the *Providence*.

The *Bellona* was a West Indiaman homeward bound from Surinam to London was reported lost "on the Bolt Head" in Lloyds List of Tuesday 29 September, 1807, so presumably the wreck was a few days earlier. Captain Ferris and four of her crew were drowned.

The *Providence* was wrecked on 19 November, 1808. Even Stonehouse Pool at Plymouth was not safe from the "very violent gale from the west-north-west", which struck the south coast of Devon that day. In Plymouth a whole tier of ships broke loose and several of them grounded in the Sound. A transport called the *Enterprise* from La Coruña was driven onshore at Padstow. The *Providence*, another transport coming back from La Coruña and the Peninsular War, was wrecked that Saturday morning by the same gale. "Totally lost on the Bolt near Salcombe with only the Master saved" is the way Lloyds recorded the loss, but whether "Master" here meant that Captain Denton was the only survivor is not made clear.

Close to the south-east of Bolt Head are the Great Mew Stone (19m high) and the Little Mew Stone (5m). If you are extremely careful you can run between these two conical rocks when heading along the Bolt to the west. If you do so you are running over the remains of the *Liberta* (Site **236**).

238 Cantabria This 1803-ton Spanish steamer was bound for Newcastle from Bilbao with a cargo of iron ore on 13 December, 1932, when she ran ashore before dawn in thick fog in Steeple Cove on the Bolt. Her 24-man crew abandoned ship and reached the shore, but were then no better off because their landing place was under cliffs that were impossible to climb. Nor could the rocket team get

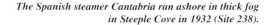

The Spanish steamer Cantabria ran ashore in thick fog in Steeple Cove in 1932 (Site 238).

Above: The Amelie-Suzanne on the rocks at Off Cove in 1972 (Site 239).
Below: The tea clipper Halloween wrecked near the Ham Stone in 1887 (Site 241).

a line to them from above because of the overhang. The Salcombe lifeboat eventually found the 263ft steamer despite the fog and, in a big ground swell, ran a shuttle service from lifeboat to shore with a small boat they found on the Spanish steamer. All the crew were finally landed at Salcombe.

Today, the *Cantabria* is completely broken at 50 12 54N; 03 48 57W, but her boilers stand upright and divers can peer into them from the top. Steeple Cove has a pretty sea bed with coloured growths in under 10m. The main debris is at the western end, just to the right of two rocky pinnacles on the shore. Lobsters hide under the plating. The wreckage of the ship, which was formerly the British steamer *Hornsey*, is scattered widely, but her anchor and winch can be easily spotted. Her iron propeller is there too, but extremely difficult to spot amid the growth. Steeple Cove is easily identified by the unmanned Coastguard hut high on the cliffs on the eastern side.

239 Amelie-Suzanne During the foggy night of 31 March, 1972, this Belgian MFV went onto the rocks at the eastern point of Off Cove. Following her distress message, the crew of five were rescued by the Salcombe lifeboat. Soon after, the fishing vessel slipped deeper. There she is today at 50 12 46N; 03 47 53W in less than 10m and very broken indeed.

240 The Ham Stone This is an important mark for many dives and has been the cause of a number of wrecks, including the *Herzogin Cecilie* and the *Soudan*. It is close to Soar Mill Cove, 11m high, and goes down about the same distance on the seaward side. There is heavy kelp on the inside. Local boatmen regard the Gregory Rocks, in line with Ham Stone but closer to Salcombe, as more of a menace as they present an unseen danger to boats hugging the coast.

241 Halloween On 17 January, 1887, this fully-rigged iron tea clipper was fighting a south-easterly gale on her way to London from Foochow (Fuzhou) with 1600 tons of tea in her holds. She was an exceptionally fast ship and carried a main yard 78ft long, which supported an immense mainsail. On her maiden voyage to Sydney she took only 69 days, and she held the Shanghai to London record at 89 days, which made her one of the fastest ships afloat.

But on this voyage no records were to come her way. Bad weather had dogged Captain Dawton from the moment he left China on 13 August. It had taken 155 days before she sighted the Eddystone Light and now in the dark she was unwittingly running straight in towards the land. Huge seas, wind and rain blotted out everything, and at 7.30pm she shot inside the Ham Stone and crunched into the rocks of Soar Mill Cove. During that night three men tried to swim ashore with a line. One drowned and the other two lost the line, but did manage to reach the shore and climb the cliffs to Southdown Farm.

The Hope Cove lifeboat was launched at 8.30am. It was 10am before they reached the wreck and took off 19 men, more dead than alive, frozen and clinging to the masts and rigging. Within three days the ship was broken by squalls and her cargo was piled 12ft high on the beach. A "gentleman" came down from London and contracted with farmers to cart the damaged tea to Kingsbridge where it was put on a train for London. The tea and the man disappeared and no one was ever paid for their trouble!

Today the ribs of the *Halloween* and some of her well-rusted plates are to be found about 100yds off the western end of the cove, amid kelp in 11m. A fine porthole was recovered in 1992.

242 Volere This 464-ton Italian barque was bound from Genoa to London with a cargo of 330 tons of marble, in blocks weighing 6 or 14 tons each, in her holds and walnut timber on her decks. She was driven into Soar Mill Cove by a south-westerly gale on 6 March, 1881.

The captain of the *Volere*, his wife and one seaman were drowned, but nine were saved. Some of the marble was salvaged by hard-hat divers in the 1920s, and more was raised in 1939. The divers drilled holes in the blocks, then used the tidal lift method to bring the blocks ashore. It could not have been easy, for 200 tons can still be found scattered in 7 to 18m of water at the foot of the cliffs, just to the east of the cove.

243 Lintor Ken This ship was also said to have been carrying marble when sunk in Soar Mill Cove in 1765. It has been said too, that she was carrying statues, which were salvaged and taken to Powderham for the decoration of the castle of the Courtenay family. No other details can be found.

The story becomes more complicated as the loss of a small Dutch vessel, the *Young Hendrick*, is recorded in Soar Mill Cove in December 1756, and there is correspondence about this wreck between the Courtenay family and the ship's owners concerning some "works of art" that were salvaged. It may be that the *Lintor Ken* never existed, but there is often a grain of truth in these handed-down tales, so divers should keep their eyes open for marble statues when diving in the bay.

244 Charter This Lowestoft wooden steam drifter of 96 tons was wrecked at 50 13 25N; 03 50 00W, on 7 January, 1933, when fishing from Plymouth. She went

These marble blocks were salvaged in 1939 from the wreck of the Volere in Soar Mill Cove (Site 242).

Fog caused the loss of the Swedish steamer Jane Rowe near Soar Mill Cove in 1914 (Site 245).

ashore at Cathole Cliff just west of Soar Mill Cove in the afternoon. She was undamaged, despite a fresh wind and ground swell, until the tide went out, when she fell over onto her side. Despite the efforts of the ten-man crew, who tried to save her on the next tide, she was found to be too badly damaged to sail again. The wreck is in very small pieces in less than 10m. Her boiler marks the site.

The date of her wrecking was exactly one year after she had been forced to put back into Plymouth with two other steam drifters after running into a massive westerly gale; three of the crew had to be taken to hospital with head injuries. In this incident the *Charter* had lost all her nets, having had to cut them away.

245 Jane Rowe This 1259-ton Swedish steamer, whose home port was Gefle, set out from Cardiff with a cargo of coal on 27 January, 1914, and delivered this to Oran on 4 February. She was in Oran for a fortnight, then sailed for Rotterdam on 18 February with her holds crammed with iron ore. In dense fog on 28 February, she went ashore at 10.29am and sat on an even keel on a sand bank among rocks near Soar Mill Cove and under Bolberry Down. She looked as though she would float off easily but though first one tug and then the *Kingsbridge Packet* tried, she stayed stuck.

By the next day there were five tugs pulling at her without success. Then it was too late. At 10.30am on 1 March all the crew were taken off by breeches buoy as the *Jane Rowe* was pushed further in onto the rocks as the tide rose. Soon she was broadside on, with the seas breaking over her. Within a short time all four of her holds and the engine room were pierced. She was soon a total wreck. A good mark for the very broken wreckage is the boiler of the Lowestoft steam-drifter *Charter* (Site **244**).

246 Ruperra Built of iron in 1877 at Jarrow, this small steamship of 835 tons left Alexandria on 7 January, 1881, with a cargo of cotton seed. She called at Gibraltar

The Blesk was the first oil tanker in the world to be wrecked; she caused widespread pollution. Here she is jammed on the Greystone in 1896 (Site 248).

and was told to go to Hull. She left Gibraltar on 21 January and headed for the Channel. By noon on 26 January her captain, John Angel Lee, was unsure where he was, but thought he was off Ushant. He stopped to take soundings, decided he was definitely ten miles west of Ushant and set off at full speed on a course reckoned to take him well clear of Portland Bill.

At 11pm he went to bed, telling the mate to report to him at midnight, when they would be in sight of Start Point lighthouse. The mate reported at midnight that the weather was clear, but that he had seen nothing. The master made no reply and went back to sleep. At 5am the Chief Officer, who was now in charge, saw "something very black" just ahead, stopped the engines and ordered the helm hard to port. He was too late. The black shape was the huge cliffs to the east of Soar Mill Cove and the *Ruperra* ran into them at almost her top speed.

The engines were put full astern, but had no effect. Then with the ebb tide pushing her, the steamer swung broadside to the rocks and within a few hours was broken to pieces. The crew took to the boats and when it was light landed at Hope Cove. Captain Lee lost his master's ticket for six months, the first mate lost his for three months and the second mate was reprimanded by the court of inquiry.

Local divers led by Neville Oldham (*see* Site **296**) have found the wreck in less than 9m, tucked under the point some 200yds to the east of the entrance to Soar Mill Cove. She is very broken with her iron plates scattered amid copper piping and anchor chain. But so far they have found no sign of her two inverted compound condensing engines, which together produced 120hp.

Just on the other side of Soar Mill Cove and about half a mile to the west of the Ham Stone lie the remains of the *Westmoreland*, a barque of 450 tons that ran ashore on the foggy night of 14 July, 1871, while carrying a cargo of rum and sugar from Jamaica. Though the crew of 17 got ashore safely, the ship became a total wreck. The wreckage is usually covered by several feet of sand.

247 Dragon This West Indiaman smashed into the spectacular sheer walls of Cathole Cliff on 23 August, 1757, in a south-westerly gale. She was homeward bound from Jamaica to London with a cargo of rum and sugar. A tombstone in Malborough churchyard reads:

> Here lye the bodies of Rhodes-Daniel, Mary, and Joseph Chambers, sons and daughter of Edward Chambers of Jamaica, who were shipwrecked at Cat-hole within this parish.

Nine people were drowned, though the captain and ten crew were saved. After an eight-year search local diver Bill Bunting believes he has found her wreckage, including cannon and shot. The site is close in; it covers and uncovers with sand, but the sand movement does not appear to follow any particular pattern.

248 Blesk One of the first ships designed to carry benzine in bulk, this oil tanker, built in 1890, was the first tanker in the world to be wrecked – and the first to bring large scale pollution to the coast of Britain. The *Blesk*, loaded with 3180 tons of petrol oil in the special tanks forward and with her engine at the stern, was 298ft long, and left the Black Sea port of Batumi on 14 November, 1896, headed for Hamburg.

On 1 December the *Blesk* had reached the English Channel. Seeing a light, Captain Adolph Deme assumed it was La Corbière lighthouse in Jersey and altered his course more to the north. The idea that the light might be that of the Eddystone never crossed his mind. It was, and the *Blesk* was now on collision

The Jebba on the rocks near Bolt Tail in 1907 (Site 249).

course with the land. At 9.08pm in blinding rain at ten knots, she ran onto the Greystone, to the east of Bolt Tail. All 43 crew were saved by the Hope Cove lifeboat.

By the following day, after being pounded by huge seas, it was clear her tanks were ruptured. The oil spread along the coast, killing fish and seabirds. The oil could be smelled in Totnes, 20 miles away. At 4pm she broke in two. She is at 50 13 51N; 03 51 33W and her wreckage is spread widely on both sides of the Greystone in less than 10m. Though there is iron plate amid the kelp-covered gullies that run out to sea from the Greystone, the major part of the wreckage is under sand on the eastern side. This cover is often removed by storms, exposing her keel, propeller shaft and engine parts.

249 Jebba Named the *Albertville* when she was built in 1896 by Raylton Dixon and Company at Middlesbrough for the Africa Steamship Company, this 3813-ton steamer was renamed *Jebba* when taken over by the Elder Dempster Line. In the early hours of 18 March, 1907, in thick fog, she ran ashore near Bolt Tail, a few yards east of the wreck of HMS *Ramillies* (Site **250**), where she finally came to rest, broadside on with her bows to the east. She was carrying ivory, rubber, palm oil, pineapples, bananas and mail from Nigeria and the Gold Coast (now Ghana).

On board were 79 passengers and 76 crew. But even though the mail steamer was filling fast, there was no panic. Her distress rocket soared high above the sheer cliffs of Bolt Tail. The Hope Cove lifeboat was launched within minutes, but the rescue of the passengers came from the land. Two local fishermen climbed along the cliffs in the dark and got close enough to rig a bosun's chair, by means of which all were saved. The fishermen, Isaac Jarvis and John Argeat, were both awarded the Albert Medal for their bravery.

For days afterwards the sea was too rough for boats to get alongside and start proper salvage, though most of the mail was later recovered. There was no chance of getting the *Jebba* off. Divers who inspected the hull reported that she was too badly rent on the rocks. Most of the cargo was saved, though some of the ivory was reported missing. A month after she was wrecked, she started to break up and by the summer was completely in pieces. The fruit washed out of her littered the beaches all around. The ship's cat, two chimpanzees and many parrots, the crew's pets, were brought off the ship safely and some of the parrots were given to local people. So every parrot in a pub in the South Hams is firmly believed to be from the *Jebba* – or a descendant of one!

The *Jebba* today is at 50 14 04N; 03 51 45W and has not moved from the position in which she was wrecked – and in which she was photographed so many times. Her stern and rudder are very close to the wreck site of the *Ramillies* (Site **250**). Swimming east in 7 to 10m of water you will find ribs and two boilers on a patch of sand.

In the kelp-covered rock gullies round about are many small pieces of broken crockery, some inscribed "Africa SS Company", and iron plating. Some idea of the force of the sea that strikes the Bolt can be seen by a porthole handle that is embedded into the solid rock. And somewhere there may be those ivory tusks, which were never recovered from the wreck! She did have a bronze propeller and a bronze spare – but those were salvaged very early on.

250 HMS Ramillies The loss of this 90-gun, 1689-ton warship was to cause one of the most terrible death tolls in the history of the Royal Navy. On 15 February, 1760, out of the 734 men aboard her, only 26 were to survive the wrecking just to the east of Bolt Tail.

The *Ramillies* was old – and leaky. She had been launched on 26 October, 1664, as the *Katherine*. She was rebuilt in 1702 and became the *Royal Katherine*; in 1749 she was rebuilt again and became the *Ramillies*. By 1760 she was repaired again, having been leaking so badly that she missed the Battle of Quiberon Bay, the great English triumph of the Seven Years' War. She was repaired at Plymouth and, captained by Wittewronge Taylor, rejoined the Channel Squadron under Admiral Edward Boscawen. Boscawen was due to join his squadron to the fleet in Quiberon Bay, but had twice been beaten back by bad weather. On 6 February, 1760, despite warnings of bad weather he tried again. With him and his flagship *Royal William* went the *Ramillies*, *Sandwich*, *St George*, *Princess Amelia*, *Venus* and *Hawke*.

It was not to be third time lucky, for although they did not know it, they were heading into a hurricane. Gales tore at them from the south-west, swung to the north-east, then settled into a violent south-westerly with squalls of sleet and rain. The ships were scattered, but Captain Taylor clung to the flagship until 14 February when, with the crew continuously at the pumps as the *Ramillies* was leaking badly again, he bore away to run before the wind. All night they ran to the eastward, heading as they thought for the shelter of Plymouth.

At 10am they saw land, but not clearly and they stood in for a better look. Through a gap in the sleet blanket, the sailing master saw an island and decided that it was Looe Island. It was a terrible mistake – the island was in fact Burgh Island, and he was in Bigbury Bay, 26 miles further east than he thought. And he was on a lee shore, with a giant south-westerly blowing him to disaster. If he had decided to ride it out in the bay all might have been well, but believing himself only a headland short of Plymouth Sound – he thought Bolt Tail was Rame Head – he set his topsails and tried to round the Bolt.

The *Ramillies* was leaking too badly for such a manoeuvre, and the great weight of water in her made her too cumbersome. Only now did the sailing master see his mistake and try to stay the ship, but the great swells pushed her nearer and nearer the 300ft cliffs. Now Captain Taylor took back his command. The mainmast and mizzen were cut away. Minutes later the foremast was chopped down too. Down went the best bower anchor and at that moment another mistake was made. The bower hung for a moment as though caught and someone, thinking it would not drop free, cut loose the small bower anchor too. Both anchors went down, but the cables crossed and at each great snub of a swell they sawed across one another. But at 2pm they held her off the shore.

Just before 6pm the cables parted and in the dusk she swung broadside. The next wall of water drove her starboard side first onto the rocks. Her bow ground round and now she was in the crushing machine between the waves and the rocks, with her stern being driven into a cave in the cliff. The *Ramillies* was not long in going, but before she was really smashed to pieces some appalling scenes took place on board. The Captain of Marines is said to have gone off his head and to have marched about reciting poetry. The ship's boatswain, who had brought his young son to sea with him, threw the child towards the shore and safety, only to see him dashed on the rocks. Seconds later, the father's body

The Maine is one of the best-known wreck dives in Devon (Site 251). This photograph was taken at Antwerp in 1913, when she was still under her original name of Sierra Blanca.

joined that of his son. So did over 700 others. Only 26 crew managed to scramble to safety into cracks and crevices where the waves could not reach them.

There was a good deal of salvage at the time, particularly of her cannon. There was more in 1906 by a helmet diver. The wreck is now owned by David Langfield, who bought her in 1964. "Ramillies Cove" is marked on some Ordnance Survey maps, but the site is further to the east near Whitechurch Cove. Looking in from the sea you will see two caves with a knob of rock separating them in the middle. The right-hand cave is where she struck and indeed there are two cannon right up inside the cave.

There is not now much to see except cannonballs and five worn cannon. This is largely due to visiting divers taking souvenirs and the archaeological excavation that went on for seven years. The archaeological divers led by Peter McBride have recovered many artefacts, such as belt and shoe buckles, and they have also found the gun lock of one of the cannon. Most of the cannon are badly eroded and they were moved to one side of the site. Some small explosive charges were used to break stubborn lumps of layers of concretion. One of the bow anchors of the *Ramillies* is to be found some distance to the south-west of the wreck site.

251 Maine The *Maine* was a dirty British cargo ship with a salt-caked smoke stack and she came zig-zagging down the Channel on a mad March day in 1917. Watching her through the periscope of his U-boat, *UC-17*, was Oberleutnant

Ralph Wenninger. Rain stopped anyone aboard the 3616-ton *Maine* spotting him and on Friday 23 March at 8.05am his torpedo struck her full in the port side, level with No. 2 hold.

The blast knocked Captain "Bill" Johnston off his feet, blew off the hatches of Nos. 2 and 3 holds, smashed the port gig and wrecked the bridge. And it made a great hole in her side through which water poured onto her cargo of chalk, horsehair and goatskins. Captain Johnston felt her already settling by the head and sent off distress calls before setting course for land.

First help to arrive was Royal Navy torpedo boat No. 99, commanded by Lieutenant-Commander Percy Taylor of the Royal Naval Reserve. He had been in command of a flotilla of minesweepers, clearing mines from the entrances to Dartmouth and Teignmouth – some of which had been laid by Wenninger in *UC-17* – and was now on his way home to Devonport. Commander Taylor put his boat alongside the *Maine* and took off most of the crew.

Captain Johnston told him that his ship was now completely out of action, with the central area fully flooded, but Taylor thought there might be a chance of beaching her in Bigbury Bay and passed a towline to the stricken ship. Other patrol boats now arrived and took on the tow too, but progress was very slow. At

*Divers Peter Williams and Nick Jewson with the bell
from the Maine (Site 251).*

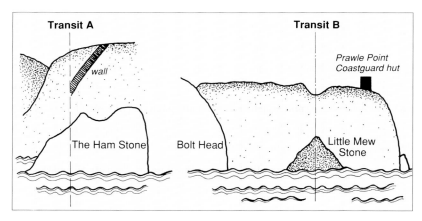

Transit A

wall

The Ham Stone

Transit B

Prawle Point
Coastguard hut

Bolt Head

Little Mew
Stone

Transit marks for the Maine (Site 251).

noon the first tug arrived and took over the tow. It was too late. Soon after the new tow was established, the internal bulkheads of the *Maine* collapsed and at 12.45pm she sank. She did so, in Taylor's words, "gracefully, upright and on an even keel". By then Oberleutnant Wenninger had headed his submarine away to the north-east, heading homeward for Zeebrugge, base of the Flanders Flotilla.

For a long time the position of the *Maine* was quite clear. Her two masts stuck up 12ft clear of the surface and the Admiralty issued a Notice to Mariners about this hazard. In time both her masts collapsed, and for some reason the local fishermen called her "the Railway Line Wreck".

She was first dived in 1961 by Torbay BSAC, who bought her for £100 and salvaged her bronze propeller for which they received £840. Then the gun was salvaged from her stern, and in 1983 another diving team from Torbay BSAC raised the spare iron propeller from her deck, which is now displayed at the front of the Victoria Shopping Centre at Paignton.

The *UC-17* was sunk by a mine when going through the Dover Barrage on 22 April, 1918. Wenninger and 20 of his men made a free ascent from the crippled submarine in 30m. Only six survived, including Wenninger, who spent the rest of the war in a prison camp for officers at Donnington Hall, Leicestershire. When last heard of in 1929 he was the executive officer of the German cruiser *Berlin*.

The *Maine* today is one of the most popular dives in Devon, probably because she is easily accessible and is still very unbroken. She is at 50 12 45N; 03 50 53W, upright on an even keel on a shingle sea bed at 37m from which she is 15m proud. Though both her propellers and the gun have been salvaged, divers should remember she belongs to Torbay Branch. Although they do not mind anyone diving her, they would object most strongly to anyone taking souvenirs.

Thousands of divers have the *Maine* in their log books, but in 1987 two divers from Bracknell BSAC, Nick Jewson and Peter Williams, on their first dive on her, found her bell! It is two feet high, 77lb of solid brass. All those other divers who missed it since diving on her started in 1961 can take some comfort that it was in the bottom of a hole near the big deck anchor winches and only the tip of the tang (the very top of the bell) was showing. The two divers presented the bell to Torbay BSAC.

The *Maine* was built for the Sierra Shipping Company of Liverpool and was called *Sierra Blanca* when launched in 1905. She was 375ft overall, and 361ft between perpendiculars as she had an overhanging counter stern of 14 feet. Her beam was 46ft. She was renamed in 1913 by the Atlantic Transport Company. She was swept of her superstructure in 1920 and what remains of that now lies a short distance away on the starboard side. There are big congers in the main wreckage. Beware of jagged edges – the hull plating is now thin in places. She lies across the tide in strong streams of several knots at spring tides. It is essential to dive her 2 hours after high water or 2½ hours after low water. Latest reports say her counterstern is broken and falling away and her poop deck is collapsing inwards.

Transit marks for the *Maine* are shown in the diagram opposite.

A block of "patent fuel" sits on a wreck diver's bookshelf. He has outlined the stamped letters in white. One diver died trying to recover one of these coal briquettes from the Skaala (Site 253).

252 Ambassador This 300ft steamer was first found by Kingston BSAC when they were looking for the *Skaala* (Site **253**). She left Odessa in 1891 for Hamburg with a cargo of grain and fertiliser. Off the Devon coast on 19 September she struck something and sank in 50m. She is upright, 3m proud and has an iron propeller. Her position is 50 11 30N; 03 49 48W.

253 Skaala Reported as loaded with "patent fuel" (coal briquettes) when she sank, this Norwegian steamer of 1129 tons was 229ft long, with a beam of 35ft and was built in 1906 by Bergens Mek. Vaerksted of Norway. On 26 December, 1917, she was on her way from Port Talbot to Rouen when Oberleutnant Stöter torpedoed her at 2.45pm from one of the two bow tubes of *UB-35* as he lay in wait on the surface for coastal shipping. He had been ordered to patrol between Start Point and the Eddystone and the *Skaala* was his first victim on that patrol, which lasted from 22 December, 1917, to 1 January, 1918. One man died in Stöter's attack; the other 16 crew landed safely at Dartmouth.

There have already been two diving deaths on the *Skaala*, which lies about a quarter of a mile from the *Maine* at 50 11 12N; 03 50 20W (not at the charted position). Sadly, at least one of the diving deaths is due to the coal briquettes, which look like good souvenirs. They are stamped "Cardiff" and bear a royal crown mark. But they are very heavy and one diver who later died was seen struggling upwards carrying one of these heavy items. So if in doubt, dump the coal!

The *Skaala* is a deep dive, 43m to the sea bed and 33m to her deck. She is upright with a list to port. Her superstructure – she has not been swept – is collapsing around the engine room. She lies with her bows to the north-west on the sand-shingle sea bed. Her propeller is iron. The damage to her starboard side is from the torpedo of *UB-35*. The builder's plate has been recovered.

Do not think that the boat lying across No. 2 hold is one of her lifeboats. It is a small fishing boat of 20ft with its own engine and propeller, which has settled across the wreck!

254 Wreathier Identified by her bell, this wreck is intact and upright at 50 10 40N; 03 49 39W. Three of the crew died when she was torpedoed on 3 December, 1917, by *UB-35*, commanded by Oberleutnant Stöter, who had been given the area between Start Point and the Eddystone to patrol on this mission. The 852-ton *Wreathier* was steel-built by Craig Taylor and Company at Stockton-on-Tees in 1897. She was 200ft long with a beam of 31ft and was armed with a gun on her stern. She was carrying coal from Barry to Rouen when she sank. The depth to her deck is 41m and a further 9m to the sea bed. She lies north-north-east to south-south-west.

255 Uskmoor An unarmed British steamer of 3189 tons, the *Uskmoor* was heading for Barry in ballast from Dunkirk when torpedoed by Kapitänleutnant Viebeg in *UB-80* on the morning of 5 March, 1918, three miles south-west of Prawle Point. All the crew were saved. This 331ft steamer is now at 50 10 25N; 03 47 10W, lying north-west to south-east on a very rippled sand sea bed at 54m from which she stands 12m proud.

256 Catherine Allen She overturned in a flat calm while hauling in a full cockle dredge on 28 October, 1973. The 60ft boat later sank at 50 10 14N; 03 48 10W onto the sea bed at 48m, from which she is 11m proud, and lying north–south.

257 Wreck, name unknown At 50 10 10N; 03 50 54W, she is 110ft long, lying east-north-east to west-south-west. She is silted and sinking into the 54m sea bed, from which she stands 5m proud.

258 HMS Stockforce A "special service" ship was how the Navy described her in their records, but in fact she was a Q-ship. This 732-ton small coastal steamer had, until the beginning of 1918, been the *Charyce*. The Navy requisitioned her

The Wreathier, seen here at Stockton-on-Tees in 1897, was torpedoed and sunk by UB-35 in 1917 (Site 254).

in Cardiff and fitted her with two four-inch guns, plus a 12-pounder and a 3-pounder, all hidden behind screens and looking like ordinary deck housings. Her captain was Lieutenant Harold Auten.

On 30 July, 1918, HMS *Stockforce* was steaming along innocently to the west when Kapitänleutnant Oelricher in *UB-98* put a torpedo into her. It struck on the starboard side, putting the hidden forward gun out of action and wounding four of her crew. The decoy abandon-ship party, showing all signs of panic, launched their boat and rowed desperately away from the ship. Meanwhile the hidden Navy gun crews waited at their stations for the submarine to surface, even though water was pouring into the *Stockforce* between decks. After five minutes *UB-98* surfaced, but lay half a mile off for another 15 minutes waiting for any suspicious move. Finally she moved in to just 300yds away. As she did so, the Q-ship dropped her screens and opened fire with both four-inch guns. The first round carried away one of the periscopes. The second shot hit the conning tower dead centre, blowing it away and sending the man in it high in the air. Another shot hit the submarine where the conning tower had been and just below the waterline. Blue smoke poured out of the submarine as round after round hit her. After twenty hits the U-boat sank by the stern.

The *Stockforce* was in a bad way and Auten set course at full speed for the land, but the ship was awash forward and seemed unlikely to travel far. However, after transferring half the crew and the wounded to a trawler, the *Stockforce* got within a few miles of Bolt Head before sinking at 50 09 47N; 03 50 14W. She now lies upright in 57m and it is 49m to her decks. She is very broken, lying east–west, and is about 120ft long.

Lieutenant Auten was awarded the Victoria Cross and there were decorations for most of the crew. Amazingly, the *UB-98* managed to make her way home and was handed over to the Royal Navy at the end of the war by Kapitänleutnant Oelricher when the surviving U-boats surrendered at Harwich.

259 Wreck, name unknown At 50 09 45N; 03 50 19W this one is either very small or well sunk into the sea bed, standing only 1m proud of the sea bed at 57m.

260 Ternefjell A Norwegian steamer of 1451 tons, this ship was on her way from Antwerp, via London, to Chicago. On 24 May, 1953, she was in collision with the 1494-ton British steamer *Dotterel* and sank at 50 09 14N; 03 50 02W. She lies north-west to south-east with her bows to the north-west where collision damage is clear. The depth to her deck is 52m; to the sea bed 60m.

261 Big wreck, name unknown At 50 06 24N; 03 51 13W, this wreck is certainly large and lies north-east to south-west. There is some small wreckage, about 2m high, close by to the west, but the main wreckage is of a large ship, standing 14m proud of the sea bed at 68m.

262 Molbo This is the wreck of a 300ft steamer lying north–south in 68m of water. She stands 8m proud at 50 03 01N; 03 51 08W.

AREA 6:

Bigbury Bay

This area runs from the tip of Bolt Tail in the east (03 52 18W), curves round into Hope Cove and then runs along Bigbury Bay to Stoke Point (04 01 18W). It is difficult from any point on land, except from the top of Bolt Tail, to identify Bigbury Bay as an entity – it is a long stretch of coastline, and has bays within it. Seen from the sea on a summer day, Bigbury Bay seems to be a smiling land of green fields sloping up from sandy beaches and inlets, or running down to little coves among the cliffs. But for sailing ships of olden times it was a deadly trap in any south-west gale. Few sailing ships caught in the bay in that onshore wind survived – which makes the area one of great interest to divers.

There is no coast road running around the shores of Bigbury Bay, so each site must be approached by narrow lanes. Divers towing boats should bear this carefully in mind and try to avoid holiday rush hours, or be prepared for long waits between passing places.

The 20m depth contour runs roughly a mile offshore, but the sea bed is rocky in many places with steep cliffs and holes. Diving, for example, off Bolt Tail can produce depths in excess of 30m. This is good crab country – and crayfish can be found in deep water – so the fishermen of HOPE COVE pot mainly for crabs.

Divers should note that this has always been one of the most sensitive places in Devon for confrontations between divers and fishermen, and they would be well advised to stay as far away as possible from crab pot markers. Diving groups have descended on Hope Cove in huge numbers in the past, particularly over Easter and other bank holidays, and caused friction – largely through carelessness rather than deliberate bad behaviour. Much as it may amaze some divers, local people do not take kindly to the sight of divers changing in the road outside their homes! Yet it is perfectly possible to have a wonderful diving holiday here – conditions generally are superb with visibility often over 15m – all it takes is a little common sense.

Approach is made from the A381 Kingsbridge to Salcombe road. Two miles out of Kingsbridge, a right turn is clearly marked to "Hope Cove". This road is very

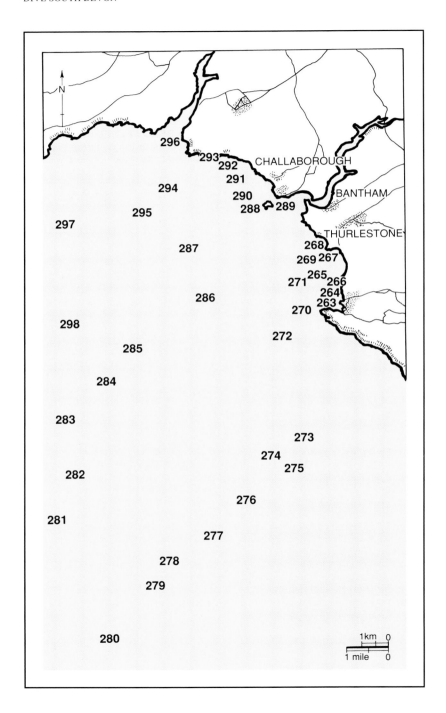

Opposite: Dive sites in Area 6: Bigbury Bay. This area is covered by Admiralty Chart 1613 (Eddystone Rocks to Berry Head); Ordnance Survey map 202.

narrow indeed, with passing places. Inner Hope is the older part of the village, closer to Bolt Tail, and is signposted left as you enter Outer Hope.

If you wish to launch a boat you must take this road; divers should not stir up trouble by using the slipway at Outer Hope. The BSAC have agreed with the Harbour Master that, in return for unrestricted access to the concrete slipway at Inner Hope – the BSAC made a major contribution to its repair – divers will not use the Outer Hope slipway.

The slipway in front of the old lifeboat house at Inner Hope is for launching dive boats, and the BSAC have installed a notice there. Cars and trailers should then be driven round to Outer Hope car park; loading and unloading of gear should be done on Mouthwell Beach (*see* below). When launching, divers should keep their eyes down – for it is around the Inner Hope slipway that silver coins, possibly from the *San Pedro el Mayor* (Site **264**) have been found.

If you plan to leave your inflatable moored in the cove overnight make sure it is anchored very firmly; the sea bed is poor holding ground. In a recent salvage claim for a large inflatable, the trawler skipper who brought it in said he found it floating four miles out.

263 Hope Cove Many a beginner has made their first sea dive in the sheltered waters here. Most of these have been along the steep rock formations of Bolt Tail on the east side of the cove. Depths vary with the distance from shore, but 15m is common the further out you swim towards Bolt Tail. There are gullies and overhanging ledges with plentiful marine life, some congers, and the odd flatfish on the sand base near the foot of the rocks.

For a shore dive, MOUTHWELL BEACH is easily reached from the Outer Hope car park, but be warned that this is a very popular beach in season for families with

Below: Inner Hope slipway, with the Shippen rocks and Outer Hope in the background.

151

Left: The Chalice. This tiny communion cup, only about 2½ inches across, was found crushed into the Shippen Rock at Hope Cove. Below: Outer Hope, looking across Bigbury Bay towards Bolt Tail. Dive boats should be launched at nearby Inner Hope.

small children. Take care not to spread gear about, and take care in the water. There is heavy lilo traffic! Immediately off the beach the sand gives way to shingle banks and there seems little reason for diving here – except, of course, for the *San Pedro el Mayor*, believed by many to have been wrecked on the Shippen Rock close to Mouthwell Beach.

264 San Pedro el Mayor Now here is a mystery wreck just waiting for some diver to discover signs of it. This was a hospital ship of the Spanish Armada and carried 20 cannon, 30 sailors and 100 soldiers. On 21 July, 1588, she was with the rest of the Spanish fleet off Plymouth – and soon the wounded from the first skirmishes with Drake, Howard, Hawkins and Frobisher were transferred to her. Then, when everything went wrong and the Armada was forced into that dreadful circumnavigation of the British Isles, the *San Pedro el Mayor* went too. At the end of October she was back off Plymouth, but in terrible shape after being battered by gales almost all the way.

There was now no one aboard her strong enough to fight the winds; a south-westerly gale blew her into Bigbury Bay and straight, they say, into Hope Cove. There, at the beginning of November 1588, her voyage of misery ended and the looting and pillaging began. An eye-witness wrote: "The ship is not to be recovered; she lieth on a rock and full of water to her upper decks." Another report read: "The ship being run upon the rocks by the Spaniards, is now through the tempestuous weather broken in pieces and scattered on the seashore." So even though there is no intact wreck to find, you would think there would be something to see. But there is no trace, and surprisingly not even a shard of pottery from all the "drugs and pothecary stuff as came to 6000 ducats" that was aboard.

So where should the diver start looking? Let us assume that all the cannon were saved – we know they were iron, but valuable all the same. That leaves woodwork, pots, bowls and coins. There are reports by divers over the years of ancient timbers showing from time to time near the Shippen, but being covered up

Thurlestone and Hope Cove, showing the positions of the Louis Sheid (Site 268) and the Empire Harry (Site 271). Also marked is the probable wreck site of the San Pedro el Mayor (Site 264).

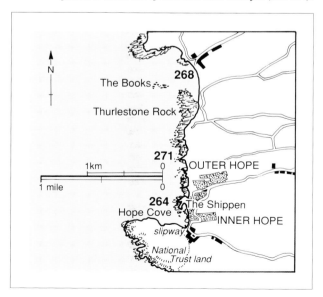

again by storms. And there have been coins, though they were not found near the Shippen, but right over by the Inner Hope slipway, down which divers should launch their boats.

The prevailing wind in the area is the south-westerly. It is the south-westerlies that put the sand on the beaches, but when the wind moves round to the north-west and blows hard for a few tides, the beach surface is removed by a scouring action. It is this that tells us that the *San Pedro el Mayor* most likely did hit the Shippen. When this scouring takes place great quantities of sand and shingle are removed and a stiff clay base is exposed. In this clay, coins have been found that bear on one side the Maltese cross and on the other the Spanish arms surmounted with a royal crown and King Philip's name. Several of the older local inhabitants have them and they have always been found on Inner Hope beach, mostly very close to the slipway.

It is likely that these coins were not washed up from the wreck, but were lost in the confusion of the Spaniards coming ashore. A letter of the time tells us: "There hath been some plate and certain ducats rifled and spoiled at their first landing, both from their persons and out of their chests." This implies that some of the Spaniards came ashore in boats, bringing their chests with them. In the prevailing weather, the only way to have landed a boat would have been to run with the wind and take a chance of beaching close in to Bolt Tail. This suggests that the ship was to the west of the landing spot and out on the Shippen.

Is there nothing at all to see of the *San Pedro el Mayor*? Well, yes – in the Village Inn at Thurlestone above your head in the saloon bar are some ancient timbers they swear came from the ship!

265 Portuguese Coin Wreck It may be that there were two wrecks in Hope Cove long ago, for not all the coins found by the Inner Hope slipway were Spanish. When the slipway was being repaired for the RNLI in 1912, some cruzados of King John IV of Portugal were found. The idea that these had been carried by the *San Pedro el Mayor* was quickly dispelled by the dates: John IV reigned from 1640 to 1656.

There is one old report of another wreck in the area. It describes the wreck of the *San Pedro el Mayor* before continuing:

At a later date a foreign ship went upon the rocks, and the inhabitants of the village were soon aboard. Having found there a Roman Catholic priest, they concluded he was a Jesuit, come as in Elizabeth's time to conspire against the government of the country, so they locked him up in the cabin and sent for the Malborough dogs – that is the local pack of hounds – to hunt him about the country, this being a form of insult offered in former days to unpopular people. The unfortunate man was saved from this outrage by the intervention of the local gentry.

266 The Chalice The diving sensation of 1990 was the underwater find by Stephen George of an Elizabethan pewter chalice crushed into a crevice of the Shippen rock at Hope Cove. Was this from the *San Pedro el Mayor* or the poor priest on the Portuguese coin wreck? The pewter is described by experts as a travelling communion cup.

Neville Oldham (left) and the author examining the cannon recovered
from the wreck of the Chanteloupe (Site 267).

Just off the beach at THURLESTONE SANDS – 1000yds of coarse reddish material – is its trade mark, the great arch of natural stone that rises 10m above the sea. So distinctive is this stone that it appears in the Domesday Book as "Torlestan". The first part of the name comes from the Saxon "thyrl", meaning a hole, so giving us "Holestone". Thurlestone Rock stands sideways on to the shore so that the hole cannot be seen from the beach in front of it, nor can you see the arch in it from the best launching site in the area close by at the eastern end of the beach. The Admiralty Pilot seems to imagine that, from the seaward side, it resembles the hull of a stranded vessel, but this does not leap immediately to mind when you are out at sea.

The approach to Thurlestone Sands can be difficult because following the signs for "Thurlestone" will land you up at the western end of the beach where the Links Court flats sit on top of some small cliffs and overlook a little car park. There is no direct road through from the western to the eastern end and Thurlestone Rock. The best way out is via South Milton and to follow the signposts for Thurlestone Sands from there. The only direct approach to Thurlestone Sands is from the A381 from Kingsbridge. Two separate turnings on your right as you head towards Salcombe will take you there. The first is signposted "South Milton" and provided you bear left in that village will bring you to the right place. The second turning is signposted "Thurlestone Rock" and takes you there via South Huish. Both roads are extremely narrow, and both take you down to the dunes at the back of Thurlestone Sands.

There is a car park for over 100 cars, for which there is a charge. The land belongs to the National Trust, who call it South Milton Sands. The diver should aim to get as close to the eastern end as possible, where there is a big building labelled Rock House Marine Apartments. It is not often that divers are handed

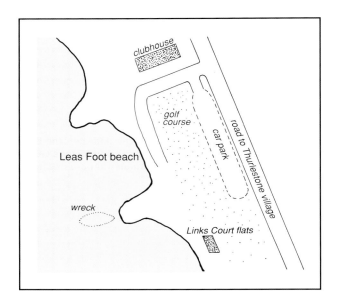

How to find the wreck of the Louis Sheid (Site 268), off Leas Foot Beach.

access on a plate, but they are here! There is no ramp, but just in front of Rock House the road leads past an opening to the sea and it is easy to manoeuvre boats down to the sand. From the end of this access to the beach and slightly to the left a natural channel, which can easily be seen through the water, runs straight out to sea through the eastern end of the reef that connects Thurlestone Rock to the shore. The channel is called New Way Gut for some reason. Much of the reef dries at low water.

267 Chanteloupe On 24 September, 1772, this barque, homeward bound from Grenada for London, was dashed onto the reef that links Thurlestone Rock to the shore. Hurricane-force winds and giant seas soon started to break her up, but one woman passenger put on all her jewellery hoping that if she reached the shore the locals would make extra efforts to save her. The jewels had the opposite effect. Though she reached the shore alive, the locals cut off her ears and fingers to get at the jewellery and she died. Neville Oldham found the wreck in 1988 – cannon, musket and pistol shot are buried under several feet of sand just by the rock itself, on the seaward side. A cannon raised from the wreck can be seen on the green near Thurlestone Church.

At the foot of Thurlestone Village by the golf club, Leas Foot Beach is the launch site for the *Louis Sheid* (Site **268**). The road that runs across the face of the club house is a dead end; there is no parking in it but boats can be towed up to a gap in the railings and lifted over the low posts that stop you driving onto the sand. Once your boat and gear have been unloaded, you must return your car and trailer to the public car park near the golf club.

To the right of Leas Foot as you face the sea is Warren Point. It was here that the *Hawthorn*, a barque of 296 tons, was wrecked on 8 March, 1881, after being abandoned by her crew. Divers have found her anchors welded into the rocks by marine growth. Also found were copper nails, a square porthole, and the letters L, O and D in lead.

268 Louis Sheid Though no torpedo even came near her, the blame for this ship running ashore on 8 December, 1939, close to Thurlestone Golf Club, must go to Korvettenkapitän Gunther Prien, the German war hero decorated by Hitler with the Knight's Cross with Oak Leaves for sinking the *Royal Oak* in Scapa Flow less than two months earlier. It was fear of Prien in *U-47* that sent the *Louis Sheid* into the shelter of the coast.

The *Louis Sheid* was a big ship – 6057 tons, 418ft long with a beam of 55ft. She was built in 1920 by Nord Werft of Wesermunde as the *Ultor* for the Rickmers Line before being renamed *Kendal Castle* for the James Chambers Lancashire Shipping Company of Liverpool, and then renamed *Louis Sheid* for the Belgian National Shipping Line.

In the early morning of 7 December, 1939, there was no doubt about the ship's allegiance. Homeward bound for Antwerp with a cargo of grain and a crew of 46, the word BELGIE was painted in huge white letters on her sides, together with a large Belgian flag. Britain was at war with Germany, but Belgium was not. Nor were the Netherlands, but neutrality did not save the 8159-ton cargo liner *Tajandoen*, bound from Amsterdam for Batavia (now Jakarta) with 14 passengers and a general cargo of cement, iron, glassware, mild steel sheet, aniline and pharmaceutical products. Prien started to line up on her at 5.24am and hit her with

Only weeks after the Louis Sheid was wrecked at Thurlestone in 1939
(Site 268), the south-westerly gales broke her in two.

one torpedo at 5.30. The great explosion could be heard on board the *Louis Sheid* and the Dutch ship began to sink almost at once. The explosion had split her fuel tanks and fuel covered the sea around her. Six crew did not reach the lifeboats when they were lowered and probably died in the torpedo hit. The 62 who did make the boats had no sooner done so than the fuel oil around the ship ignited. The men rowed madly across the blazing sea and, scorched and singed, managed to reach the safety of the *Louis Sheid*.

Once the captain had these survivors safely aboard, he feared that he might share the Dutch ship's fate, as Prien and *U-47* were obviously no respecters of neutrality. So the *Louis Sheid* made off at full speed for the nearest land and shallow waters where the U-boat might not dare to go. By nightfall she was running close in along the south Devon coast. Heavy rainfall was blocking out the shape of the land and the wind was increasing to a full southerly gale. There were no friendly shore lights to guide her – blackout regulations made sure of that – and soon the ship was heading nearer and nearer to the shore. Finally, just missing the rocks called the Delvers, stretching out from Warren Point, she ran into the tiny bay of Leas Foot in front of Thurlestone Golf Club. On the south side of the little shingle beach another small headland with a tiny reef at its foot was waiting. There the *Louis Sheid* struck, very hard, just as the tide was dropping.

The ship was within a few yards of the Links Hotel, now a block of flats called Links Court. She did not strand unnoticed. Jack Jarvis, the former coxswain of the Hope Cove lifeboat, saw it happen and telephoned the Salcombe lifeboat. The Salcombe boat had a hellish journey round the Bolt in enormous seas and finally found the *Louis Sheid* two hours later. It was only when they came alongside – rising and falling 20ft with the waves – and 40 men jumped into the boat, that coxswain Eddie Distin found he was rescuing not one crew but two. All the first 40 men came from the *Tajandoen*!

The lifeboat made two trips, taking off all the Dutchmen first and landing them at Hope Cove, where local fishermen dared enormous waves to set up a ferry service between lifeboat and shore. When the Salcombe boat went back for the third time, the *Louis Sheid* had been moved by the wind and sea and the rising tide. She was now broadside under the cliffs.

The rocket apparatus was set up on the cliff overlooking her and the team soon had a line aboard. All her crew came off safely that way. Eddie Distin was awarded the RNLI silver medal for the rescue and each of his crew received the bronze. The *Louis Sheid*, despite many attempts to shift her, never moved again. The grain was washed out of her onto the nearby beaches. Salvage was tried, but abandoned in 1940 after south-westerly gales broke her in two. More salvage was attempted in 1942, after which the bow collapsed, and from time to time after that. For one attempt an aerial ropeway was set up the cliffs and was driven by a traction engine. Lots of metal was cut off her. After the war she was sold for £400 and more salvage took place.

At 50 15 48N; 03 52 12W, the *Louis Sheid* is a good dive for novices. It is not a long snorkel out to her, though she is more often dived by boat. At low tide her stem post sticks clear of the water, which is 10m deep. The remains lie amid kelp on rock. The boilers are still there and house some very large wrasse. The rest is ribs and masses of plates. A small part of her bow, which it is possible to enter, was found recently by Peter Mitchell on the south side of Leas Foot Bay.

Within a few yards of the part of Leas Foot Beach from which all those divers have snorkelled out to the *Louis Sheid*, diver Stephen George discovered a great broken anchor of wood and iron, with an 11ft stock, 14ft shank and 15-inch diameter ring. This is now in the Salcombe Maritime Museum and though some suggest it may have come from the *San Pedro el Mayor* (Site **264**), it is more likely that it dates from the 1780–1820 period.

Divers will be delighted to know that the sewer pipe at the west end of the beach is no longer operational! A new arrangement for Thurlestone pipes sewage to a reed bed system near South Milton.

At the mouth of the River Avon (pronounced "Awn") is the village of BANTHAM. It is possible, but unwise, for diving boats to launch here. The tiny access road – on your right after driving through the small village towards the sea – is very steep with a difficult turn back on itself before emerging on the river bank near an elegant thatched boathouse. Exit to the sea is only possible two hours either side of high tide. Low tide, due to some peculiarities of the river, is 1½ hours later than the tide table would have you believe.

The sea way is tricky and many an outboard propeller has been lost here. Take local advice, and remember that the entrance is just as difficult on the return, which must be made no later than two hours after high. Consult the Harbour Master at the boathouse before attempting a launch.

The best launching site for the *Persier* (Site **294**) is at CHALLABOROUGH. Approach is by the A379, turning off onto the B3392 towards Bigbury. At the Pickwick Inn turn right for Ringmore and Challaborough. The road is steep, narrow and winding, and divers towing boats should sound their horn on every corner – Challaborough is a popular caravan and camping site. Launching is off the beach and at high tide is easy. There is parking space available close by. When launching beware of the swell, which has overturned quite a number of boats here. There is a seaward current at low water spring tides on the right of the beach, where there is a deep pool. To the left, where Burgh Island looms close, there can be a similar current. Diver coxswains running along the coast towards Beacon Point should keep an eye open for two rocks charted as coming close to the surface, which can take off a longshaft propeller. One of these rocks is Wells Rock (Site **291**).

On the map, WONWELL looks a likely place to launch, but do not waste time trying to launch there. It is possible, but the mouth of the River Erme has been known as a poor harbour since ancient times. The river tends to change its course and the greater part of it dries. At high water and with a totally calm sea, small boats can get about three-quarters of a mile up. Beware of the reefs across the mouth at other times – one runs 900yds to the west from Fernycombe Point on the east side.

The roads to the river become packed in the holiday season. The whole of this area is best dived from boats launched at Challaborough, though much of the inner mouth of the Erme is covered by two historic wreck protection orders (*see* Site **296**).

Boat diving sites

269 The Books What gives this reef its name no one knows, but it may originally have been the "Brook Rocks" as this outcrop of granite lies directly off the mouth of the brook that flows into the sea through Thurlestone Sands. Part of the reef dries out at low water and many kelp-covered rocks then stick up out of the sea. The rocks cover a huge area and for as much as shows there is the same again underwater, weed-dark through the usually clear sea. Divers who pass this dive by in search of deep water are missing an interesting experience. Great gullies run through the reef and there is a wonderland of marine life.

Not only are crabs and the occasional lobster to be found, but also traces of the numerous ships that this reef has claimed. For example, divers have reported seeing huge ancient anchors among the rocks and some people think that these are evidence of the last desperate attempt to stop the *San Pedro el Mayor* from being driven ashore at Hope Cove. Any diver finding these anchors should examine them closely. Old Spanish anchors were notoriously unsound and the discovery of a large broken one might confirm the 16th-century saying "as rotten as a Spanish anchor". But so many ships have hit the reef that the anchors on the rocks might have come from many another wreck.

Divers might find evidence, for example, of the wrecking of the *George and Ann* of Exeter and a French lugger privateer, both lost here on Sunday 23 October, 1808. The story goes that Captain Hodder in the *George and Ann*, when chased by the French privateer, lured the Frenchman onto the reef, but unfortunately ran on himself in doing so!

270 Cannon It is not the fact of a cannon on the sea bed at 50 14 47N; 03 52 05W that might make this find important, but the position. The cannon may have come from HMS *Ramillies* (Site **250**), but there is a chance that it might have something to do with HMS *Orestes*. This 16-gun sloop was caught in Bigbury Bay on 29 January, 1812, and had to dump all her guns before she could beat her way out and get into Plymouth. However, as the cannon is reported to be 10ft long it is probably too large for the *Orestes* and is much more likely to come from the *Ramillies*, having been lost during salvage operations.

271 Empire Harry This tug of 479 tons was launched in October 1942 and went into Admiralty service in March 1943. She was one of the Empire Larch class built by Goole Shipbuilding and Repairing Company as part of a Government programme to meet the wartime demand for tugs of all kinds. All these tugs were 136ft long with a beam of 30ft and triple-expansion steam engines of 1200hp. Today the boiler for those engines shows at low water at 50 14 59N; 03 51 42W.

The *Empire Harry* was a victim of that strange combination – fog and a gale. She was towing two laden U.S. Army barges from Falmouth to Antwerp when she went ashore on the rocks running out from Beacon Point, near Hope Cove. The two lighters were smashed to pieces along the coast and the 19 crew of the tug were saved by the Salcombe lifeboat from the wreck some 400yds offshore. The tug broke up and there are plates and ribs in 5m in the area around the boiler.

Two hundred yards north of the boiler is the wreck of the 28ft steel fishing boat *Rampager*, which sank in 1984 near Soar Mill Cove, was raised, stripped and re-sunk off Beacon Point.

272 The Three Pinnacles These three rock towers are charted about 1¹/₂ miles east of Bolt Tail. The tallest reaches to only 15m from the surface in a general depth of 23m at 50 13 54N; 03 54 00W, and an echo sounder must be used for precise location. The pinnacles, though not as spectacular as those of the East Rutts, are a great dive and the sea bed itself is interesting, with many rock shelves under which lobsters and crabs and, in season, crawfish are to be found. A diver descending the steep face of the rocks will without doubt be surrounded by vast schools of large pollack, which seem to make the pinnacles the centre of an unending circular swim.

273 Tasmania This Italian steamer of 3662 tons was built in England in 1900 by W. Doxford and Sons. On 3 October, 1917, she was heading from Hartlepool for Torre Annunziata, near Naples, and was some miles west of Prawle Point when Kapitänleutnant Klaus Lafrenz in *UC-65* spotted her. The *Tasmania* did not see his periscope, nor the torpedo he fired from a bow tube. It struck the ship on the port side by No. 2 hold, completely destroying the nearby stokehold. However, the 342ft steamer did not sink at once and the crew had time to take to their boats. They were picked up by Naval patrol boats and landed at Plymouth.

Lafrenz, who was homeward bound, continued eastwards and reached Zeebrugge safely on 5 October. He was captured and lost *UC-65* and 23 of his crew on his next mission in probably the most stupid action of the whole submarine war. Spotting a British submarine on the surface, he told his No. 2 that it was easy to dodge torpedoes and to demonstrate let the British submarine fire at him. He did dodge the first torpedo but the British captain had fired two, and the second blew Lafrenz into the sea and his boat to pieces!

The *Tasmania* is now at 50 09 58N; 03 52 27W. It is 48m to her deck and 55m to the sea bed. She is upright, but the torpedo damage to her port side has let a deal of her 5100 tons of coal onto the sea bed. She lies north-west to south-east and is very broken in places.

274 Five Mile Reef Located at 50 09 36N; 03 53 30W, this reef is excellent diving, with some very rough ground on a sort of plateau at 25m. The sides of the plateau fall away strikingly swiftly all around and provide some self-service shelves for lobsters and crabs!

275 U-1063 This 871-ton U-boat commanded by Oberleutnant Stephan was 220ft long with a beam of 20ft and a draught of 16ft. She was one of the last produced during World War Two, but was caught by HMS *Loch Killin*, a Navy Loch-class frigate, on 16 April, 1945, and destroyed with depth charges. Today she lies in the same spot – 50 08 54N; 03 53 24W. This is a rocky area and her depth is 58m, from which she stands upright and 6m proud.

276 The River Barge Lost when under tow by the Polish tug *Koral* on 2 January, 1975, this is no little barge. She is 269ft long with a beam of 33ft and is now to be found lying at 48m to the top of her and at 59m to the sea bed. She is upright, with her bows to the east and no sign of damage at 50 08 13N; 03 55 32W.

277 Wreck, name unknown At 50 07 25N; 03 56 36W, this wreck is 250ft long with a beam of 31ft and lies almost north–south. She is partially buried and her bow is so damaged that it is broken and pointing straight up. The wreck has been trawled into many times. The depth to her highest point is 53m; the depth to the sea bed is 63m.

278 Wreck, name unknown At 50 06 38N; 03 58 04W and located only by echo sounder, this one lies amid a collection of large rocks on the sea bed at 64m. The wreck stands 6m proud.

279 Yewforest Attacked by both German aircraft and E-boats, this British steamer of 815 tons was the first victim in a convoy of coastal shipping on 19 November, 1942, and was sunk on the same day as the *Brigitte* (Site **350**). The 199ft Greenock-built ship was torpedoed by an E-boat at 3.10am and sank swiftly. Out of her crew of 12 and three Naval gunners, nine crew and two gunners were lost.

The *Yewforest* had been in various convoys since leaving Hull for Newport. Her cargo was important for the war effort – 900 tons of steel billets. Today she is at 50 05 46N; 03 59 09W, 7m proud of the sea bed at 67m, with a 2m scour on both sides of her. She lies south-east to north-west and is shallowest at the south-eastern end.

280 Wreck, name unknown At 50 03 21N; 03 58 57W this is a large wreck some 380ft long with a beam of 40ft, well sunk into the sand, standing 7m proud of the sea bed at 68m.

281 Wreck, name unknown At 50 07 38N; 04 00 22W this is another well-known "fastener" of local fishermen's nets, even though the sea bed here suffers from sand waves. She stands 12m proud of the sea bed at 63m.

282 East Point The *East Point* was "ten miles east of the Eddystone" on her way from London to Philadelphia on 9 March, 1917, when *U-48* put a torpedo into her. She was British, a steamer of 5234 tons, 390ft long with a beam of 51ft, and today she lies at 50 08 57N; 03 59 52W on a flat bottom of coarse sand at 57m, from which she stands 7m proud.

283 Wreck, name unknown Nothing is known about this wreck at 50 12 30N; 04 09 45W except that she shows as quite small at 48m.

284 HMS Untiring This 740-ton U class Royal Navy submarine was built by Vickers Armstrong and launched on 20 January, 1943. After war service the 197ft submarine was loaned to the Greek Navy in July 1945 and renamed *Zifas*. On her return in 1952 she was obsolete and on 25 July, 1957, was scuttled to the south-west of the East Rutts for use as an echo sounder training target. She is at 50 12 46N; 04 00 36W 8m proud in 50m.

285 The East Rutts These are over five miles from shore and need an echo sounder to locate them at 50 13 24N; 03 58 48W. The East Rutts are several pinnacles of rock rising from the sea bed in 33m to within 8m of the surface. They are usually heavily potted, but when first visited by divers in the late 1950s they were abundant in crawfish and lobsters. Since divers talked about this, they have been heavily fished and there are now few shellfish to be seen; they are however a spectacular dive. There is talk – where is there not? – of an old submarine being seen here by divers, but no confirmation is to be found.

286 Oregon About the same size as the *Cutty Sark*, the 801-ton steel-hulled sailing ship *Oregon* now lies at 50 14 41N; 03 56 22W. She was homeward bound for Newcastle from Iquique in Chile with a cargo of sodium nitrate when, on the evening of 18 December, 1890, she struck The Books (*see* Site **269**). Captain Lowe got her off and appears to have set a course to seaward, but found his ship was now leaking badly and was forced to abandon her. The first boat lowered was swamped by the high seas, but the second was successfully launched. In the pitch dark, the boat drifted for twelve hours before making out the land.

It was not until 6am that "guided by the light from a labourer's lantern on the shore the sailors succeeded in reaching the fishing village of Hope, where they were treated with great kindness" (from *The Times*). The *Oregon* sank as soon as the second boat was launched and is now in 30m, standing 7m proud. She is very broken and rusting away. Her sides have already collapsed. She was first dived by Kingston Branch and was identified by the date of her building, 1875, cast into the boss of her wheel.

A large anchor is on the site near the bow. Some of her blocks are of lignum vitae, and polish up beautifully even after their long stay underwater. Transit marks for the *Oregon* are shown in the diagram on page 165.

287 Sidney H At 50 15 20N; 03 58 43W. This British fishing boat sank on 4 November, 1982, after striking something underwater and tearing out her propeller shaft. One diving report says that she is intact but so far over on her port side at 30m that she is almost capsized.

288 The Aircraft Graveyard A mile out to sea from the westerly tip of Burgh Island at 50 16 25N; 03 54 49W are the wings and aluminium frames of several aircraft. John Plummer of Bigbury BSAC, who dived there recently, reports "lots of aluminium, but no engines". Depths on the site vary from 15 to 20m. It would seem that the wreckage was dumped deliberately and may be of World War Two aircraft such as the Catalina – but the author can find no record of such dumping.

289 Burgh Island This was known in olden times as "Burrow Island", "Burrough Island" or "Burr Island" and those are the ways you will see it spelt on old maps and in many old wreck reports: "Hit Burrough Island", "Struck edge of Burrow Island". It was quite common for sailing ship masters in poor weather to mistake Burgh Island for Looe Island, much further to the west, and a wreck often resulted. A classic example of this error was the sinking of HMS *Ramillies* (Site **250**). It was left, however, to Captain Little of the *Villa Nova*, a brigantine in ballast from St Malo to Cardiff, to make the biggest error of all about the lie of the land in these parts. In 1879, he thought Bolt Tail was Land's End and in attempting to round it went ashore on Burgh Island itself.

At low tide a causeway of firm sand leads from the shore at Bigbury to the island and you can walk across for a drink at the Pilchard Inn there. Beware of leaving the return too late: the tide sweeps through at an amazing rate. A tractor-wheeled passenger wagon, with the passenger compartment perched high out of reach of the sea, makes crossings every half hour when the tide is up in all but really bad weather. But the lifeboat did once have to rescue the passengers when even the tractor became stuck. The sand is firm – until the tide starts to soften it. Under the causeway is at least one Army truck that left it too late!

Do not try to cut through by boat between the mouth of the Avon and Challaborough. You will not make it and boats stuck there do look silly when people walk out past them!

Burgh Island is a boat dive. During the season the rocks round the island can be heavily potted and some nets are in use. Further out the ground continues as slate ledges and ridges with sand and shingle floored gullies running seawards and to the south-west.

Large shoals of pollack are a very common sight and there are crabs in the deeper water. It is a good place to see rose coral in large clumps. Big bass are often around and the occasional salmon has been spotted heading for its home waters of the Avon. Off Burgh Island are inshore mackerel fishing grounds. There are persistent reports of worn iron cannon being seen close in to the island.

Burgh Island is owned by Tony and Beatrice Porter. They have restored the 1920s-style hotel and its restaurant, where it is necessary to book, especially during the summer season. It is said that the hotel was a getaway for Sir Noël Coward and that Agatha Christie wrote *Ten Little Niggers* there. The Beatles stayed there and many film and television programmes have featured the island.

New diving discoveries (*see* Site **296**) show that the island may have had a very much bigger claim to fame in the very distant past. It now seems likely that this was the fabled island of Ictis, the Bronze Age centre for Britain's tin trade with Mediterranean countries and continental Europe. Divers found stone anchors close to Burgh Island in 1993. A settlement dating back to the Bronze Age is know to have existed on nearby Bantham Ham.

290 The Challaborough Cannon In 20m of water off Challaborough, divers have, on four completely separate occasions, found beautiful little bronze cannon, which must mean an old wreck in the area. Roy Wardle, a keen South London diver, found one in 1974 – lying on the sand with the muzzle sticking out from under a flat rock. The bright green told him that it was bronze. When cleaned it was just under two feet long, with little lifting dolphins. Unfortunately the crest on it was too badly worn to be made out. The touchhole had been re-bushed at some time and the latch cover was missing. But the cascabel is a great work of art, completely circled by beautiful little bronze leaves clustering round the acorn of the handle. The bore is 1½ inches in diameter.

About the same time and in exactly the same area, a Guildford diver found its twin! And then in 1977, Geoffrey Moles, a founder member of St Albans BSAC, found yet another bronze gun – a bigger relative 30 inches long, weighing 60lb, and dated 1670. This one had the right-hand dolphin (looking from the cascabel forward) missing, as well as the latch cover over the touchhole. Geoff Moles says that he was diving in gin-clear water over slate gullies in 20m. He saw the "bright green" gun from 25 feet away. It was out in the open on top of one of the slate ridges. He clipped the caribineer of his SMB to the remaining dolphin and searched around for anything else. He found nothing. On examination the cannon was found to be unloaded. The bore was once again 1¹/₂ inches. It seems almost unbelievable, but later another St Albans diver found this bigger gun's twin, matching even down to the same missing dolphin, not far from the site of the first, lying on sand in the bottom of one of the slate gullies.

The cannon have been identified from the coat of arms on the two larger guns as "probably Dutch". This and the date on them rules out the two ships of Philip of Castile that were lost in the mouth of the Erme or the Avon in January 1506.

There was a Dutch ship lost in the area on 29 November, 1691 – we do not know her name, only that five or six of her crew were lost, that she was registered in Holland, and was on passage from the Canary Islands. There was another Dutch ship, the *Annatiere Helena*, wrecked and looted at Thurlestone in 1738. And a Hamburg-bound Dutch galiot laden with wine, brandy, coffee and indigo was stranded at Thurlestone on 10 or 11 January, 1753, but as much of her cargo was salvaged it is unlikely they would have left the guns.

There is a chance that the guns came from a much later ship, and not necessarily a Dutch one. Such expensive decorated guns would last at least a century at sea, moving from ship to ship when either captured or sold. One candidate for the guns could be the *Dagger*, lost at Bantham in 1736. We know she was carrying small guns because of an Admiralty Court held at Hope Cove on

Transit marks for the Oregon (Site 286).

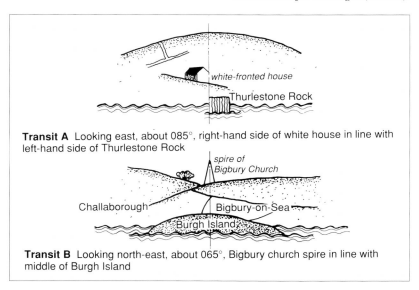

Transit A Looking east, about 085°, right-hand side of white house in line with left-hand side of Thurlestone Rock

Transit B Looking north-east, about 065°, Bigbury church spire in line with middle of Burgh Island

21 April, 1737, where people were summoned for not taking goods from the sea to Lord Devon's steward. Part of the court records read:

> We present George Hamblin of Orford Jefford for taking up of a graper about fifty weight at the place the Dagger was cast away at Bantham harbour, 1736 ... We present John Piles of Kingsbridge for taking up a small gun where the Dagger was lost ...

The description of the loss of the *Dagger* at Bantham Harbour is very vague. However, local divers have recently explored the reef of which Murray's Rock shows at low water and is marked with a beacon. This reef runs to the south-east from the south-east tip of Burgh Island and is a hazard to boats intent on entering the Avon at Bantham. The divers found a large, ancient anchor near the end of the reef furthest from the island. There may well be more bronze guns in the sea around Burgh Island and divers there should be alert for the bright green that bronze and brass take on after being underwater for any length of time.

291 Wells Rock This hidden hazard lies just off Beacon Point at the mouth of the Erme (which should not be confused with Beacon Point near Hope Cove). Though the chart shows a little over 1m of water over it, at least one longshaft propeller has been damaged here. The rock acts as a mark for good diving directly off it, where the sea bed slopes quickly to the 20m mark and there is excellent shellfish country of gullies and ledges.

292 Alpha The wreckage of this 50-ton trawler ketch lies in Ayrmer Cove in 7m of water. She hit Toby's Point at the mouth of the cove in fog at 7pm on 26 October, 1899. The *Alpha* had been built at Brixham in 1897 and her crew tried hard to save her. With the Hope Cove lifeboat standing by, they got her off the rocks of the point, but she started filling with water and they had to put her ashore again in the cove. The light westerly of that murky evening turned into a full blown gale and she became a total wreck. Much of her ironwork and timbers are buried in the sand at 50 17 39N; 03 55 07W.

293 Thrush You can tell this one by her cargo – hundreds of slates are on the bottom at 50 17 35N; 03 57 05W – and as she was a wooden barge there is not much else to be seen. She was lost on 6 August, 1904, when her anchors dragged. The crew of two were taken off by the Yealm lifeboat.

Found by divers on 25 January, 1977, her wreckage covers an area about 100ft by 35ft. She is in 12m, inshore from the wreck of the *Persier* (Site **294**) and close to Beacon Point. She may have been anchored off the Erme for the transfer of slates to small boats for building work locally.

294 Persier Although she was torpedoed by Oberleutnant Werner Riecken and his crew of 34 in *UB-1017* on 11 February, 1945, he did not see her sink – and nor did anyone else. It was not until Plymouth Sound BSAC found her in May 1969 at 50 17 00N; 03 58 09W that anyone knew where she was.

The story of her last voyage begins on 8 February, 1945. She left Cardiff on a mercy mission – to take food to the liberated but starving people of Belgium. There were 63 people on board the ship when she sailed, some of them survivors of the *Leopoldville*, torpedoed and sunk off Cherbourg on the night of Christmas Day 1944. These survivors had asked to be repatriated and as the *Persier* was the first ship to head for a Belgian port, they were put aboard.

For this voyage, the 5382-ton Belgian steamer, which had been called the *War Buffalo* when she was launched at Newcastle in 1918, was to be part of Convoy BTC 65. The convoy commander, Commodore Edmund Wood, and his staff of three signallers were aboard. On 11 February the convoy was between the Eddystone and the shore when Commodore Wood received a message from one of the small escorts that a periscope had been seen. Not long afterwards a column of water shot skywards on the port side of the convoy. Older hands guessed that it was the premature explosion of a torpedo. They were right.

Within seconds another torpedo hissed past the stern of the *Persier* from port to starboard and disappeared. On the bridge Captain Mathieu, First Officer Lardinoy and Commodore Wood braced themselves. They knew what was coming, and at 5.25pm precisely it did. The torpedo struck the port side opposite No. 2 hold and just forward of the bridge. The explosion flung Lardinoy to the deck and broke his nose. On board *UB-1017* the crew believed they had hit two ships – the premature explosion of the earlier torpedo, they thought, was another hit. Riecken later reported two ships sunk.

On board the *Persier*, as the sea poured into the damaged hold, the cargo of powdered egg, baby food and meat broke loose and five tons of woollen blankets soaked up the sea. The ship started to list to port. Abandon ship drill took only six minutes, but it went terribly wrong. Lifeboat No. 1, with Commodore Wood and ten others, was launched correctly, but the enormous seas unhooked the bow and left it suspended by the stern, spilling everyone into the water. Lifeboat No. 3 was drawn into the ship's propeller and was chopped to pieces. Lifeboat No. 1 was then righted, but as three men slid down the falls to her, one, a stoker, caught his foot and was left hanging, smashed against the side of the ship by every wave. The two other men fared little better – they reached the boat safely but it was then also drawn into the propeller.

The ship was now about four miles from the Eddystone in winds of Force 7. The seas were colossal. Rafts were launched and men managed to cling to them. The *Persier* had stopped moving, with her propeller still. But she was obviously not

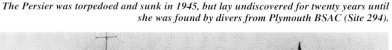

The Persier was torpedoed and sunk in 1945, but lay undiscovered for twenty years until she was found by divers from Plymouth BSAC (Site 294).

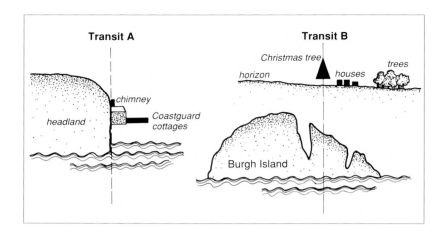

Transit marks for the Persier (Site 294).

long for the surface. Her stern was right out of the water. Still aboard were her captain, Lardinoy, and five others. It was then that Lardinoy put forward a desperate idea. He would swim to a nearby small cargo ship, the *Birker Force*, and ask the captain to come alongside to rescue them. To get him away from the ship, he asked the other men to throw him as far out as they could. That is what they did.

Despite being thumped by nearby depth-charging, Lardinoy managed to swim to a lifeboat that had been launched from the *Birker Force* and gasped out his message. As the ship moved in on the *Persier*, the men on board flung an old unseaworthy raft into the sea and jumped for it. They were all picked up. In all, 44 were saved. The *Persier* was last seen drifting into the night, stern high, bow down. Tugs sent out from Plymouth searched in vain.

She sank in the dark and no one saw her going. And no one would know where she was today if Colin Hopkins, then chairman of Plymouth Sound BSAC, after being told by a sea-angling friend of a place he was always losing tackle, dived the site and found the wreck of a large armed merchantman with a 4.7-inch gun on her stern and two sets of Oerlikon guns, one on the stern and one on the bridge. She had a bronze propeller. Plymouth Sound BSAC confirmed her name when they recovered her bell – still clearly marked *War Buffalo*. They bought the *Persier* for £300, and twelve members of the branch put up the money. Remember, they still own her.

The *Persier* today is right off the mouth of the Erme with her bows to the south-west. Her bow is her highest point about 10m above the sea bed at 28m. She is over on her port side and very broken amidships, where she is lying over rock outcrops. Her centre has collapsed inwards. The three boilers are clear to see. Nearby is an 8ft anchor. Her propeller and three guns have all been salvaged.

Diver coxswains should approach from the east (the Burgh Island side) then drag an anchor or grapnel until hooked in. Try the same tactic from the west and you will certainly hook into the big reef before the wreckage. Transit marks are shown in the diagram opposite: open up the bluff at the mouth of the Erme until you can see the old Coastguard cottages. Line up on the first chimney. The east–west mark is: on the skyline near Thurlestone there is a large Christmas-tree shaped tree. Put this slightly to the right of the fork between the main two peaks on Burgh Island. The best launch site is from Challaborough.

WARNING A net has been reported on her stern.

295 The Other Persier In May 1980 a diver reported that he had missed the wreck of the *Persier* and had found himself on another wreck – that of a steel vessel complete with portholes and two boilers 20ft high, on a reef some 2m off the a bed at 25m. He estimated that he was about 380m east-south-east of the wreck of the *Persier*, at 50 17 00N; 03 58 22W. This might have been thought to be part of the *Persier* and local dive boat skippers searched the area in vain.

Quite independently a highly respected underwater expert, Jim Gill, has also reported being on a wreck that "was clearly not the Persier" with a bow section standing well proud. This report put the new wreck some 500m south of the *Persier*.

296 Erme Estuary wrecks The River Erme flows from Dartmoor into Bigbury Bay. Heavy silting means that today there is only a small navigable channel upstream from the mouth and then only at high tide. From the sea, the mouth

Challaborough is the best place to launch when diving the Persier (Site 294). Also marked is the aircraft graveyard off Burgh Island (Site 288).

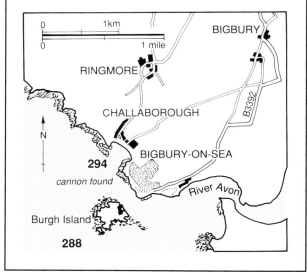

of the Erme looks like a haven. Once in, it can provide shelter. But getting in is the problem and the only safe approach is by hugging the coast on either side where there are narrow entrances. The rest of the mouth is blocked by the East and West Mary Rocks. These rocks are part of a reef right across the obvious entrance and only show at low water. The rest of the time they are a deadly trap as they lie only just under the surface and have ripped the bottom out of many craft over the centuries.

Just how many the divers of the South-West section of the Nautical Archaeology Society were to find out when, in 1990, one of their members, Stephen George, reported his discovery of a cannon site in the Erme Estuary. During the following days the archaeological divers, led by Neville Oldham, located two swivel guns, possibly from the 1490s. These suggested that they had found the two ships of Philip of Castile, reported in old documents as being lost in the Erme mouth in 1506.

However, a later discovery on the same site was a Swedish finbanker cannon, 2.69m long, dated between 1690 and 1750. Then the divers found a silver coin, a French half-écu minted between 1610 and 1640, pan weights, a pestle, sounding weights, lead shot and a little bronze figure of a goddess.

But the most sensational finds came last of all as the divers widened their search – 42 ingots of almost pure tin, crudely shaped in earth moulds, typical of Bronze Age work. This meant that the divers had found one of the oldest shipwrecks in Britain, and probably the remains of three or four others, all victims of the reef across the bay. Their ingot discovery also suggests that nearby Burgh Island is the island of Ictis, to which tin-traders sailed to buy tin from the ancient Britons, written about in 10 BC by the Greek historian Diodorus Siculus. He wrote that Ictis was left dry at low tides and the tin was brought out to it from the shore

Neville Oldham with the Swedish finbanker cannon recovered from the Erme estuary (Site 296). The cannon is about to be lowered into a preservation tank.

in carts – the resemblance to Burgh Island could not be more striking. It would also explain the Bronze Age swords found at Moor Sands (Site **230**).

Both Erme sites are protected and this effectively stops all diving in the mouth of the river.

297 Bayawahha This is a real mystery ship, said to be at 50 15 54N; 03 59 57W and also said to have been carrying a cargo of wheat from Plymouth to Dartmouth when she sank on New Year's Eve 1916. There is also a tonnage for this mystery ship – 1150 tons. The trouble is that there is no trace of any such ship in Lloyds records. Nor can she be found elsewhere, not even on the sea bed!

The mystery does not end here. At the same position is said to be the *VYC-18*, a lighter sunk on 18 February, 1956, carrying a cargo of wheat! The trouble is that the area in which they lie is a dizzying underwater landscape of crags and canyons and echo sounders go a little crazy there. The bottom depth varies from 30 to 40m give or take a peak or two.

Nearby at 50 16 40N; 04 01 50W is what appears to be a barge. This small wreck was located in 1984 in a depth of 35m. It could of course be the *VYC-18*!

298 Totnes Castle This 91-ton paddle-steamer was built by the famous Philip yard at Dartmouth in 1923. She was 108ft long with a beam of 17ft and drew only 3ft. She was powered by two-cylinder compound diagonal engines, had a steel hull, and took holidaymakers on trips up the Dart to Totnes and back until the end of the summer season of 1963. An inspection then revealed that she needed expensive repairs, which would make her unprofitable. Her wheelhouse and lifeboat were transferred to a new motor vessel named *Cardiff Castle*.

The *Totnes Castle* was then sold and became a floating hostel and sailing school on the Dart. But the venture failed and she was up for sale again, slowly deteriorating at her mooring until 1967, when she was sold for breaking at Marrowbone Slip in Plymouth's Sutton Harbour. She never reached the breakers.

On Thursday 9 November she set out on her last voyage. She was being towed by the Plymouth tug *Antony*, whose captain expected the trip to take five hours in good weather, but when he was off Burgh Island the wind and sea came up and she foundered. None of the seven crew of the *Antony* were aboard the *Totnes Castle* at the time and they were able to cast off and retrieve their towing hawser before she went down.

Today she is at 50 15 20N; 03 58 44W and sits upright in a hollow in the shingle sea bed at 40m from which she is 3m proud. Her superstructure is missing, but her engines can be clearly seen, together with many of the gauges. Divers have recovered portholes, but if they search for her bell they are wasting their time – it was removed when she was converted to a hostel and can be seen in Totnes Museum.

The Longroom at Plymouth.

AREA 7:

Plymouth Sound

This area runs from Stoke Point (04 01 18W) in the east to Plymouth Sound (04 11 12W) in the west, which is the end of south Devon waters and where Cornwall takes over. It includes those yachtsmen's delights Newton Ferrers and Noss Mayo, sweeps on to Wembury, with its voluntary marine reserve, and round into Plymouth Sound, with Fort Bovisand, the most important diving centre in the South West on the eastern side near Plymouth Breakwater. The area is rich in wrecks and marine life. Most diving here is from boats and there are several good launching sites.

The approach to NEWTON FERRERS is by the A379 Kingsbridge–Plymouth road, turning off near Yealmpton onto the B3186. When Newton Ferrers is reached, the fjord-like harbour is clear below you. Almost all of it dries at low water, but has a depth of 3.5m at high water. The village across the arm of the Yealm is NOSS MAYO, which needs a turn back to Bridgend to reach it.

The Newton Ferrers public launching site – for which, as at Noss Mayo, there is a charge – is straight down the steep hill marked as a no through road. Divers towing inflatables should take great care, but there is easy access after the road bends sharply to the right. You can drive right down to the mud. Public moorings are available and harbour dues are payable.

The Harbour Master should be consulted before launching for advice about moorings and the use of the river itself. To find his office, do not turn down the steep road to the launch site, but carry on round by the road that runs along the side of the estuary until you come to the Yealm Hotel on your right. The Harbour Office is under the hotel and you can park in the forecourt of the hotel and walk across to it. The office is open from 10 to 12 noon and from 2.30 to 3.30pm (tel. 01752 872533).

There is a strict six-knot speed limit within the harbour for safety reasons, not wake disturbance. Saying that your inflatable makes less wash on the plane is no excuse! Newton Ferrers is much used by divers and the Harbour Master can help you in many ways. For example, if the weather is too rough outside the river, only he can give you permission to dive from Cellars Beach, which is inside the sand bar, an extensive shallow bank that dries and extends south from Bar Point, just to the east of Season Point. CELLARS BEACH provides interesting shallow diving with much fish life, particularly mullet.

Approached by turning off the A379 about 14 miles west of Kingsbridge or by leaving Plymstock in the direction of the gunnery school HMS *Cambridge*, WEMBURY has a small, sandy cove. On either side of the beach are rocky reefs. The beach is backed by a low cliff and most of the land belongs to the National Trust or the Ministry of Defence. The latter also own the Great Mew Stone, which dominates the view out to sea – landing on it is forbidden. Boats can be launched at Wembury. The approach roads are steep and narrow, but access to the beach and the launch is easy, provided the traffic to the car park does not jam up!

Wembury is at the heart of the Wembury Bay Marine Conservation Area. The seaward boundaries if this voluntary reserve run in a line from Gara Point near the mouth of the Yealm across to the Little Mew Stone, then to the Shag Stone, and finally to the jetty at Bovisand Harbour. Divers may look and photograph, but are asked not take marine life from the area. The same applies to the wrecks that fall within those boundaries (Sites **324**, **326**, **327**, **332** and **334**). Wembury has a warden, who will be delighted to help divers.

299 Wembury Bay To the east (the left of the beach looking out to sea) is the rocky reef known as Church Ledge and to the west the mass of the Wembury Ledge, which at one time connected directly with the Great Mew Stone. The Mew Stone protects Wembury from south-westerlies, so there is sheltered diving off the beach down to 11m in gullies in the slate reefs, with crevices and overhangs amid the kelp. A really powerful swimmer on a very calm day could snorkel out and dive the Great Mew Stone, but this is more sensibly regarded as a boat dive. The waters inside the Mew Stone are much used for novice training and first sea dives. Just off Church Ledge is Porchopen Shoal, 3.4m deep.

Most of Wembury Bay is under 11m deep, but has a prolific fish life. It is famed among marine biologists because almost all United Kingdom species of wrasse can be found here. The corkwing wrasse regularly breeds here and has been extensively studied in the bay by scientists from the Marine Biological Association. The sea bed further out consists of large boulders and deep gullies with sand flooring.

300 Heybrook Bay This lies just around Wembury Point to the west and is approached through Down Thomas. There is a car park. Entry to the water is by walking down to the little pebble bay directly below the car park. The bottom is boulders and sandy gullies in 10m with abundant fish life. There are crabs – but remember you are in a marine reserve!

Opposite: Dive Sites in Area 7, Plymouth Sound. Note that distances from offshore sites to the land are not to scale. This area is covered by Admiralty charts 95 (Wembury and the River Yealm), 1613 (Eddystone Rocks to Berry Head), 1900 (Approaches to Plymouth) and 1967 (Plymouth Sound); Ordnance Survey map 201.

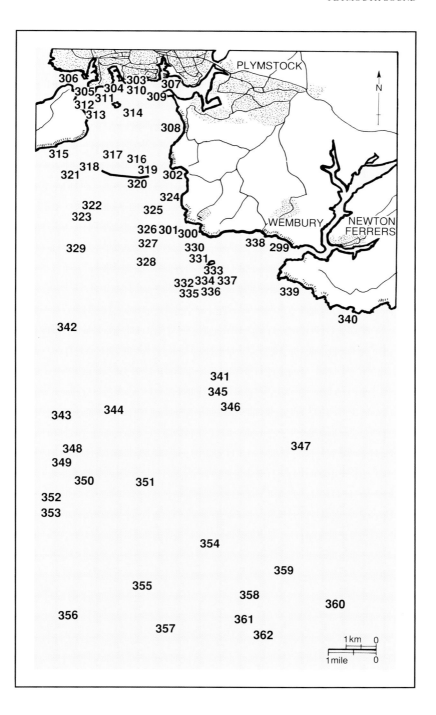

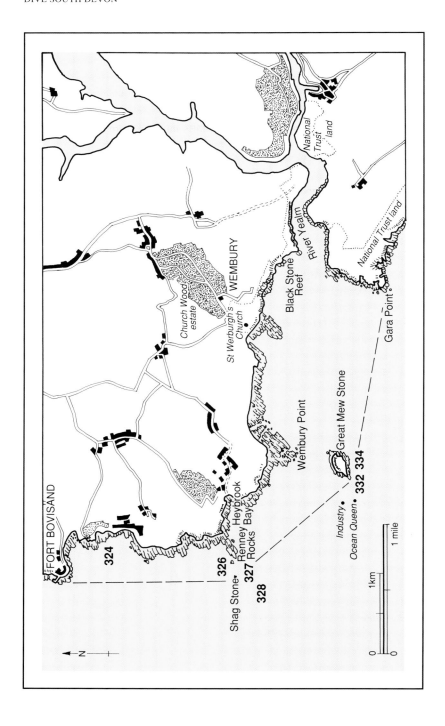

301 Renney Rocks Entry is just to the west of these rocks from a small sandy beach. It entails a five-minute walk with your gear along a footpath, but this will not worry the fit. Kelp abounds on this dive in less than 10m, but there is a great deal of wreckage spread around the rocks themselves. They have been the scene of several shipwrecks, including those listed as Sites **326** and **327**.

302 Fort Bovisand Shore diving involves walking down the slipway and moving out of the harbour to either east or west. SMBs must be worn and great care taken due to the boat traffic. This is a good first sea dive area for novices. Fort Bovisand is the diver's Mecca in the South West and the most important diving centre in the whole of southern England. Designated as a National Diving Centre by the BSAC, the converted fort was built in 1847 to defend Britain against Napoleon and can sleep over 100 divers at a time.

Fort Bovisand was opened in 1970 by Plymouth Ocean Projects Ltd and is the largest diver training school in Britain. The grounds cover several acres. The two founders of the centre, Alan Bax and Jim Gill, are divers of great experience and are in control of the day-to-day running of the fort. It has its own L-shaped jetty and a harbour that provides sheltered water for novices and training and pick-up facilities for dive boats. A 4m wide slipway provides easy launching and there is a boat and trailer park close at hand.

The fort, which is visited by divers from all over Europe, is reached from Plymouth by following the A379 for Kingsbridge. Follow this road over Laira Bridge to the first roundabout, then turn right and follow signs for Plymstock until you reach a set of traffic lights. Turn right into Dean Cross Road; continue on this road as it changes to Radford Park Road, then to Hooe Road. After 1½ miles there is Lakeside Garage on your left. Continue past the garage and up the hill. Take the left fork into Jennycliff Lane, which will eventually follows the coastline up the hill. Stay on this road until a sign indicates right for Fort Bovisand, the beach and car park.

Cars may be taken through the narrow gate of the fort for unloading. Afterwards they must be parked outside the fort gate in the car park or alongside the massive walls of the casemates. Charges are made for parking at busy times, but not for residents.

The Underwater Centre has classrooms with modern teaching aids. These are used for basic and advanced diver training.

At the fort there is a fully operational diving medical centre with four chambers for emergency use – the Diving Diseases Research Centre run by Dr Maurice Cross. There are plans to move the research centre to Plymouth's Derriford Hospital, where when not required for treating diving emergencies the chambers could be used for pressure therapy for other illnesses.

Underwater photographers are catered for, with a darkroom and large lecture room, fully equipped with 16mm cine, video and 35mm slide projection facilities. There is a drying room, air charging and a hire and repair shop. There is a large training tank, which is used for basic underwater cutting, welding and power tool

Opposite: Wembury Bay marine conservation area: the boundary of this voluntary reserve is marked with a dotted line. The numbered dive sites are the Vectis (324), the Nepaul (326), the Constance (327), the Glen Strathallan (328), the Ajax (332) and the Rothesay (334).

Fort Bovisand, on the eastern edge of Plymouth Sound. Plymouth Breakwater and Penlee Point can be seen in the distance.

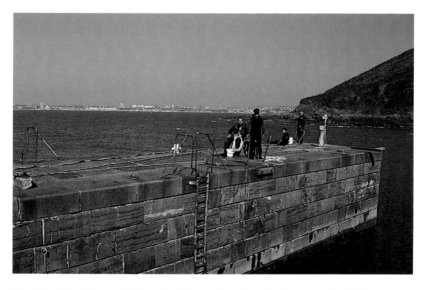

The jetty at Fort Bovisand. The city of Plymouth can be clearly seen on the skyline.

lessons – 18ft in diameter and 10ft deep, it can be used for basic scuba training by arrangement.

Bovisand Harbour belongs to the fort and is the gateway to excellent and varied diving. The area of the harbour provides depths down to 10m and is sheltered by the solid limestone blocks, topped with granite, of the L-shaped jetty. The reason for building the harbour was not just to supply the fort but to ease the difficulty in supplying fresh water to Naval ships. In Drake's time the great warships anchored off the little stream that runs down to Bovisand Bay and sent their longboats ashore with casks to collect drinking water. By 1816 supplying ships in this way was no longer good enough and Sir John Rennie designed and built a reservoir in the valley. From this, water was piped down a 9-inch cast-iron pipe to Staddon Point, where the fort now stands, and out along the jetty.

The jetty now acts as a diving platform and an embarkation point for boats. It has a built-in air supply that can feed low-pressure air to six diving stations simultaneously. The A Flag is flown at the fort to show that diving operations are in progress in some part of the Bovisand area, entrance channel or harbour.

There is a Bovisand Code of Conduct aimed at safety and the preservation of wildlife and archaeological material in the immediate vicinity. The following rules should be observed:

Power boats should enter and leave the harbour by the approach channel at all times.

The speed of boats in the approach channel and harbour must not exceed four knots.

Permission must be obtained from the Training Office on weekdays between 8.30am and 5.30pm (otherwise from the Hire Centre) for any diving in the harbour area and approach channel or diving areas (whether for sport, training or trials), mooring in the harbour and use of the jetty steps, ladders or slip for loading, unloading or launching. Diving in the harbour area and approach channel should generally be kept to a minimum. Priority will be given to divers under training and trials groups.

Divers swimming in the Fort Bovisand diving areas should remain on the surface until they are well clear of the harbour and approach channel.

All diving groups in the area are to be clearly marked by a buoy carrying the diving flag and where possible this flag should be of a rigid material. SMBs are provided free by the fort against a refundable deposit.

A blue and white chequered flag (International Flag N) is flown when the harbour steps are in use. Approaching boats should not go alongside until the steps are clear and people using them should move away as soon as possible.

No conventional swimming is allowed from any part of the jetty.

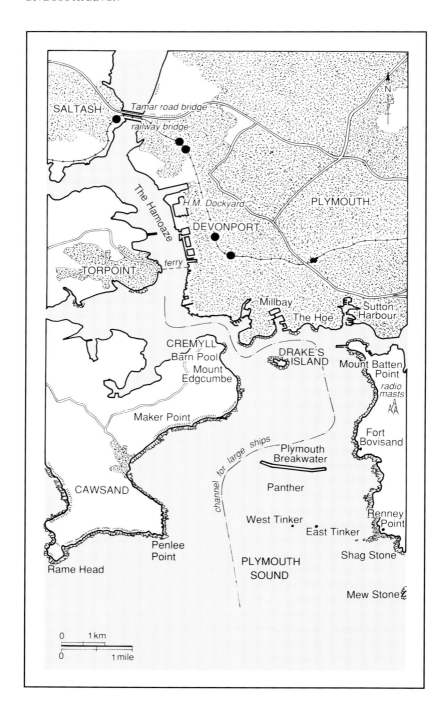

No wildlife is to be collected from above or below water in the Bovisand areas without the permission of the directors of Fort Bovisand. No spearguns are to be carried or used.

The code also requests divers in the Plymouth area to take only items required for the use or consumption of the individual, and asks them to report any archaeological finds thought to be more than 100 years old to the directors, or to the curator of Plymouth Museum.

The code contains other information and sensible advice for all divers, to help them to understand the fishermen's use of the Plymouth area:

The only conflict of interest likely to occur is between divers and shell fisherman, of whom there are many full-time skippers in this area. They will probably visit any given spot only a dozen or so times a year and will leave their gear down for a maximum of about 48 hours.

Two types of gear are used: conventional lobster or crab pots and tangle nets (vertical nets with their bottoms on the sea bed, some 2m high with a mesh of 20 to 25mm). Both types of gear are laid in lines that may be up to 500 yards long, marked with a float at each end.

Because the skippers and their crews rely on the sale of their catch for their living and because that the tangle nets provide a very real danger, divers are asked not to dive between the buoys that mark each end of a net or pot line, nor close to the end markers.

The local fishermen have agreed to mark their floats or buoys with the registered number of their boats, and also to use buoys of such size that they are readily identifiable from one end of the line to the other. When you see one, look for the other – it may be several hundred yards away – and then do not dive between them.

Other Plymouth launch sites are at Phoenix Wharf (near the Mayflower Steps, from which the Pilgrim Fathers sailed), at Richmond Walk, at Oreston and at Queen Anne's Battery marina. Most hard dive boats use Sutton Harbour to take on divers, though a few use Queen Anne's Battery.

Diving within PLYMOUTH SOUND is a matter of trust between divers and the Queen's Harbour Master – please do not break that trust. You must always seek permission to dive. You must dive where you said you wanted to – not somewhere nearby. You must have boat cover. You must use SMBs. Your boat cover must be ready to haul divers up by their SMB lines at the approach of any large ship. Ideally your dive boat should be equipped with VHF radio, so that your diving party can be notified if you are in the way of a ship or liable to be in the near future. There is a speed limit of ten knots.

Opposite: Detailed map of the Plymouth area.

The bell of Die Fraumetta Catharina von Flensburg, sunk in Plymouth
Sound in 1786 (Site 313), was presented by the divers who found the wreck
to the Prince of Wales, President of the BSAC. The presentation was made
at the BSAC's twenty-first anniversary dinner in 1974. Sir Harry Secombe
is singing "I'm for ever blowing bubbles".

The Queen's Harbour Master can be contacted at the Longroom at Stonehouse (tel. 01752 663225). His jurisdiction covers the whole Sound and extends seaward roughly to a line drawn from Penlee Point in the west to HMS *Cambridge* and Wembury Point in the east. The area is policed by the Ministry of Defence and there is closed-circuit television coverage from Drake's Island.

Divers who wish to dive close to the dockyards should be aware of the Port of Plymouth Diving Regulations, which state:

> No diving shall take place within 100m of the walls, slipways or boundaries of Her Majesty's Dockyards, floating Docks or other Crown Establishments, or within 150m of any of Her Majesty's vessels, or anywhere within the fairways of the Dockyard Port, save with the licence in writing of the Queen's Harbour Master.

That sounds as though it makes general diving difficult, but this is not so. To dive elsewhere, divers must follow a proper procedure and will generally find permission easy to obtain.

Divers wanting to dive in the Sound should telephone the Longroom or call "Longroom" on VHF Channel 16. The diver will then be asked to state the time of dive and proposed location, number of divers, dive duration, and details of the dive boat, including VHF identification if any. When permission is given, the diver will be advised of any signals required or any special information about the area in which the dive is to take place.

Divers should be aware of the HMS *Cambridge* firing range – this shore establishment at Wembury Point has firing areas that extend 15 miles to seaward. All gunnery training for the Royal Navy is carried out here; normal firing times are 8.30am to 5pm Tuesday to Friday. When firing is in progress or about to start, three large red flags are flown at Wembury Point and across the Sound at Penlee Fog Signal Station. All vessels have normal navigation rights during this time, but any vessel making a slow way across the range, or stopped on it, can interrupt firing. Yachts and small boats are asked to keep within one mile of the shore when crossing the area and to keep to a steady course and speed.

There are two main degaussing ranges in the Sound – one to the east of Penlee Point and the other to the south. Naval ships use these areas three or four times a week. A small boat in the area could hold up their work. If you are diving near these places keep a sharp look-out for any ships wanting to operate there.

High power sonar trials occasionally take place in the area. The Harbour Master tries to inform all concerned, but if you hear or your divers report any strange noises under water, abandon diving at once and contact the Harbour Master for information. Trial underwater explosions are sometimes carried out – cover boats are always present and will tell you if diving should be abandoned.

Mill Bay is a cannon site and has been the subject of an archaeological survey. Just 25yds from the modern breakwater are nine Swedish cannon. They date from the late 17th or early 18th century, when Sweden was a source of marine armaments for many countries. There is also chain shot. There was some embarrassment in 1973 when four Royal Marines of 42 Commando on a recreational dive raised one of the cannon and then found out that they had visited an archaeological site. The cannon was replaced very quickly!

Diving in Plymouth Sound is as varied as you like to make it and continues throughout the entire year. Only heavy rain inland colouring the Tamar and other rivers and streams that exit through the Sound puts a stop to divers finding reasonable visibility in some sheltered spot, even in the worst weather. This run-off from the land does, however, generally affect visibility. Sunlight rarely penetrates more than 4m, so sea life is that much higher in the Sound than in the open sea.

Spring tides rise just under 5m, neap tides just under 4m. A southerly gale can raise that by nearly 1m; northerly winds have the opposite effect. Generally, the tide stream is about 1½ knots, but it can reach nearly 3 knots over the Cremyll Shoal and 2 knots in the Hamoaze. Tides can be exceptionally strong between Drake's Island and Ravenness Point, an area known as The Bridge.

Slack water in the Sound is usually at high and low water and lasts for no more than 30 minutes. Visibility is better on the flood slack, because the ebb tide brings down silt from the Hamoaze and Tamar.

WARNING When shore diving, like diving anywhere in the Sound, SMBs must be used. All shore diving here would be safer with boat cover.

303 Promenade Pier This pier is below the Hoe, but you will look for it above the water in vain, even though when it was completed in 1884 it was 420 feet long, complete with a ballroom and café, and was supported on 140 iron columns. A direct hit from German bombers in 1942, together with some salvage, mean that today its remains are in less than 9m. Bottles, coins and pieces of "what the butler saw" slot machines are often found by divers. There is parking on Hoe Road; steps lead down to a short concrete pier. A compass course of 220° will take the diver to the wreckage.

WARNING Tripper boats are a hazard.

304 The Walls These lie almost beneath the Longroom in Firestone Bay and are sheer rock cliffs underwater, plunging down to 40m. Approach from the west end of Union Street, turning into Durnford Street at the Stonehouse roundabout, to reach the car park right at the water's edge. The rocks are covered with jewel and plumose anemones and dead man's fingers.

The site of the former Promenade Pier on Plymouth Hoe. In the background is Smeaton's lighthouse of 1759, which originally stood on the Eddystone Rocks.

305 Devil's Point This is a continuation to the west of The Walls. Here the underwater cliffs drop down to 38m, but you must take care as you become exposed to the very strong tides of The Narrows and could be swept into the main shipping channel. This makes boat cover almost essential, even though entry can be made from the shore. There is no exit from the water at Devil's Point, and further up is Devonport naval base where all diving is banned.

Boat diving sites

306 Mashfords Shoal When all other sites are weather bound, particularly in winter, Plymouth Sound divers take part in a strange ritual – they call it "having a skrange off Mashfords". This is a rummage dive in the mud off Mashfords Shoal, named after the boatyard at Cremyll.

Before the Breakwater was completed in 1844, this area was one of the few really sheltered moorings for shipping using the Sound and the Hamoaze. The debris of centuries lies among the small boat moorings. It is Plymouth Sound's "bottle bank", with some really old specimens brought up.

But not all discoveries here are small: one local diver "skranging" here found an intact diver's hard-hat helmet, another a complete masthead lamp, and yet another a very old bronze ship's cooking pot.

The edge of Mashfords Shoal is a wall of mud on stony ground where the channel starts. Divers have seen ancient wooden wreckage emerge from the wall only to disappear on a later dive when the wall has moved and changed shape due to the river currents.

The presence of such wreckage is not surprising, as Plymouth has been a Naval and commercial port for centuries. The main anchorages of today were not sheltered enough for early shipping, which hid up the Tamar or in the Cattewater at the mouth of the River Plym.

307 Cattewater Historic Wreck This wreck at 50 21 41N; 04 07 37W is just off RAF Mountbatten. No diving is allowed within 50m of that point. The Cattewater – which means "ship water" and was presumably a mooring place in ancient times – is the last reach of the River Plym before it flows out through Cobbler Channel into the Sound proper.

The wreck was discovered when a dredger brought up wood when deepening the area around the old flying boat moorings. Parts of two small breech-loaders were brought up at the same time. A third gun was later raised by divers. By a process of elimination of shipwrecks recorded in Plymouth archives, there seems a possibility that this wreck is the *St James of the Croyne*, which sank "in great winds" during the night of 17 January, 1494.

308 Fylrix Diving is banned on this 637-ton British motor vessel, which is on her starboard side at 50 21 05N; 04 07 30W in Plymouth Sound. As she is in only 5m of water in Jennycliff Bay, her whole side dries at low tide and she breaks surface at half tide. She is 203ft long with a beam of 28ft and is now used as a site for explosives courses.

The *Fylrix* was on her way from Dean Quarry at Porthoustock on the Lizard Peninsula with a load of granite chippings destined for London's roads. Divers will know Porthoustock as the beach from which many dives on the Manacles have begun. During the voyage a gale caught her off the Eddystone during the night of 21 November, 1984, and in the large seas her cargo shifted and she developed a pronounced list to starboard. Her master radioed for help and headed for Plymouth. He was escorted into the Sound by a Royal Navy frigate and anchored in the shelter of Jennycliff Bay. During the early hours of the morning the list grew worse and the crew abandoned her just before she capsized.

The *Fylrix* was visited by hundreds of amateur divers and she has been stripped of all possible souvenirs; the bronze propeller has gone. Before the diving ban was put into operation an amateur diver died when trapped inside the wreck.

309 Mallard Shoal This is a scenic dive when visibility is good. Dive with care as you are on the edge of the main channel. Some divers report having found a cliff face here, which drops from 20 to 30m and is good for lobsters. Watch for ships coming out of the Cattewater via the Cobbler Channel. You may also find a sailing club mark here if you didn't check the yacht racing calendar!

310 Asia Knoll On this drift dive north of Drake's Island you must keep inside the marker of the main channel in depths of 10 to 12m. This is flatfish country. There is also a deal of rubbish on the bottom. Beware of the large passenger ferries, which sometimes take a short cut!

311 Battery Bay At Wilderness Point there is a cliff face dropping down to 40m. Very tidal, best dived on slack half an hour before high water, when you have a 45-minute window.

312 Barn Pool This is almost a shore dive on the banks of the Mount Edgcumbe Country Park. Fort Bovisand has a training platform moored nearby. Barn Pool has been an anchoring place for centuries, which means that there are interesting items to be found on the bottom. The water increases rapidly from 7m to 30m as you move offshore. At 30m and balanced almost on the edge of another drop is a World War Two military barge, possibly an ammunition carrier. The site is part of a Plymouth University project.

313 Die Fraumetta Catharina von Flensburg The chance find of a bronze bell poking out of the mud bottom of Plymouth Sound at 30m near Drake's Island in October 1973 led to the discovery of this wreck of 1786. Divers of Plymouth Sound BSAC made the find at 50 21 06N; 04 09 46W.

The night of 10 December, 1786, threatened disaster for all the shipping then in Plymouth, for the wind that night was a southerly gale, blowing straight into the Sound. The *Catharina* had arrived that day, seeking shelter from the worsening weather. She was on the way from St Petersburg to Genoa with a cargo of hemp and leather hides. At 10pm the wind broke the ship from her moorings, hurled the 53-ton brigantine onto the rocks of Drake's Island, then drove her across the foam-filled narrows towards Mount Edgcumbe before she sank in the darkness under the Raven's Cliffs. Somehow the crew struggled ashore, but the ship went down in deep water.

The bell the divers raised bore the full name of the ship and the date 1782. From Flensburg (now in Germany but in the 18th century part of Denmark) the divers were able to establish that the ship had been built there in that year. Her owners were Hinrich Lorck and Knut Andersen and her captain was Hans Jensen Twedt. Further exploration of the wreck site turned up her anchor and a few rolls of leather. Each roll contained six complete reindeer hides, complete with tails, with Russian lettering cut into them. The silt had preserved the hides, assisted by their tanning with willow bark and currying with birch oil.

Since those first few discoveries, an archaeological survey by the Plymouth Sound divers of the site using airlifts has revealed that there is 75 per cent of the ship below the mud and that her holds are packed with rolls of hides, hundreds of them! Some hides have been made into bags, belts and shoes, and sold to fund the continuing survey. No diving is allowed without the permission of Ian Skelton of Plymouth Sound BSAC.

314 Drake's Island At 50 21 30N; 04 09 10W, this used to be known as St Nicholas Island. A prominent island, with a peak height of 21m, it is surrounded by rocky ledges, some of which dry at low water. On the south-east corner among the ledges, divers have found traces of the 70-gun HMS *Conqueror*, wrecked when almost new after hitting the island during a gale on 26 October, 1760. The traces are mostly cannonballs, as she was heavily salvaged before she finally broke up.

In 1972, a diver found a magnificent bronze cannon in very shallow water just off the island. Nearly five feet long, it was fully charged with ball. It has been identified as a light field gun of the reign of Frederick II of Prussia, and dated between 1752 and 1780 but no one can explain how it came to be on the sea bed there.

315 Queen's Grounds Off Picklecombe Point and Fort Picklecombe, a western version of Fort Bovisand now converted into flats, is a fine ground for flatfish in less than 10m. It is essential to make sure that you do not drift dive into the main channel.

316 Plymouth Breakwater The first and centre stone of the Breakwater – a structure 1700yds long – was laid on the Shovel Rock on 12 August, 1812, and the structure was completed in 1840. The Breakwater Fort is 50yds north of the centre of the Breakwater and there is 7.3m of water in the passage between them.

Plymouth Breakwater Lighthouse is at the west end of the Breakwater and was established in 1844. The tower is 23m high, with the height of the light 19m above mean high water. It has a range of 15 miles, with a white and red flash every ten seconds.

There is a conical light beacon with a black framework ball topmark 15m high at the east end of the Breakwater. The topmark is meant to be a refuge for shipwrecked sailors and can take six people. There are four stone shelters at intervals along the Breakwater and the landing pier is half way along, on the north side.

The Breakwater provides protection for the northern part of the Sound from southerly gales, which have been powerful enough to toss a ship completely over the Breakwater. Diving on the southern edge provides depths down to 9m where the rocks and boulders of the wave-breaking material dumped to protect the construction gives way to a sea bed of rough ground with sand, shale and rocky outcrops.

In 1993, a diver was exploring the area just off the Breakwater when a bright green glow told him that he was looking at a tube of brass. He thought at first that he had found a naval shell case, but its weight told him it was more than that. In fact, he had discovered a two-foot long brass gun made, according to the inscription on it, by the well known gun founder Thomas Pyke of Bridgwater and dated 1787. It was on its own, lying in the open on the sea bed and not apparently associated with any wreckage.

Water depths around the Breakwater Fort are 12 to 15m. The fort is 144ft long and 114ft wide. It was planned to have two storeys of iron and to house fourteen 12.5-inch guns and four 10-inch guns. It soon became obsolete and spent most of its early life as a Naval signal station. The fort is used by Fort Bovisand for commercial diver training courses, which are Government approved for those who want to enter the diving industry and work on such operations as the North Sea oil rigs. It is also the national examination centre for diver inspectors.

317 Hopper Barge No. 42 At 50 20 06N; 04 09 30W. On 13 September, 1913, this 150-ton self-propelled barge was returning from a dredging contract at La Coruña in Spain when she smashed into Plymouth Breakwater. The eight men aboard were saved. The barge was raised and taken in tow but sank. She is now in two parts. To the north-west lie her boiler and firebox; to the south-west is most of the upturned barge, though a large part of it is buried under the sand sea bed in 15m.

WARNING This wreck is in the main shipping channel and like all diving in the Sound needs the permission of the Queen's Harbour Master to dive.

318 Lancaster Bomber Returning from a raid on the U-boat pens at Lorient in Brittany, this Lancaster Mark III, ED 450 G of 49 Squadron RAF, is believed to have been so badly damaged that the pilot, Flight Sergeant G.B.C. Miller, was trying to make a landing anywhere. The Lancaster took off from Fiskerton in Nottinghamshire at 7pm on 13 February, 1943, and in the early hours of the next day hit the steel cable of a barrage balloon protecting shipping in Plymouth Sound. The aircraft crashed onto the Breakwater at 50 19 58N; 04 09 10W.

None of the bodies of the seven crew were found and they may all have baled out over the sea some time earlier. Today the wreckage is mostly in small pieces and is scattered among the blocks of the Breakwater at the western end of the seaward side in 15m. An aircraft recovery group raised one of the Rolls Royce engines, a propeller and other pieces.

319 Yvonne This four-masted barquentine of Marseilles left Jamaica early in August 1920 with a cargo of wood for Le Havre. On 3 October, in the early evening, a southerly gale dashed the *Yvonne* (of over 1000 tons) onto the eastern end of Plymouth Breakwater. Eighteen of her crew were saved by scrambling onto the Breakwater and over it to the lifeboat. But one man, the cook, was lost.

Today, the little that is left of the *Yvonne* is at 50 20 00N; 04 08 15W at the bottom of the Breakwater a short distance to the west of the eastern beacon. The most prominent item is her large anchor and chain at 9m among the blocks of stone placed there to break the force of the waves striking the Breakwater.

320 HMS Abelard What is left of her is at 50 19 53N; 04 08 27W. *Abelard* was a 187-ton steam trawler built in 1909 in North Shields. She was requisitioned by the Navy as a drifter-minesweeper at the start of World War One. On Christmas Eve 1916 she was wrecked "two cables 240 degrees from the Breakwater Beacon" and her masts stuck up eight feet above the water at low spring tides. Salvage operations started at once, but by 11 January were postponed and then abandoned. There was talk that she had hit a mine, but there is no conclusive evidence of this. Today she is well broken. Her bows face south and her boiler stands 5m proud of a sandy sea bed in 10m. The iron propeller is still to be seen. The rest of the flattened wreckage lies among boulders and kelp.

321 Two trawlers At 50 19 42N; 04 10 14W are the remains of two trawlers, which stand 4m high in 15m. Very little is known about this wreckage except that some salvage was carried out in 1946.

WARNING The wreckage is heavily netted.

Transit marks for the Poulmic (site 323).

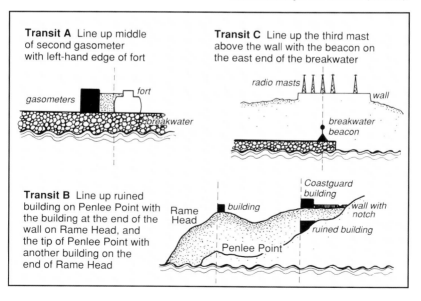

189

The Poulmic (Site 323) was a victim of a parachute mine in 1940, just outside Plymouth Sound.

322 Encourage This 45-ton MFV is at 50 19 25N; 04 09 57W where she sank after hitting a mine on 25 October, 1940, while leaving Plymouth for the fishing grounds. The crew of four were lost. The mine is believed to have been one of many dropped by parachutes from German aircraft. The fishing boat's mast was visible at low water for some time "6.8 cables from the Breakwater Fort 210 degrees", but she is now totally broken up with little more than a few timbers remaining in 12m.

323 Poulmic Another victim of a parachuted sea mine, this French transport ship of 350 tons was in Plymouth when France surrendered in 1940 and was taken over by the Royal Navy. Manned by Free French forces, she was used as a patrol vessel. The 122ft ship, with a beam of 27ft, could do 12 knots and was being used as a minesweeper in the entrance to Plymouth Sound off Penlee Point on 6 October, 1940, when she struck a mine herself.

The ship was blown apart and you will now find her remains at 50 19 05N; 04 09 38W. The largest section is her double bottom. Deck winches are to be seen, as are parts of her engine. The highest point of the wreck is a rib that stands 5m high on a rocky sea bed varying from 15 to 20m. There are many Oerlikon anti-aircraft shells lying around in the gullies in a bad state of preservation and they should be considered dangerous. There are one or two larger shell cases amid the wreckage, and two large cannonballs that appear to be practice shots from the large guns used at Fort Bovisand in its early days.

Transit marks for the *Poulmic* are shown in the diagram on page 189.

324 Vectis On 15 February, 1912, this 907-ton steamer was wrecked on her return run to Cardiff after unloading a cargo of coal in the Cattewater. After passing the western end of the Breakwater, the steamer suddenly altered course and steamed at full speed onto the rocks of Andurn Point. She was stuck there until the Christmas hurricane that year broke her into small pieces. The shattered wreckage is to be found over a wide area around the point in under 10m.

325 Tinker Shoal This can make a good drift dive over a broken reef in 20m. During the course of such a dive you will pass over a great deal of small wreckage.

326 Nepaul This 375ft P&O liner of 3550 tons was homeward bound from Calcutta for London when she ran onto the Shag Stone in the dark evening of 10 December, 1890. She had landed most of her passengers at Marseilles and the small number that were still aboard were taken off by one of the Plymouth pilot boats. It was hoped to refloat her on the next high water, but when the tide came back, all it did was to fill her up inside. Her bottom had been badly ripped open. She became a total loss and is now very broken at 50 19 02N; 04 07 28W.

Her wreckage is mixed with that of the trawler *Baroda*, whose skipper thought he was safe following in the liner's wake. The *Baroda* was wrecked less than 100yds from the *Nepaul* and it is difficult to tell which wreckage is which, particularly as the steamer *Constance* (Site **327**) is there too. It is safe to say that the large winches and anchor belong to the *Nepaul*, as do most of the steel plates and ribs that lie amid kelp in less than 10m. There is a good deal of broken pottery in the area, but unless it bears the P&O crest it could belong to any ship.

327 Constance This British steamer of 850 tons was on passage from Antwerp to Plymouth on 21 January, 1888, when she ran into the Shag Stone in fog. The 209ft ship was carrying a cargo of hides and she now lies, very broken, at 50 19 02N; 04 07 28W just south-east of the Shag Stone in 13m. Three of the crew were killed when they were thrown out of the lifeboat after abandoning the *Constance* in heavy seas.

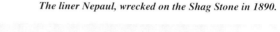

The liner Nepaul, wrecked on the Shag Stone in 1890.

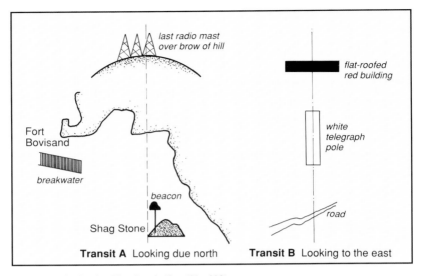

last radio mast over brow of hill

flat-roofed red building

white telegraph pole

Fort Bovisand

breakwater

beacon

road

Shag Stone

Transit A Looking due north   **Transit B** Looking to the east

Transit marks for the Glen Strathallan (Site 328).

328 Glen Strathallan Once a trawler, then a millionaire's plaything, then a training ship and finally the only ship in Britain to be sunk especially for divers. She is now to the south of the Shag Stone at 50 18 56N; 04 07 37W and is very broken in 14m.

The *Glen Strathallan* was built as a 330-ton trawler in 1928, 150ft long with a beam of 22ft, and was converted for £30,000 into a pleasure yacht by the multi-millionaire Colby Cubbin. In World War Two the *Glen Strathallan* went to war with the Navy as an escort ship. At the end of the war Mr Cubbin got his yacht back and used it for cruising until his death. In his will he stipulated that she should be used as a training ship for boys (which for years she was) and that when too old for that, the ship should be sunk in deep water.

So on 27 April, 1970, she was scuttled in her present position for use as an underwater classroom for divers training at Fort Bovisand. Not all that deep, though, the wreck had to be dispersed a year later. The bows are still recognisable and her large boiler stands clear in a sand patch. Otherwise the wreckage has a heavy kelp covering.

Transit marks are shown in the diagram above.

329 HMS Elk This 181-ton former Grimsby fishing trawler was built in 1902. In 1915 she was hired by the Navy as a minesweeper and served until 1919, when she returned to fishing. In 1939, she was called up again and used as a dan layer (to handle the large nets and buoys laid across the entrance to Plymouth Sound). On 27 November, 1940, she struck a mine and sank at 50 18 24N; 04 10 12W. All aboard were saved. In 1981 she was found by amateur divers lying upright without her superstructure on a sand bottom and since then has been a popular dive from Plymouth.

She is 5m proud of the sea bed at 27m. The port side shows more damage than the starboard. She is 108ft long and the bows are complete. A hole gives entry to the engine room, but much of the plating is rusting and there are some very sharp edges. Lobsters are under some broken off plates. There are large congers inside her. She has been stripped of all items of interest, with the portholes and the telegraph going first. Outside the *Elk* in 34m there is a sudden drop-off of 10m down to 44m. This steep bank may be the sign of a former coastline of thousands of years ago. The steep bank is covered with gorgonias.

330 Cannonball Gully North of the Great Mew Stone in 9m of water at 50 18 30N; 04 06 52W is a gully with heavily concreted cannonballs in it.

WARNING Do not dive if red flags are flying from the HMS *Cambridge* gunnery school.

331 Great Mew Stone This rocky island, with its remarkable steep-shelving face, is 59m high. The Little Mew Stone, 15m high, sits on the middle of the Mew Stone Ledge, which runs out 400yds to the south-west of the Great Mew Stone.

Though the Mew Stone is now uninhabited and belongs to the Ministry of Defence, people have lived on it. In 1774 a local Plymouth man, guilty only of some minor crime, was sentenced to be transported to the island for a term of seven years. The man lived there with his family and completed his sentence without once setting foot on the mainland. When the sentence ended the family moved off the island but the daughter, known as Black Joan, opted to stay. She married and raised three children on the Mew Stone until her husband fell from one of the steep rocks and was drowned.

In the early 1800s Sam Wakeman and his wife Ann lived there in a hut – now in ruins – with a garden, and kept chickens and pigs. He lived rent free in return for protecting the island's rabbits for Mr C. Calmady, the owner, to shoot. Wakeman later gave up the island and became a boatman at the Barbican steps. In the late 1920s the island changed hands for £575.

It is certain that at one time it was possible to wade out to the Mew Stone at low tide, though not always successfully, judging by this entry in the Wembury Church register:

Burials, 1720. May 15. Richard Cragg, Robert Sampson, Mary Avent, Mary Hake, John Tingcomb, 17, Josias Avent, 21, Walter Avent, 29, Mary Beer, 30, Elizabeth Taylor. Drowned between the Mew Stone and the Continent on a Sunday.

The Mew Stones and The Ledge have claimed many ships. An extraordinary number of sailing ship captains seemed to think it easy to sail between the Mew Stone and the shore, but that narrow passage is only 50yds wide and the rocks running out from the shore to Culter Rock or north from the Mew Stone itself proved they were wrong.

There are plenty of wrecks for divers to look out for. The Norwegian barque *August Smith* was wrecked on Wembury Beach in 1895. In 1897 the brigantine

St Pierre of Le Havre, bound for Madagascar loaded with coal briquettes, struck the Mew Stone and foundered. Divers have found some of her cargo. Earlier victims were the smack *Industry* in 1851 and a year later the 206-ton brig *Ocean Queen*, which went down on the Little Mew Stone with the loss of all but one of her 15-man crew.

332 Ajax This 800-ton London-registered paddle steamer ran a regular service between London and Cork, calling at Plymouth on the way. On 12 October, 1854, she left London with 350 passengers and, in her 206ft hull, a general cargo, chests of tea and tons of guano fertiliser. Captain Rochford was standing in for the regular captain who was ill. On 13 October the *Ajax* was approaching Plymouth – much too close in. The captain rejected the advice of Chief Officer Steel to give the Mew Stone a wider berth, and held his course. It was flat calm and visibility was perfect, but the *Ajax* ran straight onto the Little Mew Stone and ripped her bottom open on the Mew Stone Ledge. Despite panic among the passengers, all were safely taken off by boats from Plymouth. The *Ajax* became a total wreck.

A Coastguard report recorded that the wreck was "either done purposely or else from sheer culpable negligence". Captain Rochford had lost another steamer, the *Minerva*, only two months earlier on the Skerries near Holyhead! There is plenty of wreckage to be found on the site in 12m of water just to the South of the Little Mew Stone, though some of this wreckage may be that of the *Rothesay* (Site **334**). In the gullies amid the kelp are decking and winches, with one piece sticking up above the kelp to a height of over 3m.

333 Matilda This fishing vessel was a casualty of the engines of the *Ajax*, onto which she ran on 1 March, 1866, when passing the Mew Stone. She sank so swiftly that only William Bunce, a boy, survived from her crew of three.

334 Rothesay A 332-ton coaster, this steamer was in ballast heading home to Cardiff from Caen when she was caught in near hurricane winds and decided to run for the shelter of Plymouth. Just before midnight on 15 October, 1877, the *Rothesay* was blown onto the rocks surrounding the Mew Stones. When she struck, one of the crew was washed overboard and carried unhurt onto the Great Mew Stone. With his help the remaining crew managed to get a line ashore and escaped along it as the ship began to break up.

In the daylight at low water the *Rothesay* presented an amazing sight – a dozen holes could be seen in her hull and the stem and stern posts had been torn completely off. The wreckage of the *Rothesay* appears to be mixed with that of the *Ajax* (Site **332**). It is spread over a wide area and in many of the gullies in shallow water amid the kelp.

335 The Nillus Cannon Wreck This lies on the south side of the Great Mew Stone, among the gullies on the Ledge. The sea bed is all steep-sided gullies and mounds and over a dozen iron cannon lie in them, among heavy growth. The site was discovered by Dick Middlewood of Croydon BSAC in 1968. Two huge anchors – one nearly 10ft long – and much broken pottery were found later in a combined survey of the site by the Croydon divers and Slough SAC in under 10m. Dating of the cannon, the anchors and the red pottery, possibly from Spanish oil jars, point to a ship of the middle or late 18th century. Divers from Chester SAC found a ship's bell in the area, which could be 17th or 18th century. It bore just the word "Nillus". The *Ajax* wreckage encroaches on this site.

336 The Mew Stone Drop-off Further to the south, the gullies follow the run of the steep face of the Great Mew Stone going down and out. They drop down swiftly to 30m. Here there is some evidence of an aircraft wreck and in 1984 David Swales and the author found part of a very corroded belt of 0.5-inch tracer bullets, similar to those used in Flying Fortress bombers. From the bottom of the gullies in 30m there is a sudden cliff face falling sheer to 40m.

337 The Mew Stone Submarine It is possible that the 1984 report of a World War One U-boat jammed into a gully of the Little Mew Stone was a hoax. But if so, it was an elaborate one. A position of 50 18 12N; 04 06 30W was given, placing her about 100yds south of the Little Mew Stone. She was said to be about 100 feet long, lying at an angle of 45° in the gully, which runs down from the submarine's bow in 12m to her stern in 26m. There were no periscopes to be seen and no propeller, though the boss was still there. She was described as about 12ft high and it was said that divers had been inside her, though this had entailed taking off their gear to enter the hatch. Plymouth diving experts expressed grave doubts about her existence soon after publication of the report. One diver said that he had found a huge length of piping in that area. The author would welcome any detail to either prove or disprove the submarine's existence!

338 The Astrolabe The waters inside the Mew Stone are sheltered and ideal for training dives. The depth is rarely more than 11m, with sand patches leading to gullies running north-west into the face of the Mew Stone reef. The floor of these is coarse sand and shingle and the gullies are roofed with kelp.

An extraordinary find was made here by Wilf Jenkin of Plymouth Sound BSAC. Among the sea growth in one gully he found a bronze astrolabe, one of the early instruments used in navigation. His discovery of this ring of brass was only the 25th astrolabe known to exist and experts dated it to the first quarter of the 17th century. If there was a navigation instrument, where is the wreck? A good question, but despite extensive searches of thousands of square yards by Plymouth Sound BSAC, nothing else has been found.

339 Black Stone Reef This area of rough ground starts 800yds south-west of Blackstone Point and rises to within 3m of the surface. A very pretty area of good diving ground, it consists of rocks, some six or seven metres high, with many gullies to 18m. Fish life is very plentiful and dead man's fingers, jewel anemones and soft corals provide the background. This is a large area at least 100yds square and it can be spotted easily by the tidal turbulence over it.

340 Hilsea Point Rocks Reckoned by some local divers to be the best scenic dive in this part of Devon, the rocks are 800yds south-east of Hilsea Point and almost directly south of the old Coastguard lookout, which is a quarter of a mile east of the point, 90m high on the cliffs. The rocks are seven or eight pinnacles and the tallest rises to within 2m of the surface from the sea bed at 24 to 26m.

Rocks and sand lie between the pinnacles, one of which has a hole in it that divers can swim through.

These tall and slender pinnacles are a wonderful sight in good visibility with hard corals, soft corals, sea fans and large sea urchins decorating them and clouds of fish surrounding them, parting to let large ling swim through. There are sometimes large edible crabs and lobsters at the base of the pinnacles. The only drawback is the fierce tide runs, which reach 1$^1/_2$ knots at times. Diving must be done on slack or after half tide, which means three hours before high water or three hours 20 minutes after high water.

341 The West Rutts These rocks lie four miles west of the East Rutts (Site **285**). Between these two groups of rocks and to the south is a strange area of sand waves, some with crests 5m high. The run of the waves is north–south with 100 to 300yds between the crests.

The rocks of the West Rutts are not so dramatic as those of East Rutts, rising only from 36m to 25m, and are not as good a dive. Most of the ground is rough with gravel and sand patches among the rocks. There are some large rocks with crabs, lobsters and crawfish in season.

342 HMS Foyle When this destroyer torpedo boat was mined in the Dover Straits on 15 March, 1917, 27 Navy men were killed out of her crew of 70. Her bow was blown right off and sank. However, the stern section stayed afloat and was taken in tow for Plymouth. It nearly sank it, but sank at 50 16 42N; 04 10 48W.

HMS *Foyle* was built by Cammell Laird in 1903. The 550-ton ship was 225ft long with a beam of 23.5ft and had 7000hp engines, which would have given her over 25 knots. She had four 12-pounder guns and two torpedo tubes, but there is only one gun left on the stern section now. Divers recovered her nameplate in 1972. The wreck is on a sandy bed at 46m, upright with a list of 30°, and 6m proud. Her boilers are clear. She is now very broken and some reports say that she is sinking into the sea bed.

343 Submarine, identity unknown Located only by magnetometer, and previously thought to be a submarine-shaped rock, this wreck is at 50 10 43N; 04 10 02W. It may not be a submarine, but it does stand only 3m proud of the sea bed at 59m. No diving information is available.

344 Stanhope This is yet another victim of *UB-31* and Oberleutnant Bieber. On 15 June, 1917, he torpedoed the *Teesdale*, but she managed to beach. Bieber went on hunting. On June 17, he found the 2854-ton *Stanhope* and shadowed her for a while before firing a torpedo from periscope depth. The 333ft British steamer went down like a stone and 22 of her crew were lost, though her captain survived. She had been heading for Dunkirk from Barrow with a cargo of steel rails.

This ship, which was built by Ropner and Sons in 1900 for the English Steamship Company, now lies at 50 11 09N; 04 08 21W. Depth is 58m to the sea bed and 47m to her deck. She is very broken and is in two amidships. She is on a slope with the southern end the shallowest part.

345 Australbush This British armed steamer of 4398 tons was torpedoed by *UC-31* while travelling empty from Le Havre to Cardiff on 13 November, 1917, and is now on the bottom at 50 12 12N; 04 05 15W. Two men died in the sinking. The depth to the top of the wreck is 44m, and 56m to the sea bed. She is known locally as "The Coal Boat" and lies north–south. She has been trawled into many times and there are nets on her. Her bell has been raised.

346 Lord Stonehaven Though listed by the Admiralty as an "unknown", Plymouth Sound divers are certain that the trawler sitting upright in 58m at 50 11 43N; 04 05 31W is the *Lord Stonehaven*, an Admiralty-requisitioned trawler sunk by E-boats during an attack on a convoy off the Eddystone on 2 October, 1942. The 444-ton craft, which was built in 1934, is intact. The shell cases, small arms cartridges and batteries are dated no later than 1941.

WARNING This wreck is netted with tangle and gill nets.

347 "Eastern Coal Boat" That is what local fishermen and divers call this small wreck of a steamer. Only 52ft long, lying east–west and very broken, she is at 50 10 21N; 04 03 01W. She has been trawled into many times, so watch out for nets. Depth is 59m and she is 6m proud.

348 Wreck, name unknown At 50 09 37N; 04 10 54W, this is a small wreck standing 10m proud of a 60m sea bed of mud and sand.

349 Claverley In the morning darkness of 20 August, 1917, Oberleutnant Umberger manoeuvred the *UB-38* so that her bow was pointing directly at the even darker patch that was the 3829-ton British steamer *Claverley*, bound for Genoa from the Tyne, crossing right in front of the surfaced submarine. Ten men died when Umberger's torpedo struck home and the 350ft steamer sank swiftly at 50 08 37N; 04 10 21W.

Today the *Claverley*, built in 1907 by W. Doxford and Sons, is described by Plymouth Sound divers as "big and upright". She is on a flat sand and mud sea bed at 62m from which she stands 7m proud. Her stern gun is still in place.

350 Brigitte Travelling in convoy on 19 November, 1942, this 1595-ton British steamer, bound for Barry from Southampton in ballast, was at the centre of two E-boat attacks during the dark early hours. In addition to her crew she carried two Naval gunners and the Convoy Commodore and his staff, making 23 on board in all.

The first attack on the convoy, from E-boats based at Cherbourg, came shortly after 3am, preceded by an attack from aircraft. The *Yewforest*, another ship in the convoy, was sunk (Site **279**), but then the E-boats withdrew and the convoy steamed on down the Channel.

Six miles further on, the E-boats attacked again. This time it was the *Brigitte* that took a torpedo in her port side. Seven crew, the two gunners and one of the Convoy Commodore's staff were lost. The ship is still intact at 50 08 11N; 04 09 11W on a black mud sea bed at 64m. Her highest point is her bridge at 51m.

351 Wreck, name unknown At 50 08 03N; 04 07 54W, this wreck has long been known as a "fastener" by Plymouth trawlermen, but they have no idea of her identity, and nor does anyone else. The depth to the sea bed is 62m. The depth to the highest point the of wreck is 58m.

352 Lab A Norwegian steamer of 1118 tons, 226ft long with a crew of 21, the *Lab* was on her way for Mumbles from Southampton in ballast on 18 November, 1942, when an E-boat torpedoed her in the dark. Three of the crew were lost when she sank. Today she is at 50 07 39N; 04 10 09W. Plymouth Sound divers describe her as very broken up and in several pieces, only 5m off the flat sand and mud sea bed in 63m.

353 Wreck, name unknown At 50 06 05N; 04 11 12W is a small wreck on a flat sea bed of fine sand, standing 8m proud in 68m.

354 Visborg At 50 05 32N; 04 06 03W and too deep for most divers in 68m standing 13m proud, this Norwegian steamer of 1311 tons is interesting as she was one of the last victims of Oberleutnant Erich Noodt in *UB-19* just three days before he was sunk in a famous action by the Q-ship *Penshurst*.

The 245ft *Visborg* was laden with 1760 tons of coal from Barry and heading for Cherbourg on 27 November, 1916, when she was stopped by Noodt, who planted bombs that sent her to the bottom. All the crew were saved. *UB-19* motored on and the same day sank the 1884-ton *Belle Ile*, a Norwegian steamer carrying iron ore from Spain to France.

On 30 November Erich Noodt was lured within range by the 1191-ton Q-ship *Penshurst* – with her low freeboard and funnel aft looking very much like an oil tanker – by the simple device of her stopping and all the crew apparently abandoning ship. When the unsuspecting U-boat came within 250yds on the surface, the Navy gun crews left aboard pumped shells from their hidden 3-pounder and 12-pounder guns into the submarine. They hit her with over 80 rounds and the 118ft U-boat sank bow first. Noodt and thirteen of his crew were captured but seven died. Captain F.H. Grenfell and the crew of the *Penshurst* sank another submarine on 14 January, 1917 – the *UB-37*, which was commanded by Oberleutnant P. Gunther.

355 Robin John This British wooden MFV sank after a collision with the Dutch fishing boat *Care Beka* on 5 July, 1972. She is lying upright on a flat bottom at 50 04 30N; 04 07 47W, 4m proud of the sea bed at 69m.

356 Wreck, name unknown This is located at 50 03 29N; 04 10 16W, though the position is approximate and is that of a fisherman's "fastener" in a depth of 70m. It may of course be a rock.

357 Wreck, name unknown At 50 03 28N; 04 07 33W is the wreck of a steamship about 230ft long with a 33-ft beam, lying nearly north–south and is very broken. She is at 64m and it is another 6m to the sea bed.

358 Wreck, name unknown At 50 04 25N; 04 05 19W, this wreck lies in an area of sand and mud waves. She has a high bow and stern and is 8m proud of the sea bed at 69m.

359 Dragmea, Tregenna or Benito At 50 05 12N; 04 04 39W, standing 12m off a sea bed at 68m, this wreck has not been dived and could be any of the three MFVs named. She is in an area of sand waves.

360 Wreck, name unknown Too deep for amateur divers, this one at 50 04 23N; 04 03 28W is well known to the Plymouth trawlermen as a "fastener" and must be well draped with nets. The depth to the sea bed is 70m.

361 Bell Virtue This West German container ship of 499 tons was in collision with the Panamanian bulk carrier *Maritime Pioneer* in thick fog on 27 April, 1973. The *Bell Virtue*, fully loaded and on passage from Waterford to Rozenburg, sank swiftly and now lies upright at 50 03 30N; 04 05 40W. She is 265ft with a beam of 41ft, and stands 13m proud of the sea bed at 70m.

362 Wreck, name unknown At 50 03 24N; 04 05 32W, just 200yds south of the *Bell Virtue*, is a fishing vessel about 148ft long with a beam of 33ft. She lies north–south on a flat sand and mud sea bed at 70m, from which she stands 9m proud.

The slipway at Whitestrand Quay, Salcombe, at high tide.

APPENDIX 1:

Dive Services

Dive boats

Boats available are listed in order from east to west. *Diver* magazine is a good source of information about other operators in this area.

Seaton Three hard boats and three RIBs are operated by Seaton Marine Services (tel. 01297 23344).

Exmouth *Grace* (skipper Maurice Webb, former D.O. of Exedive), 10 divers, 36ft boat with full electronic gear (tel. 01395 264193).

Brixham *Deep Mystery* (diver skipper Stephen Sargison), 12 divers, 38ft, all electronic gear, magnetometer (tel. 01803 855772).

Dartmouth *Maureen* (diver skipper Mike Rowley), 12 divers, 67ft with full electronic gear, compressor on board (tel. 01860 571012 or 01602 655033).

Hallsands Two inflatables (one an RIB), 14ft6in and 15ft6in, with trailer. For hire from Hallsands Hotel, on production of a boat handling certificate (tel. 01548 511264).

Salcombe *Dunedin* (diver skipper John Kempton), 10 divers, 65ft, compressor, all electronic gear, live-aboard and cruises (tel. 01548 842057).
  Likely Lad (diver skipper Richard Clarkson), 10 divers, 31ft with electronic gear (tel. 01548 852934).
  Nirvana (diver skipper Bill Bunting), 10 divers, 31ft with electronic equipment (tel. 01548 857102).
  Panther (diver skipper Pat Dean), 12 divers, 52ft with electronic gear, compressor, lifting winch (tel. 01548 843319).

Challaborough 5.5m RIB (diver skipper John Plummer), 6 divers, electronic gear (tel. 01548 810701).

Fort Bovisand Inflatables for hire and hard boat charter arranged (tel. 01752 408021).

Plymouth *Amoco* (Diver skipper Dave Booker), 10 divers, 33ft, all electronic gear (tel. 01752 666576).
   Beatrice (diver skipper John Holman), 12 divers, 35ft, all electronic gear (tel. 01752 790605).
   Cee King (diver skipper Richard Kings), 12 divers, 32ft, all electronic gear (tel. 01752 663247).
   Excalibur (diver skipper Roger Webber), 10 divers, 30ft, all electronic gear (tel. 01752 405403).
   Freedom (diver skipper John Dance), 10 divers, 33ft, all electronic gear (tel. 01364 3300).
   Jem Express (diver skipper Ernie Palmer), 12 divers, 36ft, all electronic gear (tel. 01752 401807).
   Maid Maggie (diver skipper Glenn Lindsay), 12 divers, 32ft, all electronic gear (tel. 01752 491544).
   Storm (diver skipper Rod Davies), 10 divers, 31ft, all electronic gear (tel. 01752 862165).
   UK National (diver skipper Dick Linford), 12 divers, 36ft, all electronic gear (tel. 01752 862488).

Air supplies

Seaton Seaton Marine Services, The Harbour, Axmouth. Owners are Ray Kirkland and John Ledger. Air to 5000psi, 7 days per week, 9am to 5pm. Other times by arrangement (tel. 01297 23344).

Exmouth Diver Training School, The Quayside. BSAC School No 9. Proprietors David Lea and Robin Hawkins. Air to 3700psi. Monday to Friday 9am to 5pm; Saturday 9am to 12 noon (tel. 01395 266300).

Exeter Aquanaut, 17 Clifton Road. BSAC School No. 110. Air to 4000psi. Monday and Tuesday 9am to 5pm; Wednesday 9am to 1pm; Thursdays, Fridays and Saturdays 9am to 5.30pm; Sundays 8am to 8.30am (tel. 01392 218825).

Torquay From Torbay Branch at their store on Beacon Quay opposite Haldon Pier. Air to 3600psi. From 6pm in summer.

Paignton Venture Sports and Watersports Centre, 371 Torquay Road. BSAC School No. 156. Proprietor Geoff Sharp. Air to 4000psi. Open 9am to 5.30pm Monday to Saturday (9am to 1pm on Wednesdays); on Sundays in June, July and August open until 12 noon (tel. 01803 523023).

Nautique, Unit 5, South Quay. Proprietors: Pete and Sandra Inger. Air to 4000psi. Open 8am to 8pm seven days a week in season, in winter 10am to 5pm (tel. 01803 550278).

Brixham Breakwater Beach Café and Restaurant. Air to 4000psi. Open mid March to 31 October, 8am to 10pm, seven days, including bank holidays (tel. 01803 856738).

Hallsands Hallsands Hotel. Air to 3600psi and from air banks. During season open seven days a week, 9am to 10 pm. The hotel, on the cliff overlooking the beach, is fully licensed with 18 bedrooms. Proprietors David and Caroline Light are former members of Bristol Aerospace BSAC and welcome divers. Special rates for club parties include free air (tel. 01548 511264).

Kingsbridge Kingsbridge Watersports, 39 Fore Street. Proprietors Richard and Jane Clarkson. Air to 3800psi. Open 9am to 6pm Monday to Saturday in summer. Fills outside hours by arrangement (tel. 01548 852934).

Salcombe Pat Dean will supply air to 4000psi from the compressor on board his boat *Panther* by arrangement. At Furzehill, Moult Road, Salcombe, he has special bunkhouse accommodation and rooms for 16 divers, usually reserved for those using his boat (tel. 01548 843319 or call *Panther* on Channel 16).

Challaborough J.P. Leisure. Air to 4400psi. Open Easter to mid October, 9am to 6pm, other times by arrangement (tel. 01548 810701).

Plymouth Fort Bovisand. Air to 4000. Open 8.30am to 5.30pm seven days a week. (tel. 01752 408021).
   Sandford and Down, 24, Pier Street, West Hoe. Air to 4400psi. Open 9am to 6pm Tuesdays to Saturdays, 9am to 11 am (tel. 01752 266248).
   Sound Diving, Queen Anne's Battery, Coxside (in the marina). Air to 4000psi. Open April to September 8am to 7pm seven days a week, October to March weekdays 1pm to 5.30pm (closed Thursdays), Saturdays 9am to 5pm, Sundays 9.30am to 11.30 am (tel. 01752 670674).

Diving equipment and services

See under Air Supplies above for details of the opening hours, addresses and telephone numbers of the following suppliers.

Seaton Seaton Marine Services have a dive shop selling a wide range of equipment. Workshops do all servicing, bottle testing, and maintenance. The firm operates a decompression chamber accommodating 12, with lock-in-lock-out facilities, qualified operators and medical support. A 20ft tank offers an introductory course in hard-hat.

Exmouth Diver Training School supplies diving equipment and teaches to Advanced standard.

Exeter Aquanaut have a wide range of new and second-hand equipment. Test bottles, all servicing.

Paignton Nautique has a full range of equipment, suits, general servicing, bottle testing. Boats and instruction can be arranged.

Venture Sports and Water Sports Centre is well stocked with equipment and suits. Bottle testing and valve repairs available.

Kingsbridge Kingsbridge Watersports stock all diving equipment, suits, repairs, servicing, bottle testing.

Challaborough J.P. Leisure sell diving equipment, repairs, servicing.

Plymouth Fort Bovisand Dive Shop is open every day except Tuesdays, from 9am to 5pm – range of diving equipment, accessories, bottle test (tel. 01752 406646).

Sandford and Down have a large range of diving equipment, hire equipment, all servicing, bottle test.

Sound Diving offer a wide range of diving gear, hire all equipment, servicing, shot-blasting, bottle test, depth-gauge testing.

Local BSAC branches

Most branches welcome visiting divers and provided there is room will let them join in branch dives. Visiting divers should therefore carry proof of their qualifications.

Places to contact each branch are given below, but current telephone numbers for branch secretaries are available from BSAC headquarters (tel. 0151 357 1951).

Exeter Branch hold "wet" meetings at Exeter City Swimming Baths, Heavitree Road on Wednesdays from 8pm.

Exmouth Exe to Sea Branch meet at Longrange Swimming Pool, Honiton on Mondays at 7.30pm.

Exedive Branch meet at Exeter City Swimming Baths, Heavitree Road on Fridays at 9pm.

Exeter Aquanaut Branch meet at Exeter City Swimming Baths, Heavitree Road on Fridays at 9pm.

Tiverton Branch hold their "wet" meetings at Tiverton Swimming Pool on Thursdays from 8.15pm.

Totnes Branch meet at Meadowbrook, Dartington Community Centre, Shinners Bridge, Dartington on Wednesdays at 8pm.

Torbay Branch is a veteran branch of the BSAC. "Wet" meetings are held during the winter only at Plainmoor Swimming Pool on Fridays from 9pm. Torbay have a small premises at Beacon Quay, which house their compressor (*see* Air Supplies) and they can be found there most summer evenings from 6pm.

Bigbury Bay Divers Branch hold their "dry" meetings at Bigbury Memorial Hall, St Ann's Chapel on Mondays at 7.30pm.

Plymouth Fort Bovisand Branch meet in the bar at the Fort on Wednesdays at 8.30pm.

Plymouth Sound Branch hold "dry" meetings on Mondays from 8pm at the Mayflower Sailing Club, Phoenix Wharf, The Barbican.

The 30-inch bronze cannon found off Burgh Island.

APPENDIX 2:

The Diver's Code of Conduct

Divers must at all times adhere to the BSAC code of conduct. It is reproduced here with the kind permission of the British Sub-Aqua Club, and has been extracted from the BSAC *Safe Diving Practices* booklet, available from BSAC Headquarters.

THE DIVER'S CODE OF CONDUCT

More and more people are taking to the water. Some for recreation; some to earn their living. This code is designed to ensure that divers do not come into conflict with other water users. It is vital that you observe it at all times.

Before leaving home

Contact the nearest British Sub-Aqua Club Branch or the dive operator local to the dive site for their advice. Seek advice from them about the local conditions and regulations.

On the beach, river bank or lakeside

1. Obtain permission, before diving in a harbour or estuary or in private water. Thank those responsible before you leave. Pay harbour dues.

2. Try to avoid overcrowding one site, consider other people on the beach.

3. Park sensibly. Avoid obstructing narrow approach roads. Keep off verges. Pay parking fees and use proper car parks.

4. Don't spread yourselves and your equipment since you may upset other people. Keep launching ramps and slipways clear.

5. Please keep the peace. Don't operate a compressor within earshot of other people – or late at night.

6. Pick up litter. Close gates. Be careful about fires. Avoid any damage to land or crops.

7. Obey special instructions such as National Trust rules, local by-laws and regulations about camping and caravanning.

8. Remember divers in wetsuits are conspicuous and bad behaviour could ban us from beaches.

In and on the water

1. Mark your dive boats so that your Club can be identified easily. Unmarked boats may become suspect.

2. Ask the harbour-master or local officials where to launch your boat – and do as they say. Tell the Coastguard, or responsible person, where you are going and tell them when you are back.

3. Stay away from buoys, pots, and pot markers. Ask local fishermen where not to dive. Offer to help them recover lost gear.

4. Remember ships have not got brakes, so avoid diving in fairways or areas of heavy surface traffic and observe the "International Regulations for the Prevention of Collisions at Sea".

5. Always fly the diving flag when diving, but not when on the way to, or from, the dive site. Never leave a boat unattended.

6. Do not come in to bathing beaches under power. Use any special approach lanes. Do not disturb any seal or bird colonies with your boats. Watch your wash in crowded anchorages.

7. Whenever possible, divers should use a surface marker buoy.

On conservation

1. Never use a speargun with an aqualung. Never use a speargun in fresh water.

2. Shellfish, such as crabs and lobsters, take several years to grow to maturity; over-collecting in an area soon depletes stocks. Only take mature fish or shellfish and then only what you need for yourself. Never sell your catch or clean it in public or on the beach. Don't display your trophies.

3. Be conservation conscious. Avoid damage to weeds and the sea bed. Do not bring up sea-fans, corals, starfish or sea urchins – in one moment you can destroy years of growth.

4. Take photographs and notes – not specimens. Shoot with a camera not a speargun – spearfishing makes fish shy of divers. Never spearfish wrasse or other inshore species since once an area is depleted of such fish, it may take a long time for them to re-colonise.

On wrecks

1. Do not dive on a designated wreck site. These are indicated on Admiralty Charts and marked by buoys or warning notices on the shore nearby.
2. Do not lift anything which appears to be of historical importance.
3. If you do discover a wreck, do not talk about it. Pinpoint the site, do a rough survey and report it to the BSAC Archaeology Adviser and the Council for Nautical Archaeology who will advise you.
4. If you do not lift anything from the wreck, it is not necessary to report your discovery to the Receiver of Wreck. If you do lift, you must report.
5. If your find is important, you may apply for it to be designated a protected site. Then you can build up a well qualified team with the right credentials and proceed with a systematic survey or excavation under licence without outside interference.

Don't Let Divers Down – Keep To The Diver's Code

Burgh Island and the tractor taxi.

Index

The bold numbers in parentheses are dive site numbers.